SUPERSTARS OF
THE 21ST CENTURY

SUPERSTARS OF THE 21ST CENTURY

Pop Favorites of America's Teens

Kathleen Tracy

GREENWOOD

AN IMPRINT OF ABC-CLIO, LLC
Santa Barbara, California • Denver, Colorado • Oxford, England

Library of Congress Cataloging-in-Publication Data

Tracy, Kathleen.
 Superstars of the 21st century : pop favorites of America's teens / Kathleen Tracy.
  p. cm.
 Includes bibliographical references and index.
 ISBN 978-0-313-37736-5 (hardcopy : alk. paper) — ISBN 978-0-313-37737-2 (ebook)
1. Celebrities—United States—Biography. 2. United States—Biography.
I. Title. II. Title: Superstars of the twenty-first century.
 CT220.T63 2013
 305.5'20922—dc23
 [B] 2012025002
ISBN: 978-0-313-37736-5
EISBN: 978-0-313-37737-2

17 16 15 14 13 1 2 3 4 5

This book is also available on the World Wide Web as an eBook.
Visit www.abc-clio.com for details.

Greenwood
An Imprint of ABC-CLIO, LLC

ABC-CLIO, LLC
130 Cremona Drive, P.O. Box 1911
Santa Barbara, California 93116-1911

This book is printed on acid-free paper ∞

Manufactured in the United States of America

CONTENTS

PREFACE

For as long as there have been celebrities, there have been cultural role models that teens either relate to, look up to, or aspire to be. These pop-culture superstars are not determined by age, nationality, gender, or specific talent but by their ability to spur imagination, impart the belief that any goal is achievable, or even just make it okay to be who you are. The pop favorites overviewed in this book are all 21st-century role models for teens in one fashion or another. They both entertain and inspire but, mostly, they provide living proof that dreams really do come true. Some, such as Ellen DeGeneres, cross generational lines in their appeal and influence; others, such as Miley Cyrus, have attained success in a variety of professional roles.

Written in an engaging manner for high school students and general readers, the chapters in this reference work feature popular athletes, such as Shawn Johnson, Nastia Liukin, and Shaun White; singers, such as Lady Gaga, Rihanna, and Taylor Swift; and actors, such as Blake Lively, Dakota Fanning, and Chace Crawford. Most of the chapters treat a single pop-culture superstar, while a few discuss several figures together because of their personal and professional relationships. Many of the chapters provide sidebars highlighting interesting people and related topics. Since this reference work is meant to support student research on the celebrities who interest them, each chapter provides notes and some chapters cite works for further reading. The volume closes with a selected, general bibliography of print and electronic resources.

To keep his physique in top shape, Lautner says he carries around bags of meat to make sure he eats enough protein and calories.

1 TAYLOR LAUTNER

Although Kristen Stewart and Robert Pattinson have received the lion's share of the *Twilight* film series media coverage, Taylor Lautner has quietly positioned himself to be Hollywood's next breakout movie star. While girls may swoon over Pattinson's soulful vampire, Lautner has big-screen, action-hero potential and could become the Tom Cruise of his generation—minus the erratic behavior and Scientology.

Taylor Daniel Lautner was born on February 11, 1992, in Grand Rapids, Michigan. His mom, Deborah, worked at the Herman Miller chair company and his father, Dan, was a commercial airline pilot. When Taylor was four, his family moved to Hudsonville, which is located about 15 miles southwest of Grand Rapids.

Taylor grew up loving sports and when he was six years old, he began taking martial arts at Fabiano's Karate in the nearby town of Holland. "A lot of boys that age are bouncing off the walls, but Taylor was always deliberate, focused," Fabiano reported to the *Grand Rapids Press*. "He wasn't a typical kid. He always worked extra hard."[1]

Within the year, Taylor competed in a national tournament in Louisville, Kentucky. While there he met Michael Chaturantabut—better known as Mike Chat, the actor who formerly played the Blue Power Ranger. Chat, who lived in Los Angeles, specialized in extreme karate, which incorporates stunts and flips. He ran a camp at the University of California, Los Angeles (UCLA) and invited Taylor to attend.

"I fell in love," Taylor told mlive.com. "By the end of the camp, I was doing aerial cartwheels with no hands."[2]

He trained with Chat for the next several years, earning his black belt while competing on the martial arts tournament circuit where he won three Junior World

Championship gold medals. He also participated with an Extreme Martial Arts (XMA) performance team.

Chat saw more than just athletic ability in Taylor, he also saw a natural performer. So on one of Taylor's visits to Los Angeles, Chat convinced him to go on an audition for a Burger King commercial. The experience led to Taylor getting an agent. Since Taylor's father worked for an airline, family members could fly standby for very little money. So when Taylor's agent would call with an audition, Taylor and his mother would leave early the next morning, get to Los Angeles around noon, go to the audition in the afternoon, take the redeye back to Michigan, and arrive in time for Taylor to get to school.

They made the trip a couple times a month for several years. "Then we decided, *This is insane. We can't keep on doing this,*" Taylor told the *Grand Rapids Press*. The family decided to move to Los Angeles for a month to let Taylor try auditioning full time. "I got one call-back—it happened on our very last day there. That gave me the drive to keep going."[3]

Taylor's parents then committed to staying in Los Angeles for six months and during that time he was cast in his first job—a *Rugrats* movie commercial for Nickelodeon. In 2003, the Lautners decided to relocate permanently. "My parents said to me, *Look, if you want to continue doing this, we can't do it from Michigan— we have to live in L.A.,*" Lautner told *The Los Angeles Times*. "I think it was when I was, like, 10 years old. It was a really difficult decision for me and obviously an extremely difficult and risky decision for my parents but, luckily, I have a very supportive family behind me. Thank goodness it worked."[4]

Taylor says it was a big deal to leave Michigan because all of his family was there. It was also difficult because acting success was slow in coming, but Taylor says the confidence he had from doing karate kept him from getting discouraged. His persistence began to pay off: he appeared on *My Wife and Kids, Summerland, The Bernie Mac Show,* and *The Nick and Jessica Variety Hour.* He also did voice-over work, playing Youngblood on the *Danny Phantom* cartoon, plus characters on *What's New, Scooby-Doo?,* and *Charlie Brown.*

His first major breakthrough was getting cast in the 2005 3-D movie *The Adventures of Shark Boy and Lava Girl.* Directed by Robert Rodriguez, who also helmed the *Spy Kids* movies, *Shark Boy* came from an idea by Rodriguez's son, Racer, then six. It tells the story of a boy who was raised by sharks and, in the process, acquired some of their physical characteristics.

In an interview with UltimateDisney.com, Taylor said he was excited to work with Rodriguez "because he was so much fun to work with. He's great to be around because he plays video games with you and he's really, really nice. And he's also a great director because we're shooting on a green screen and he helped us a lot. Ninety percent of the movie was done on green screen. We just had three days at a house, three days at a school, and that was about it. And we had one day at a playground. All the other 55 days were on the green screen."[5]

Taylor told the Disney website that his favorite part of being in a movie was getting to meet the other actors and crew. He thought it was fun playing characters not like himself and being someone totally different "for about three months. And then my least favorite part is school. Unless it's summer, you gotta do school three hours a day and sometimes more because they want to bank hours. At the end of the movie, if you don't have enough time or if you want to relax more, you're going to be leaving in a couple of days, then you get to use some of your bank hours."[6]

Taylor also admitted that acting has usurped karate because he is too busy. "You have a tournament once a month, where you got to miss a weekend for that. And you also gotta be training two hours a day. Karate is just a horrible mix with acting. So I had to pick either karate or acting, and I picked acting. But I still sometimes train at my house, just to keep up the skill."[7]

Shark Boy didn't set any box office records but it did put Taylor on the public's radar screen. "Ten-year-old boys were the ones who first recognized me," he said on mlive.com. "I'd be in the store, and boys would whisper to their moms. Then the moms would say, *Excuse me—are you Shark Boy?* I just thought it was so cool. I couldn't believe people wanted my picture."[8]

After his next film, *Cheaper by the Dozen 2,* girls started noticing him. But the reaction among some of his schoolmates was a little more frosty. "I was never extremely confident," he told *Rolling Stone* magazine. "Because I was an actor, when I was in school there was a little bullying going on. Not physical bullying but people making fun of what I do. I just had to tell myself I can't let this get to me. This is what love to do. And I'm going to continue to do it."[9]

Although he considered Los Angeles his adopted home, Taylor still made regular trips back to Michigan to visit relatives. "I love coming back here," Taylor told the *Grand Rapids Press.* "In L.A., whatever you do for fun, you gotta spend money. Here, you go jet skiing on a lake. It's such a fun place for me. I go fishing with one set of grandparents, I go quad riding with the other set. We go trap shooting. It's so much fun."[10]

In early 2008, Taylor was cast in *Twilight* as Native American teenager Jacob Black, Bella Swan's platonic best friend. A modestly budgeted film adaptation of the popular young-adult book series, *Twilight* was shot mostly on location in Oregon and took six weeks to film. Taylor had minimal screen time and was on location for only a week, appearing in just four scenes.

In the film, he was required to wear a wig because Jacob initially has hair down to the middle of his back. He told *Teen Mag* he was excited at first to change his look but after the first day of filming he was through with it. He says it was really itchy and "it was always getting in my face. I'd be trying to eat lunch and it's in my mouth and, yeah, even when were filming the scenes and I'm talking and it's in my mouth and agh! It was quite the adventure with the wig."[11]

As soon as he finished filming the movie, he prepared to begin work on the NBC series *My Own Worst Enemy,* in which he played the son of series star Christian Slater. But the series was canceled after just seven episodes, which in hindsight turned out to be a blessing for Taylor.

"Nobody knew what *Twilight* was going to be—nobody," he said in a *New York Daily News* interview. "We thought we were making it just for passionate fans of the book. People just kept telling us, *Oh, yeah, the movie is going to do so good.*

And we were like, *All right, whatever. We'll see.* But when the movie came out, I was just blown away. That's when I realized, *Boy, what am I getting myself into?*"[12]

Most of the reviews were similar to the following from *Salon*: "The movie hits one of its most exhilarating beats when Bella, in voice-over, utters the movie's thesis statement: 'About three things I was absolutely positive. First, Edward was a vampire. Second, there was a part of him—and I didn't know how dominant that part might be—that thirsted for my blood. And third, I was unconditionally and irrevocably in love with him.' *Twilight* is, by its very nature, all about unfinished business, the story of a brooding, caring romantic hero and the woman who cannot—although she wants to—yield to him. Only his eyes penetrate her. For now, that's enough."[13]

If Taylor was mentioned at all, it was in passing. Even so, just to be associated with a hit movie was a good position to be in. Just prior to the movie's premier, Taylor told *Teen Mag* that he was looking forward to playing Jacob again. "If there happen to be sequels, I really like Jacob's character when he's serious, because he gets so different. He almost has a split personality. When he is his normal self he's that happiest, friendly kind of guy, and then when he's a werewolf he's all intense and grumpy and so I look forward to that, as an actor, challenging myself to be able to show those two sides. And also the motorcycle scenes, they would be fun."[14]

When *Twilight* was released in November 2008, it made instant stars out of Pattinson and Stewart. Although it's hard to imagine now, the *Twilight* producers considered recasting the role of Jacob, thinking that Taylor's then-slender physicality didn't fit with the transformation Jacob undergoes between the first and second book when Jacob discovers he's a werewolf and matures into a strapping man-wolf. Rather than fire him outright, the studio informed Taylor he would have to audition, again, for the role.

Despite some initial insecurity, Taylor rose to the challenge. He hired a personal trainer and read self-realization books by Tony Robbins to get a positive mindset. "I'm just saying to myself, *I want this role. I love this role. I'm not gonna lose it. And I'm gonna know it better than anybody, and I'm gonna do that extra rep, because I'm gonna be Jacob Black.*"[15]

Lautner told *Interview* he was in the gym five days a week, two hours a day. "At one point, I was going seven days straight. I had put on a lot of weight, and then I started losing it drastically . . . It turned out I was overworking myself. My trainer told me that I couldn't break a sweat, because I was burning more calories than I was putting on. The hardest thing for me was the eating. At one point I had to shove as much food in my body as possible to pack on calories. My trainer wanted me to do six meals a day and not go two hours without eating. If I would cheat on eating one day, I could tell—I'd drop a few pounds."[16]

In order to pack on muscle, he ate a high-protein diet, consuming meals every two hours. The result was 30 extra pounds of near pure muscle. He did a screen test with Stewart, who was very vocal in her support of Taylor, and was recast as Jacob. The actress says he literally became a different person because he had grown up. She called him one of the nicest guys she has ever met.

By the time the sequel began filming in the summer of 2009, Taylor had tested out of school and no longer needed to be tutored on the set. He and the actors playing the werewolves hung out together to develop camaraderie. Unlike Stewart and Pattinson, Taylor had not personally been subjected to either stalking fans or intrusive media coverage, so going into *New Moon,* he was just as enthusiastic, and open, as he had been before *Twilight.* And his experience with fans was more even keeled.

> What I've found is all *Twilight* fans are the same anywhere you go. I've been all over the world in Australia, Japan . . . and everybody asks me, *Which ones are better which ones are more passionate?* and I can't answer. They are all the same: very passionate dedicated fans everywhere you go.[17]

Playing both man and wolf created some interesting mental jumps, Taylor admitted to *Fansite Friday.* "Sometimes you will film a pre-transformation Jacob and a post-transformation Jacob on the same exact day. So you do have to click over, but it's really cool because it's challenging and I like challenging myself as an actor. So I just hope I can bring both sides of Jacob alive for all the fans."[18]

More challenging, he said, was Vancouver's Pacific northwest weather. "It's actually starting to warm up now and it's a lot nicer than it was at first, but when we got up here towards the end of March it's snowing and I was like when is this gonna stop! And obviously I'm not wearing that much clothing for most of the film so that doesn't help either, but the weather is definitely starting to warm up now so that's nice."[19]

Whereas *Twilight* was all about Bella and Edward, *New Moon* was all about Bella, Edward, and Jacob. Taylor was featured prominently on the movie poster and the pre-release hype put him firmly in the media—and fans—crosshairs. The attention brought out the protectiveness of his parents. His father told the *Grand Rapids Press,* "Because of all that's happening for him, we want him to do normal things. We kept him in public school as long as we could, so he could be with his peers. We give him responsibilities at home—chores he has to do. He gets an allotted allowance and he has to budget it. We're trying to teach him things, so that when he goes out on his own, he'll be prepared."[20]

But for Taylor, his attention was on the work and bringing Jacob alive on film. He told *Box Office,* "I love Jacob and Bella's relationship. It's very different from Edward and Bella's. Jacob and Bella start off as really good friends. They become best friends—they can tell each other anything, they do whatever together, ride motorcycles. I love that. And then their relationship starts growing into more and more, and you wonder if they're going to go past friends. I love being able to do that. And work with an amazing actress, Kristen Stewart."[21]

He also enjoyed the physical transformation Jacob goes through. "Pre-transformation, the books describe Jacob as clumsy; as soon as he transforms, he's all of a sudden extremely agile. There are several scenes that show his new agility, so that was the biggest thing I had to bring out."[22]

Prior to reporting for work on *Eclipse,* Taylor costarred in a romantic comedy called *Valentine's Day,* playing Taylor Swift's love interest, a role written specifically for him. Taylor recounted a telling anecdote to *GQ* about one scene in the movie. "Originally I was supposed to take off my shirt. The script said we were walking into school and Willy takes off his shirt. I said, *Whoa, whoa, whoa. Time out. He's gonna take off his shirt in the middle of school? No, no, no.* The reason I took off my shirt for *New Moon* is because it's written in the book that way, and there's reasons behind it."[23]

Although there was speculation that the two Taylors were a couple offscreen, both maintained that they were just friends. Taylor has joked that his father forbid him to date until he was 28 but more seriously, amidst the *New Moon* frenzy, said he was too busy for a girlfriend—although he wasn't without experience. He recounted to *Seventeen* magazine his first kiss.

"It was sometime in junior high. I don't remember what year, but it was definitely in junior high with a girl from school, and we had a little thing in junior high."[24]

But he admitted to being shy at times. "I guess it just depends on the girl. Sometimes I'll feel free to completely open up, and I wish I could do that more often because that's what I look for in a girl. Someone that can open up and be herself." What he shies away from, he added, was "if a girl doesn't know how to smile or laugh or if they try to play cool all the time. Playing hard to get is not the way to win me over. I'm definitely more for the girl who can smile and laugh all the time and just have a good time."[25]

By the time *Twilight: Eclipse* was released in June 2010, Taylor's popularity arguably had equaled, if not surpassed, Pattinson's, among fans. More significantly for movie producers, Taylor was a talented actor who also had action-star potential; a thinking man's action star a la Matt Damon in the *Bourne* movies— something Taylor admits would be a dream scenario.

In the summer of 2010 that dream came true when he filmed *Abduction,* a thriller about a teen who discovers he was kidnapped as a child the same day his parents are killed. When he tries to track down his real parents, he finds his life is endangered. It was reported that Lautner has also signed a $7.5 million contract to star as superhero Stretch Armstrong, making him the highest-paid teen film actor in Hollywood.

But before he goes into superhero mode, he will finish filming the last two *Twilight* sequels, *Breaking Dawn* parts 1 and 2.

With such a busy schedule Taylor is constantly on the go. He is aware of the increased media scrutiny but largely tries to ignore it. "There's some things you just have to live with," he told *GQ.* "Like twelve cars camping outside your house, and when you wake up in the morning, they're going to follow you wherever you go." But by and large, he says, his real life hasn't changed that much. "The thing I love is that my home life hasn't changed. I still help out with the garbage. I still help out with the lawn."[26]

For all the traveling he's done to promote the *Twilight* films, Taylor expressed some frustration to *GQ* that time demands prevent him from playing tourist. "It's a tease, is what it is. You show up in Paris, and on the drive from the airport to the hotel you're like, *This is so cool! I want to see something! I want to go to the Eiffel Tower!* And then you leave the next morning. You think, *Oh, I didn't get to do anything.* I tell people: *I've been just about everywhere, but I've seen nothing.*"[27]

But he's really not complaining. Taylor goes out of his way to self-deprecatingly acknowledge his good fortune. "This could have happened to anybody who played Jacob," he told the *New York Daily News*. "I was just lucky enough to be the one that has the opportunity. I'm so grateful. It's *Twilight*. It's not me personally."[28]

NOTES

1. Terri Finch Hamilton. "Profile: Actor, Teen Heartthrob Taylor Lautner Is in the 'Twilight' Zone," *The Grand Rapids Press*, October 12, 2008, http://www.mlive.com/living/grand-rapids/index.ssf/2008/10/profile_actor_teen_heartthrob.html.

2. Ibid.

3. Ibid.

4. Gina McIntyre. "New Moon Causes Strange Changes for Taylor Lautner," *Los Angeles Times*, November 18, 2009, http://www.latimes.com/entertainment/news/la-et-taylor-lautner18-2009nov18,0,7575954.story.

5. Renata Joy. "A Bite with Sharkboy," *Ultimate Disney*, http://www.ultimatedisney.com/sharkboy-interview.html.

6. Ibid.

7. "All About Taylor Lautner," http://taylorlautnerfans.multiply.com/notes/item/1.

8. Hamilton, "Profile."

9. "Taylor Lautner: I Was Bullied as a Kid," http://www.usmagazine.com/celebrity news/news/taylor-lautner-i-was-bullied-as-a-kid-20092411.

10. Hamilton, "Profile."

11. "Interview with Twilight Actor Taylor Lautner," http://www.teenmag.com/celeb-stuff/getting-to-know/interview-with-taylor-lautner.

12. "Taylor Lautner Says, 'New Moon' Is Taken up a 'Whole Other Notch'," *Daily News*, http://www.nydailynews.com/entertainment/movies/2009/08/18/2009-08-18_taylor_lautner_says_new_moon_is_taken_up_a_whole_other_notch.html.

13. Stephanie Zacharek. "Twilight Review," *Salon*, http://www.salon.com/entertainment/movies/review/2008/11/21/twilight/.

14. "Interview with Twilight Actor Taylor Lautner."

15. Mickey Rapkin. "The Big Bet," *GQ*, July 2010, http://www.gq.com/style/wear-it-now/201007/taylor-lautner-stretch-armstrong-twilight-eclipse.

16. "Taylor Lautner," Interview, http://www.interviewmagazine.com/film/taylor-lautner/print.

17. "Fansite Friday: Taylor Lautner Interview," August 28, 2009, http://www.twilight moms.com/2009/08/fansite-friday-taylor-lautner-interview/.

18. Ibid.

19. Ibid.

20. Hamilton, "Profile."

21. Amy Nicholson. "Competing for Bella," *Box Office*, September 22, 2009, http://boxoffice.com/featured_stories/2009/09/competing-for-bella.php.

22. Ibid.

23. Rapkin, "The Big Bet."

24. Audrey Fine. "Interview with Twilight Actor Taylor Lautner," *Seventeen Magazine*, http://www.seventeen.com/entertainment/features/interview-with-taylor-lautner.

25. Ibid.

26. Rapkin, "The Big Bet."

27. Ibid.

28. "Taylor Lautner Says."

FURTHER READING

"Behind the Scenes: Twilight." *Dailies Transcript,* July 22, 2008. http://www.reelzchannel. com/article/643/interview-with-twilight-star-taylor-lautner.

Bentley, Rick. "Nice Guy Finds His Inner Wolf." *McClatchy Newspapers,* November 20, 2009. www.newsobserver.com/2009/11/20/199145/nice-guy-finds-his-inner-wolf. html#ixzz0yya9mx9t.

Carroll, Larry. "*Twilight* Actor Taylor Lautner Is Eager to Deliver 'Naked' Line, Master Driving Teen Star also Discusses His Research on the Quileute Tribe to Play Native American Character Jacob Black." May 20, 2008.

Chang, Justin. "Taylor Lautner." *Daily Variety,* November 4, 2004.

"Dream-filled 'Sharkboy and Lavagirl' Whimsical but Talky" (Daily Break). *The Virgin-ian-Pilot* (Norfolk, VA). 2005. *HighBeam Research* (November 2, 2009). http://www. highbeam.com/doc/1G1–133196327.html.

"Fansite Friday: Taylor Lautner Interview." August 28, 2009. http://www.twilightlexicon. com/2009/08/28/fansite-friday-taylor-lautner-interview/.

Interview. 2009. *HighBeam Research* (November 2, 2009). http://www.highbeam.com/ doc/1G1–203603525.html.

Koday, Dan. "Get to Know Taylor Lautner." http://www.mtv.com/movies/news/articles/ 1587744/story.jhtml.

Park, Michael Y. "Kristen Stewart: Taylor Lautner Grew Up During New Moon." *Peo-ple,* November 9, 2009. http://www.people.com/people/package/article/0,20316279_ 20318492,00.html?xid=rss-topheadlines.

R. "Male Rivalry and First Love." *The Record* (Bergen County, NJ). 2005. *HighBeam Re-search* (November 2, 2009). http://www.highbeam.com/doc/1P1–116696599.html.

Roberts, Sheila. "Kristen Stewart, Taylor Lautner New Moon Interview." http://www. moviesonline.ca/movienews_17121.html.

"Taylor Lautner and Solomon Trimble Interviews." http://movies.about.com/library/ weekly/bltwilight-premiere-taylor-lautner.htm.

"Taylor Swift Talks about SNL and 'Team Jake'"(A&E). *Seattle Post-Intelligencer.* 2009. *HighBeam Research* (November 2, 2009). http://www.highbeam.com/doc/1G1–21071 6525.html.

Taylor's generosity extends beyond family and friends. In 2012, she donated $4 million to the Country Music Hall of Fame in Nashville to fund music education.

2   TAYLOR SWIFT

For most high school teenagers, graduation or going to prom is the highlight of their year. Taylor Swift didn't get to go to prom when she was 17. Instead she was at the Country Music Television Awards, winning the Breakthrough Video of the Year for "Tim McGraw."

Taylor says since she wasn't going to prom that year, "I decided to turn the CMT Awards into my prom. I was so emotional when I won that award, because it's fan-voted."[1] At the time, Taylor thought she had achieved her dream and reached the pinnacle of her young career. What she never imagined is that her career was only just beginning.

CHILDHOOD DREAMS

Taylor Alison Swift was born on December 13, 1989, in Wyomissing, Pennsylvania. Her dad Scott was a financial advisor for Merrill Lynch; her mom Andrea was a homemaker. Taylor and her younger brother Austin spent a lot of time on the family's 11-acre Christmas-tree farm, located outside Reading, Pennsylvania, about an hour outside Philadelphia.

From her earliest memories, Taylor says she thought in terms of melody and rhyme. She would go to Disney movies and memorize the words to all the songs. Her grandmother, Marjorie Finlay, was an opera singer and Taylor loved listening to her sing. But her interest in music crystallized when her mom brought home LeAnn Rimes's debut album, *Blue.* Six-year-old Taylor was enthralled and became obsessed with country music.

"I started listening to female country artists nonstop: Faith Hill, Shania Twain, Dixie Chicks." She also discovered classic country stars like Patsy Cline, Loretta Lynn, and Tammy Wynette. But her first performing experiences were more Big

Apple than Music City. She played Sandy in *Grease* and Maria in *The Sound of Music* with a local children's musical-theater company. "When I was 9 or 10, I used to get all the lead roles because I was the tallest person," she says, adding that her singing naturally gravitated to country in both style and interest. "I was infatuated with the sound, with the storytelling. I could relate to it. I can't really tell you why. With me, it was just instinctual."[2]

Ambitious to the point of occasionally driving her family crazy, Taylor talked Andrea into flying to Nashville for vacation. Of course, Taylor brought along a demo CD of herself singing karaoke, sounding, she says, like a chipmunk. They rented a car and Andrea drove her to Music Row. "We would pull up in front of a label on Music Row and I'd walk in and talk to the receptionist: *Hi, I'm Taylor. I'm 11. I really want a record deal.*"[3]

Taylor says she felt no nervousness putting herself on the line. "I knew I could never feel the kind of rejection that I felt in middle school. Because in the music industry, if they're gonna say no to you, at least they're gonna be polite about it."[4]

Nobody took her direct approach seriously and Taylor left Nashville empty handed—which made her that much more determined to get a record deal. Part of her ambition was rooted in an innate love of music; part of it was an escape. Middle school had turned into a daily struggle. When she was 12, Taylor was ostracized by her clique because of her obsession with singing and country music, which other students found strange. The fact she was the tallest girl in class could not have helped, either. "They all decided they didn't want to hang out with me anymore. I would go sit at the lunch table and they'd move their trays to another table, which is not fun to go through."[5]

Andrea is blunter. "She was shunned," she recalls. "After school, I'd hear what nightmare had occurred that day, what awful thing was done to her. I'd have to pick her up off the floor."

Looking back she observes, "I wouldn't change a thing about growing up and not exactly fitting in. If I had been popular, I probably wouldn't have wanted to leave."[6]

The cruelty of her classmates had two positive consequences: she became even closer to her mom and it provided Taylor with inspiration. She had begun writing poetry in grade school, winning a poetry competition in fourth grade for a three-page poem about a monster in the closet.

"I think I fell in love with words before I fell in love with music," Taylor says. "All I wanted to do was talk and all I wanted to do was hear stories. I would drive my mom insane." Andrea concurs. "She had the potential to be exhausting.[7]

It was inevitable that Taylor would combine her love of music and passion for words. Songwriting was both a creative outlet and an escape. When she was 12, she wrote "The Outside," about the pain of being the odd girl out. "I used to sit in the back of class and watch these people and their interactions and really wish that I could be included,"[8] Swift says. Some of Swift's isolation was admittedly self-inflicted. While girls her age were starting to go out together socially, Taylor spent her weekends performing at open-mike nights. She also became the go-to girl when it came to the national anthem and estimates she has sung it literally hundreds of times.

"When I was 11, it occurred to me that this was the best way to get in front of a large group of people," she explains. "I'd sing it wherever I could—76ers games, the U.S. Open, garden-club meetings, I didn't care. I actually used to sing it for the Reading Phillies,"[9] the Phillies minor league team.

Andrea says prior to the trip to Nashville, Taylor had no interest in playing the guitar but when they got home, Taylor decided she needed to learn the guitar if she was going to be a successful singer-songwriter. She decided to learn on a 12 string, which her parents strongly discouraged, telling her she needed to wait until she was older because her fingers were too small.

"Well, that was all it took," Andrea says. "Don't ever say *never* or *can't do* to Taylor." She began practicing four hours a day during the week, six on weekends. "She would get calluses on her fingers and they would crack and bleed, and we would tape them up and she'd just keep on playing."[10]

The next time she went back to Nashville it was with a demo of her own songs and this time, people noticed. When she was 13, Taylor signed a development deal with RCA Records. At 14, she was signed as a songwriter by Sony/ATV Publishing, becoming the youngest person ever signed by the company.

It was clear that music was not a passing interest. And there was no doubt in Andrea and Scott's minds that their daughter possessed the necessary drive and ambition. So when Taylor begged her parents to move to Nashville, they knew it was more than whimsy. Even so, it was not a decision Scott and Andrea would make lightly.

First, Scott made sure that he would still be able to do his job and do it well in a new city. Andrea wanted to make sure the move wasn't solely about whether or not Taylor succeeded. "Because what a horrible thing if it hadn't happened, for her to carry that kind of guilt or pressure around . . . We've always told her that this is not about putting food on our table or making our dreams come true. There would always be an escape hatch into normal life if she decided this wasn't something she had to pursue."[11]

Taylor acknowledges her mom's balancing act. "[She] has never said to me, *Taylor, you're gonna be famous someday.* There are so many moms who tell their kids that. But my mom has always been practical. She didn't know whether I would succeed. She'd say, *If you want a chance at this, you've got to work really, really hard.*"[12]

Once the elder Swifts were comfortable with the groundwork they had laid, Andrea began looking at homes, but not in Nashville. She wanted to live far enough away from the city so Taylor had a normal home life and wasn't surrounded by people in the music business and their kids.

In the end, it was a house that sealed the move, Scott recalls. "Andrea and Taylor had been road-tripping to Nashville a lot for songwriting and recording sessions, and we realized it might make sense to move." Andrea found a place on Old Hickory Lake in Henderson, a Nashville suburb of 40,000 residents. Scott says when they stopped at the dock on the way up to check out the house, "I looked down the cove toward the lake, imagined my Sea Ray tied up there and said: *I'll take it.*" Andrea turned to him and asked, "Don't you want to see the house first?"[13]

Taylor says the water has always been part of the Swift family experience. Every year they would vacation in the New Jersey beach resort Stone Harbor. "At the age of four, I lived in a lifejacket," Taylor says. "We've always been able to establish and maintain a family atmosphere even when we're far from home, and I think all those years going to the shore helped that."[14]

Taylor was 14 when the family moved to Tennessee. In the morning she would attend Hendersonville High, where she was a straight-A student. In the afternoon Andrea would drive her to Music Row for her songwriting sessions at RCA. But when her deal came up for renewal, Taylor opted out of the contract. At issue was her insistence to sing her own songs rather than songs written by others.

Even though she had yet to cut a record, Taylor says it was her deal with Sony that was the real turning point in her career. "From that point on I was a paid songwriter," she says. "I would go in every day and write songs with some of the best songwriters in town. I met so many people through that and learned so many things so I really consider that to be my big break."[15]

A VIRAL STAR

After parting ways with RCA, Taylor continued honing her vocal skills at various venues in Nashville. After music executive Scott Borchetta saw her performance at the well-known Bluebird Café, he offered her a record deal with his brand new label. Even though Big Machine Records was then a small independent label, Taylor accepted the offer. If nothing else, she says, she knew she would get more personal attention than she would at a bigger label. Once signed, she began working on songs with Liz Rose, who she had met while at RCA.

In 2005, Swift showed Liz a song she had written during her freshman year in high school about an ex-boyfriend named Drew. "After the breakup, I wanted him to be reminded of me," Taylor says. "The key lines in the song are: 'When you think Tim McGraw/I hope you think my favorite song/The one we danced to all night long'."[16] The song she refers to is "Can't Tell Me Nothin'" from McGraw's *Live Like You Were Dying* album.

Taylor says she never expected the song to be released as a single, but Borchetta thought otherwise and decided "Tim McGraw" would be her first single. And it would be released well in advance on her CD. Taylor remembers sitting on the floor of the Big Machine Records office with her mom, helping stuff CD singles into envelopes. But instead of relying solely on radio play to promote Taylor, Borchetta used a multimedia strategy. He released the video before the single, arranged a cable special, and relied heavily on MySpace and other online social networks and sites.

Swift's manager Rick Barker says Taylor and her family were bullish about new media from the start. Even before the label suggested it, Taylor had her own website and a detailed MySpace page. The label put her music on MySpace prior to the release of her first CD to help determine which songs should go on the CD. And it was thanks to her early fans that "Our Song" made it onto the CD. It was the last song added and only because of the buzz it generated on MySpace.

"MySpace allowed us to tell the story about Taylor," Barker says. "And it really is her space. She wrote her bio, writes her blogs, and if someone gets commented back to, it's from Taylor. A lot of times, you can tell it's somebody else hired to sit there at a computer. Taylor's space is her space—that's our secret."[17]

By July 2006, "Tim McGraw" was a Top 10 hit in the country charts. But many in the Nashville establishment assumed she was yet another flash-in-the-pan teen performer. Country music promoter and veteran manager Jerry Bentley didn't think the 16-year old had much of a chance to break through. In a 2006 interview he suggested Taylor "get back in school and come back and see me when she's 18 . . . Even if she were 25, the odds would be against her. At 16, it's near impossible. You have to work 300-plus days for a couple of years, and there's no guarantee even then."[18]

When told of his comments, Taylor was unfazed and un-intimidated, saying the only thing that intimidated her was "the fear of being average . . . I didn't come in to this to be baby-sat . . . If you have a calling for it and are ready for it, more power to you. For me, the time is right."[19]

Taylor's self-titled debut CD was released on October 24, 2006. It would go on to sell more than 2.5 million copies, silencing Taylor's critics and making her the new face of country music.

SCOTT BORCHETTA

Scott Borchetta, the CEO and cofounder of Taylor's Big Machine Records label, knows what it's like to be a musician with a dream. He grew up in Southern California, where his father Mike was a promotion manager for many top labels including, RCA, Capitol, and Mercury. Scott dabbled in performing, playing in several bands before finding his talent as a record executive.

Borchetta's first job was working in the mail room of his father's independent promotion company. Then he came to Nashville on vacation—and never left. Following in his dad's professional footsteps, Scott eventually worked his way up the musical corporate ladder and landed a job at the DreamWorks label in the radio promotions department. There he helped promote the career of Toby Keith, Randy Travis, Darryl Worley, and Jimmy Wayne.

After DreamWorks merged with UMG Nashville, Scott decided to take a risk and start his own label. His philosophy is simple: he either loves a performer or he doesn't. And the ones he loves, he goes after, like Jack Ingram, who was the first artist Big Machine Records signed. Taylor was the second.

Borchetta, who races cars as a hobby, is a big believer in using the Internet to promote his artists. But ultimately, it always comes down to talent. His advice for anyone pursuing a career in music is to: "Work hard, be different, work harder, write great songs, be an individual, work even harder, have a vision . . . and stick to it. Don't look for a record label to 'anoint you a career'. Build a career and look for a partner to help you market your music."[20]

BREAKOUT YEAR

Success rarely comes easily and after the release of her CD, Taylor and Andrea hit the road, sleeping in motels or in the back of their car, crisscrossing the country on a radio promotions tour. It was exhausting but between the radio appearances, the MySpace buzz, and Big Machine Records's marketing genius, *Taylor Swift* reached number one. Borchetta decided to rerelease the CD, adding video content and additional songs.

In April 2007, Taylor won her first award: Breakthrough Video for "Tim McGraw" at the CMT Music Awards. The following month she performed "Tim McGraw," at the Academy of Country Music Awards, serenading the singer and his wife Faith Hill who were in the front row. She had never met McGraw before; so at the end of the song, Taylor held out her hand and introduced herself. McGraw and Hill were clearly charmed and they invited Taylor to be the opening act on their 2007 Soul2Soul 2007 tour.

"Our Song" was the third single from her first CD and the first to reach number one, staying on top of the charts for six weeks. Still 17, Taylor became the youngest person to solo write and sing a number-one country single. She was also the first female solo artist in country music history to write or cowrite every song on a platinum-selling debut CD.

Even though the media seemed fixated at times on Taylor's youth, she felt it was a nonissue, especially to her fans.

> I feel like it's been hyped the minimum amount that it could have possibly been hyped. When my label released my single to radio, they didn't say on any piece of press that I was 16. Of course people are going to talk about it because it is what it is. I am 17 years old . . . I don't have a problem talking about my age because it's never been used as something to get me ahead—ever.[21]

In November 2007, Taylor won the CMA Horizon award. During her acceptance speech she thanked her family for moving to Nashville and her fans for their support. Before leaving the stage, she blurted, "This is definitely the highlight of my senior year!"[22]

On December 13, 2007, Scott and Andrea threw Taylor an 18th birthday party in Nashville. Among the guests was Taylor's newest good friend, Kellie Pickler, who she calls a sister. Ironically, though, she admits that her success has not translated into a full social life. "It's weird—I thought I'd have so many more friends, but I feel like I'm less popular than I've ever been. It makes me value the people I can trust even more."[23]

She also valued her good fortune and found success more fun than overwhelming. "I wanted this, since the time I was a little girl," she says, recalling how she dreamed that people would care about the words she wrote. "I'm so lucky that my songs are basically my diary put to music. I'm so lucky that I get to write my own music and write my own stories, so every single time I look down in the audience and I see somebody singing the words back to me, it makes it all worth it."[24]

THE CMA AWARDS

The original CMA award was designed by Frank Waggoner in 1967. It was made of walnut and designed to look like a music chart "bullet." The base was made out of marble to represent the strength and durability of country music. The award stopped using walnut in 1983 in favor of glass. Today, CMA Awards use hand-blown glass from Florence, Italy. The award is 15 inches tall and weighs seven and a half pounds. A one-by-three-inch satin brass name-plate with beveled edges is added with the winner's name and the category of their win.

The Horizon award was introduced in 1981 and the first winner of the award was Terri Gibbs, best known for her song "Somebody's Knocking." Blind since birth, Gibbs would eventually leave mainstream country music in favor of her gospel music roots and signed with a Christian music label. After 1990, she retired to concentrate on raising her family.

Nor does Taylor worry about exposing so much of herself in her songs.

The one place where I'm allowed to not worry about censoring myself is my music. I don't need to edit names out of songs and I don't need to edit details out of my songs because I've always been able to be honest with my music. That's the one place where I'm never ever going to change how I do things.[25]

This is not a teenager who will end up the poster child of excess. The only kind of rebellion she's interested in is lyrically.

I rebelled against my record label [RCA] when they wanted to shelve me, and I've rebelled against people trying to push me around in the recording studio. To me, that's always been much more exciting than going out and getting drunk. I remember at high school trying to cheer up my girlfriends who were crying in the bathroom after some party when they couldn't remember who they'd made out with the night before. You see, I don't ever want to be that girl in the bathroom crying.[26]

Taylor says being on the road so much has taught her to write in any surroundings. It has also made her appreciate her family that much more, especially her brother Austin. She says as kids, they used to fight constantly but now they hang out when she's not on tour performing or promoting her music. "He's got a taste in music that's really eclectic and cool," she says. "He introduced me to Kings of Leon, things I wouldn't have ventured into. He likes Jack White . . . He plays lacrosse and goes to high school and gets good grades. He doesn't want to do music. He's the opposite [of me]."[27]

Taylor's nonstop schedule also made having a romantic life that much more challenging. But she still managed to find the time to have a relationship with Joe

Jonas in late summer of 2008, although while they were dating she kept discretely mum. However, after their breakup that October—Joe broke up with her over the phone—Taylor let her music do the talking, writing the song "Forever and Always" about the breakup. She also talked about it with Ryan Seacrest on his KIIS-FM radio show.

"It's tough and it's been tough," she admitted, at one point implying that Joe's management didn't want him going out with Taylor because it interfered with his sex symbol status. "I'm trying to shake it off. I'm not ready to jump in to anything with anybody. It wouldn't be fair to them. I'm not looking to find someone to fill a void." She also talked about what she looked for in a boyfriend. "If someone doesn't think my sense of humor is funny, that can be a wrong match." She also advises that if a guy mentions their ex-girlfriend within the first hour of conversation, odds are the relationship is not going anywhere.[28]

Taylor says for the most part, she tries to play it cool. "If he doesn't want to be with you, then let him do what he wants to do. The worst thing in the world to do is kick and scream and nag. The only time I lose my temper is in songs. I'm enthralled by relationships and I love the drama in them, but that's usually where it lives. I'm not a dramatic person."[29]

She also believes that being too concerned with how a relationship might affect one's career isn't wise. "When you strategize a relationship too much, like, *We're not gonna be public about it.* . . . when you think it all out, I think that complicates the relationship and I think that's unfair for the relationship . . . I think love happens when you're not looking for it, and when it happens, I'm not going to be the one to over-think it."[30]

Taylor's down-to-earth attitude also extends to her friends, many of whom are also performers, such as Kellie Pickler, Carrie Underwood, Selena Gomez, or Miley Cyrus. "I don't compete with other girls," she says. "I don't compete with other people in the industry, I compete with myself. If I looked at every other girl in the entertainment industry as competition, my life would be really lonely. I wouldn't have some of the coolest friends that I'm so glad I've gotten to know over the last couple of years."[31]

For the most part, Taylor accepts that her fans want to know about her personal life as a small price to pay for being able to do her music.

You know, I have a great life. I didn't think I was going to get to do this. I didn't think people were going to care who I go to dinner with and hang out with. The whole personal life thing, I look at it like I didn't expect to be in this position and every day is a bonus day. I can take that with all the good stuff that I've been given. It's not my favorite part, that people have a microscope on who I'm dating, but hey, whatever.[32]

Nor does Taylor have any desire to rush into adulthood.

I'm not sitting here thinking, *I wish I could go out for a drink tonight,* that's not where I am in my life. I'm not 18 wishing I was 25. I'm happy in this moment. I'm not trying to be older and get to do things that older people do. When that moment happens,

I'll live in that moment. But right now this moment is the best moment I've lived in my entire life.[33]

FEARLESS

Taylor's second alum, *Fearless,* was released in November 2008 at number one on the Billboard charts. In April 2009, Swift kicked off her 50-city *Fearless* tour, with Kellie Pickler as her opening act. Taylor met Kellie when they both toured with Brad Paisley in 2007. Pickler says they clicked right away and have a great time making each other laugh. They also collaborated on Pickler's hit single, "The Best Days of Your Life."

Fearless would eventually remain number one longer than any other album/CD released in the decade. It sold more than four million copies and earned Taylor Album of the Year at the Academy of Country Music Awards in April 2009. The success of her second CD established Taylor as a talent with longevity and also proved to have great crossover pop appeal, although she says her heart remains true to country. Instead of calling her Top 40 success a crossover, she refers to it as a spillover.

It seems that her success brings her new opportunities on an almost daily basis. In late 2008, she was approached to participate in the Body by Milk campaign. "I was really floored that I was offered it," Taylor says. "Anything that promotes good health is something that I believe in. Drinking milk is a priority for me."[34]

So is putting her past in perspective. Swift recalls playing a concert in her old Pennsylvania hometown and the girls who had so hurt her at the age of 12 showed up at the concert and after-show signing. "They waited for three hours in line and they had my shirts on. And I started to realize, wow, we were kids. And you know what? They don't remember it. I've kind of let that grudge go."[35]

"And really, if I hadn't come home from school miserable every day, maybe I wouldn't have been so motivated to write songs. I should probably be thanking them!"[36]

Perhaps because music had always been her passion and not the dream of stage parents, Swift is comfortable with the demands of success and expectations of fans. At the same time, she doesn't see herself being any different than she was before all the record sales—except for having a much busier schedule. When she has the time, she still goes to the mall with friends and is still flattered when people approach to say they love her music.

When asked what advice she would give to young people trying to break into the music business, Swift preaches individualism. "Never use the phrase *I sound just like* . . . Try to sound original, so you don't sound like anyone else. If you write your own songs that's good but if it's not your thing don't force it. Not everyone's able to do it."[37]

And very few are able to do it like Taylor Swift.

NOTES

1. Judith Newman. "Taylor Swift Style Timeline," *Allure,* http://www.allure.com/celebrity-trends/style-timeline/2010/taylor_swift_style#slide=1.

2. Judy Rosen. "Taylor Swift: Little Miss Perfect," March 6, 2008, http://www.blender.com/guide/61231/taylorswiftlittlemissperfect.html.

3. George Hatza. "Taylor Swift: Growing into Superstardom," *Reading Eagle,* December 8, 2008, http://readingeagle.com/article.aspx?id=116460.

4. Chris Willman. "Taylor Swift's Road to Fame," *Entertainment Weekly,* http://www.ew.com/ew/article/0,1567466_20010832_20176102_4,00.html.

5. *Katie Couric's All Access Grammy Special,* CBS, February 4, 2009.

6. Hatza, "Taylor Swift."

7. *Katie Couric's All Access Grammy Special.*

8. Hatza, "Taylor Swift."

9. Austin Scaggs. "Q&A: Taylor Swift," *Rolling Stone,* November 27, 2008, http://www.rollingstone.com/news/story/24375441/qa_taylor_swift.

10. Willman, "Taylor Swift's Road."

11. Ibid.

12. Newman, "Taylor Swift Style Timeline."

13. Randy Hess. "Ascending Country Music Star Taylor Swift First Made Waves Growing Up on Her Family's Sea Rays," January 9, 2009, http://tswiftfansite.wordpress.com/2009/01/02/ascending-country-music-star-taylor-swift-first-made-waves-growing-up-on-her-familys-sea-rays/.

14. Ibid.

15. Matthew Reynolds. "LIFE: Interview with Taylor Swift," *Inside Vandy,* February 23, 2007, http://www.insidevandy.com/drupal/node/3322.

16. Dale Kawashima. "Rising Country Star Taylor Swift Talks about Her Hit 'Tim McGraw', Her Debut Album and Her Songwriting," *Songwriter Universe Magazine,* 2007. http://www.songwriteruniverse.com/taylorswift123.htm.

17. Willman, "Taylor Swift's Road."

18. "Taylor Swift is Country's Youngest Star," Associated Press, November 21, 2006, http://encore.celebrityaccess.com/print.php?encoreId=51&articleId=19349.

19. Joe Edwards. "Teen Tackles Music World without Fear." *JSOnline,* November 27, 2006, http://www.jsonline.com/entertainment/musicandnightlife/29240899.html.

20. Dan Wunsch. "Music Row Movers & Shakers," *Nashville Music Guide,* August/September 2007 issue, http://www.nashvillemusicguide.com/nmg_040.htm.

21. CMT Awards, CBS, November 7, 2007.

22. Reynolds, "LIFE."

23. Lauren Waterman. "Swift Ascent," *teenvogue.com,* http://www.teenvogue.com/industry/coverlook/2009/01/teen-vogue-cover-girl-taylor-swift_090126.

24. "Taylor Swift Is Living Out Her Childhood Dream," Associated Press, May 27, 2009, http://www.msnbc.msn.com/id/30968285/.

25. Ibid.

26. John Preston. "How Did a Wholesome, Dolly Parton-Loving Teenager Become America's Biggest-Selling Artist in a Decade?" *The Sunday Telegraph London,* 2009, http://www.highbeam.com/doc/1P2-20181185.html.

27. Vanessa Grigoriadis. "Taylor Swift in Her Own Words," *Rolling Stone,* February 20, 2009, http://www.rollingstone.com/news/story/26233917/taylor_swift_in_her_own_words_the_worlds_new_pop_superstar_on_boys_and_breaking_into_the_bigtime?source=music_news_rssfeed.

28. Ryan Seacrest, KIIS-FM, November 5, 2008.

29. Grigoriadis, "Taylor Swift in Her Own Words."

30. Nekesa Mumbi Moody. "Taylor Swift Takes a Fearless Approach to Stardom," *Milford Daily News,* May 31, 2009.

31. "Taylor Swift: 'I Don't Compete' with Pal Miley Cyrus," May 27, 2009, http://www.usmagazine.com/news/taylor-swift-i-dont-compete-with-miley-cyrus-2009275.

32. "Our Interview with Taylor Swift," *Channel Guide Magazine,* November 2008, http://www.channelguidemag.com/articles/crossroadsTaylorSwift1108.php.

33. "11 Questions with Taylor Swift," *The Boot,* January 10, 2009, http://www.theboot.com/2009/01/10/11-questions-with-taylor-swift/.

34. "Country Super Star Taylor Swift Stays Fearless with a Little Help from Milk." *Health & Medicine Week,* 2008. HighBeam Research.

35. Grigoriadis, "Taylor Swift in Her Own Words."

36. Waterman, "Swift Ascent."

37. Kawashima, "Rising Country Star."

FURTHER READING

CMT Online. http://www.cmt.com/artists/az/swift__taylor/artist.jhtml.
MySpace. www.myspace.com/taylorswift.
Parvis, Sarah. *Taylor Swift,* Riverside, NJ: Andrews McMeel Publishing, 2009.
Ryals, Lexi. *Taylor Swift: Country's Sweetheart,* New York: Price Stern Sloan, 2008.
TaylorSwift.com.

Even though the *Twilight* films made him a global heartthrob, and introduced him to Kristen Stewart, Pattinson admits he was relieved once the movie series was finished so he could move on to other projects.

3 KRISTEN STEWART
AND ROBERT PATTINSON

Most authors develop a thick skin out of necessity. Rejection is the norm and it can takes years to get a book published, if you're lucky enough to get published at all. But for Stephenie Meyer, the writing and publishing of *Twilight* was a charmed experience from start to finish. A housewife and mother of three, Meyer dabbled in various creative endeavors, such as painting, before discovering a love of writing. She used whatever spare time she had in the day to work on her manuscript. Once she finished, she sent letters to 15 agents. Five did not reply and nine sent rejection letters but one requested to see the manuscript. A month later, Meyer had a three-book deal with Little Brown. And the *Twilight* phenomenon was about to begin.

A young-adult romance novel, *Twilight* was published in 2005 and tells the story of Isabella "Bella" Swan. She moves with her family from Phoenix, Arizona, to Forks, Washington, where she becomes infatuated with a mysterious boy in her high school named Edward Cullen. Bella eventually discovers that Edward and his family are vampires. But instead of feeding on humans, they drink animal blood to survive. Edward and Bella eventually fall in love but their relationship puts Bella's life in danger from a new vampire clan that moves into town.

Hollywood took notice and optioned *Twilight* to make a film version of the book. The success of the movie depended on the actors chosen to play Edward and Bella. Not only did Kristen Stewart and Robert Pattinson have incredible onscreen chemistry that made them overnight sensations, their offscreen relationship would also become to focus of rampant fan and media speculation.

KRISTEN STEWART'S UNCONVENTIONAL CHILDHOOD

The movie business was the Stewart family business. Kristen's father, John Stewart, is a stage manager for Fox, who has also dabbled in directing and producing. Her mother, Jules Mann-Stewart is a veteran script supervisor who was born in Australia. Kristen Jaymes Stewart was born in Colorado Springs, Colorado, on April 9, 1990, but grew up in the Woodland Hills area of Los Angeles. She attended Pinecrest School and one classmate remembers her being quiet and shy. "Kristen wasn't the most outgoing person in the class, but she had a few friends. She spent a lot of time hanging out with her brother [Cameron], who was a few years older but went to the same school."[1]

When she was eight years old, her parents got a call from an agent who had seen Kristen perform in a Christmas show at the school.

"My parents were both in the business so they were like, *We don't want to be stage moms.* My dad was . . . like, *Oh my God. I don't want my kid . . .* " Even though her parents were reluctant, Kristen remembers thinking, "Actually that might be really cool. I might want to go on a few auditions. I might work." She began going on auditions when she was eight years old. After a year of futility, she was getting ready to give up. "I was totally over it and the last audition I went to, which I didn't even want to go to, my mom said, *Well, this is the last one. You don't have to go to anymore.* And that was the first movie I got."[2]

Her first blink-and-you'll-miss-her film appearance was as an un-credited extra in the 1999 Disney release *Thirteenth Year.* In the fall of 2000, she was hired for her first speaking role in *The Safety of Objects,* an independent film based on short stories by A.M. Holmes about four families who find their lives inextricably intertwined. Kristen played Sam, the tomboyish daughter of a recently divorced, financially struggling woman. The movie, which premiered in April 2001, filmed for eight weeks in Toronto and New York City and the cast included Joshua Jackson, Glenn Close, and Patricia Clarkson as Sam's mom.

Later in 2001, Kristen was cast in her breakout role as Jodie Foster's daughter in *Panic Room*—a turn of events that was pure serendipity. Originally, Nicole Kidman was set to play Meg Altman, with Hayden Panettiere cast as her feisty, diabetic nine-year-old daughter Sarah. But a couple weeks into the shoot, Kidman had to drop out. She had hurt her knee while filming *Moulin Rouge* and was unable to do the physically demanding role of Meg. In *Panic Room,* Meg and Sarah hide in the panic room of their new house after burglars break in the first night they move in, unaware what the burglars want is hidden in the panic room.

The film's director, David Fincher, suggested the studio scrap the project outright. But the studio opted to recast the role of Meg. When Jodie Foster was eventually hired, the producers decided they needed to recast Sarah so Hayden Panettiere was out.

When Kristen was first sent the script, Kristen says she was "kind of freaked out at first," at the thought of possibly costarring with Foster. "I was like, *Oh my God that's huge! It's bigger than huge.*"[3] Her audition and her resemblance to Foster prompted producers to cast Kristen. Once on the set, though, even though she was aware that she was working with important people, she was not intimidated.

"I was an overly confident 10-year-old, I guess," she says. "But I was also kind of aware that I was just a kid and people don't expect anything from kids—you know, just know your lines and stay in focus. So if I did anything remotely good people would be really surprised and appreciative. That was kind of cool. But I like it so much better now. I like expectations."[4]

Panic Room was released in March 2002 and was a box office hit. Her performance earned Kristen a Young Artist award nomination for Leading Young Actress. The film was a turning point both professionally and personally. The film put Kristen on the Hollywood map and she was next cast opposite Dennis Quaid and Sharon Stone in *Cold Creek Manor*. It was around this time that Kristen decided to leave school and complete her education through a correspondence course.

"I had to stop going to school because I worked too much and my teachers resented me a lot," Kristen has said. "But I really love home school—independent study is for me. Kids typically make me really uncomfortable; put me in a room with 150 extras and I'm uncomfortable."[5]

Kristen also admits that she has issues with authority figures. "I can't deal with the structure. I don't like to be told what books to read." She observes that a lot of young actors "say that as a way of making excuses for not going to school, but I'm being entirely honest. I have that thirst; I just don't need anyone telling me what to do."[6]

Kristen's first starring role was in *Catch that Kid,* playing a girl with a passion for mountain climbing. One of her costars was Corbin Bleu, who would later gain fame in *High School Musical.* She earned another Young Artist award nomination for the 2004 film *Undertow.* But her next film, *Speak,* became her most critically acclaimed of her young career. Based on the novel by Laurie Halse Anderson, *Speak* tells the story of high school freshman Melinda Sordino, who becomes mute after being raped. By this time, Kristen knew she was never going to be cast as the goodie-two-shoes all-American girl.

"I was never trying to present myself in a certain way, but there was definitely this side that people picked up on. I was so rejected from anything that was comic or light or frivolous." Kristen says she was never the type to be chosen for a Nickelodeon series. "It wasn't like, *No, I'm not going to do a Nickelodeon series, I'm going to do cool things!* It was more like, Nickelodeon was totally uninterested, which ended up being fine. The people who are really good at that stuff are entertainers. I am so not that."[7]

Speak upped Kristen's Hollywood profile and was also a personal milestone. "I think my first *Aha!* moment was when I did *Speak.* I was just rolling with it, and ended up kind of really losing myself in it, so that I felt like I was a different person at the end. That was a big moment." *Speak* was notable in another way—she met costar Michael Angarano. Although just 13, Kristen and Angarano, who is three years older, began dating.[8]

Kristen continued to work steadily, balancing her career with schoolwork and growing up. While she had a lot of freedom compared to many teens, she says her parents were very hands-on. "Not that my parents are overbearing or anything but if my parents didn't know where I was at a given time, that's sort of unacceptable. And it's very easy to track you down, considering."[9]

Her next film of note was *The Messenger,* a thriller about a haunted house released in February 2007. Kristen says she loves horror movies and enjoyed working on one. "There's definitely some running and screaming in this [movie]," she says. "I love good horror movies, and I hate bad ones. Although, it's kind of fun to watch bad scary movies, though."[10]

Kristen admits she has been frightened of ghosts since a young child and had an unusual paranormal experience while shooting the film. She was in her room at the old hotel where the cast way staying. "It was insane, I opened my eyes and this image of this woman just filled my entire view. It was like I let out the most gut wrenching scream. I mean people called the hotel room to see if I was okay." The people she told assured her it was simply a reaction to working on the film. She didn't buy it. "I said *I totally get how you guys could think that I was just getting really into the movie and that this could be a reflection of what's going on in my work and [projected] onto my real life but it's not.* Objectively, it was not. I mean it's hard to explain. It was just there. It's not like I've ever had visions before. I don't see things that aren't there."[11]

Up to the beginning of 2008, despite having appeared in 16 films, Kristen remained anonymous to the public at large. That was about to change. On November 16, 2007, Summit Entertainment announced that Kristen had been cast to play Bella Swan in the movie adaptation of *Twilight.*

"It all happened very fast," she says. "I hadn't heard of the books and I read the script and loved it and auditioned for it, so it was very conventional in the way I got the part. But knowing Catherine (Hardwicke) was directing was definitely a draw, because I knew it would be a collaborative process—not forced, but found."[12]

The film began production in February 2008 and even before it finished shooting, there was a tremendous buzz among the book's fans about the chemistry between Kristen and costar Robert Pattinson.

Kirsten understands why the book *Twilight* had such invested fans. "Yeah it's definitely easy to become obsessed with it, because it has a very push and pull build. It's really easy to get into it and not be able to put it down." She was drawn to Bella because she's not what she seems at first glance. "My favorite thing about Bella is that she is supposed to fill this role of the damsel in distress, but in an odd way she sort of holds the power in the relationship. She is very sure of herself and is not afraid of the situation which is so much bigger than her. Bella and Edward have like a funny dynamic—he's a vampire and he would suck the last bit of blood out of her, yet she's completely fascinated by him."[13]

Kristen says some consider Bella a weak character because she gives up control. "But I think it takes a lot of courage to give up that control," she says. "That's what Catherine and I talked about, a lot, that Bella was strong enough to do that. It's a really striking story, because it's just so fundamental. What do we live for? And unless you're a total nihilist you have to say, *For someone else, for companionship.* And the story is about what you sacrifice for that."[14]

In the coming months, it would seem that Robert and Kristen were as drawn to each other as Bella and Edward.

BRIGHT TWILIGHT

Twilight was released November 21, 2008, and Kristen suddenly found herself the focus of intense fan and media attention. She was able to handle the notion of fame and celebrity much better than the promotional part of her job. "The craziness that everybody thinks that would be the difficult part to deal with, which is like, loads of people and stuff like that. But that's not what I've ever had a problem with, but the self-evaluation in interviews, and self-definition . . . I don't know myself very well." She also calls herself disjointed and not candid. "Just in general, my thoughts tend to come out in little spurts that don't necessarily connect. If you hang around long enough, you can find the linear path. But it will take a second. That is why these interviews never go well for me."[15]

Television talk shows are the worst for her. "I feel like I have nothing to say on those shows . . . I'm not good at the funny thing," she says. "Most people are really great on those shows. I don't have a contrived personality that [I can] just pump out [for] a five-minute segment, so I end up sitting there and looking kind of baffled. Embarrassing."[16]

The *Twilight* phenomenon put a crimp in Kristen's independent study and finishing her last year of high school. "It's been a bit of a rough road. I'm entirely self-indulgent and I put things off so I just took a little longer." As for any future educational plans. She says, "I've grown up saying yes I'm going to get to an Ivy League college. I definitely have a future in academics, it's just not a really conventional one. I don't know what happened but I'm going to do my own thing for a while."[17]

For the most part, Kristen remained a chameleon and despite the popularity of the film she was rarely recognized in public. "I go completely 100 per cent unnoticed in LA," she says, adding that her daily life has been largely unaffected by her new-found fame. "Nothing is really changing. I have had a consistent working life. I go from movie to movie. That may sound like a lot, but I only ever do things because I need to do them. And nothing is changing."[18]

That wasn't totally true—there was a sudden interest in her love life. For months fans and the media speculated whether Kristen and her costar Pattinson were an offscreen couple as well. At times, Kristen seemed to acknowledge there was more than just friendship between them, such as when she admitted he had proposed to her. On most other occasions, she denied they were having an affair and reaffirmed Michael Angarano was her boyfriend.

"I've acquired a good buddy and that's a big deal, but I haven't left my boyfriend for Robert Pattinson!"[19]

In August 2009, *People* ran a report indicating that Robert and Kristen had been out in the town in Hollywood and apparently spent the night together at the Chateau Marmonte. Other reports have commented on the noticeable absence of Angarano recently, but in the end, until Kristen or Robert talk publicly, the actual status of their involvement remains a mystery and may remain so.

She will appear in the *Twilight* sequels, *New Moon* and *Eclipse,* and stars as Joan Jett in the film *Runaways,* all the while trying not to let success interfere with life.

> This weird thing happens when you're in a movie that has some level of success. People start offering you all kinds of things, and they just expect you to do them because they'll be good for your career. It's not about the project's integrity or anything like that. It's about raising your profile and all that crap.[20]

She says she took a trip to Botswana, Africa, because "I wanted to learn something about the world. I just feel really ignorant whenever I leave the country. I don't know a lot of stuff, and I really want to. I figure that traveling is a good way to start if you want knowledge."[21]

As for her own future, Kristen is taking it one day at a time. "When I was younger, I worked really hard in school to give myself options, and I've literally taken those options and thrown them down the toilet—purposely. It's what I want. I want to keep doing what I'm doing."[22]

Kristen says people constantly ask her what she does for fun when she's not working. But to her, acting isn't just a job. "All it is, is self-reflection. I'm not going to school because I can't take the structure of it, but I'm not going to stop learning."[23]

SOULFUL BRIT—ROBERT PATTINSON

Some people are born beautiful; others grow into it. Then there are those who look in the mirror and simply cannot understand what all the fuzz is over. Robert Pattinson definitely falls into the latter category. When asked if he appreciates his attractiveness, he sounds genuinely flustered.

"Good-looking? Noooo," he says, admitting the pressure of expectations sometimes get to him. "Before I have to go out to face a crowd, I stare and stare at myself in the mirror until I have to tell myself to stop staring, since there's nothing I can do."[24]

Such a self-deprecating assessment finds its roots in Pattinson's upbringing. Born on May 13, 1986, Robert Thomas Pattinson was the youngest of three children and the only boy. Robert and his two older sisters, Lizzie and Victoria, grew up in Barnes, a comfortable London suburb located on the River Thames. Their father Richard was a vintage car importer and their mother Clare worked as a booker for a modeling agency.

Like many youngest children, he endured the whimsy of his older siblings. Up to the time he was 12, Elizabeth (Lizzie) and Victoria—two and four years older, respectively—would dress him up in girls' clothes to become "Claudia." But he discovered that embracing your feminine side could be a profitable asset for a young male model. So he stopped letting his sisters dress him up and began modeling professionally, including for Hackett, a well-known British clothing label. But his career ended after four years when puberty kicked in full force.

> When I first started I was quite tall and looked like a girl, so I got lots of jobs, because it was during that period where the androgynous look was cool. Then, I guess,

I became too much of a guy, so I never got any more jobs. I had the most unsuccessful modeling career.[25]

Pattinson's academic career was equally unimpressive. He began attending the all-boys Tower House Preparatory School in London when he was six. "I was quite bad," he admits. "I never ever did my homework. I always turned up for lessons as I liked my teachers but my report said I didn't try very hard." Life outside the classroom was not much fun, either. Robert was frequently bullied by other boys. "Someone stole my shoelaces once from my shoes," he recalls. "I still . . . never put laces in [my shoes]—it's like my trademark shoes now!"[26]

His career at Tower House ended in 1998 when he was expelled. It was a turning point; he enrolled at Harrodian, an exclusive coed school that emphasized the arts. But Pattinson didn't ever act in school; his future career was a matter of impulse and serendipity.

"My dad was in a restaurant and saw a bunch of pretty girls and decided to go up and ask where they had been," he recalls. "They said they went to this drama club, so he said we'd better go down too! It's the only time he's done something like that."[27] Robert and his dad went to the Barnes Theatre Company, which was located around the corner from their house, to check it out.

Robert admits that his father pushed him to be an actor. "I had never done any acting before. I really wasn't part of the acting fraternity at my school, but I joined this thing after my dad argued with me for ages. I think he had some sort of weird foresight about it."[28]

The Theatre Company put on two shows a year. Robert joined the troupe as a stage hand. "They were a very good group, and for some reason when I finished the backstage thing, I just decided to that I should try to act. So I auditioned for *Guys and Dolls* and got a little tiny part as some Cuban dancer or something and then in the next play I got the lead part, and then I got my agent. So I owe everything to that little club."[29]

Robert says the main reason he first tried acting was as a way to better meet girls. But it quickly became more than an idle pastime so when it was time to choose between pursuing a career or going to college, it was a no-brainer. "Even when I was 17 and I'd go to a student bar, I'd think, *get me out of here.* Not that I got accepted into any universities," he laughs. "Not one."[30]

Pattison says it's hard to imagine what he would have done had his dad not nudged him into joining the Theatre company. "I would have just gone to university and would have kind of just done the average thing."[31]

Without acting, Pattinson would have likely tried his luck as a musician. He plays the guitar and piano and loves making music. "That's what I wanted to do before the acting thing accidentally took off—be a musician." When he was 14, Pattinson says he fronted a rap trio, saying the group was "pretty hard-core for three private school kids from suburban London." His best friends remain musicians "and they have all got their albums and deals, and now I am acting. It is unbelievable that this stroke of luck has completely changed my entire life."[32]

Pattinson was next cast in the spring of 2003 as Rawdy Crawley in *Vanity Fair.* It was a small role and the character's scenes were cut out of the film for theatrical release, although they were put back in on the DVD. His first big screen appearance was in a 2004 German TV miniseries called *Ring of the Nibelungs*. (In Britain the film was released at *Sword of Xanten;* in the United States the DVD was released under the title *Dark Kingdom: The Dragon King*.) The film was based on the German myth *Das Nibelungenlied* that allegedly inspired Tolkien to write the *Lord of the Rings* trilogy.

Shortly before leaving for the South Africa filming location for *Nibelungs,* Pattinson was asked to audition for the role of Cedric Diggory in *Harry Potter and the Goblet of Fire.*

"I was able to get a meeting with Mike Newell and two of the casting directors the day before I left for South Africa," he says. "It was before anyone else had been seen for the other parts, so it was quite a cool position to be in. They did the rest of the casting for it afterwards. Then, the day I returned from South Africa, I got the call-back and they told me in the audition that I had got the part."[33]

Before filming began on *Harry Potter,* Robert took his final exams and graduated from high school, officially ending his formal education. His professional schooling, however, had just begun.

Pattinson says the Triwizard Tournament scenes were the most fun to shoot and also the most physically intense, especially the swimming scenes that were shot in a 60-feet-deep blue-screen tank. The scenes required the actors to hold their breath for long periods of time. "We would do a 30-second take and I couldn't let bubbles come out of my mouth because I am supposed to be able to breathe underwater in the movie," he explains. "It was strange to be underwater. It is really nice, but you can't breathe. There were divers with breathing equipment . . . You just get this breather put into your mouth after the take has been done."[34]

Not only was the *Harry Potter* production was huge, with thousands of extras, crew, and actors, Pattison was also working with well known, established actors. He admits to worrying about how he'd be received, "so I went in determined to seem like a real actor and kind of didn't speak to anyone for a while. I didn't notice the transition to being accepted, but they are all really nice people. It seems like it should have been daunting but it wasn't. We did a bonding week where we made fools of ourselves doing lots of improvising."[35]

After the extravagant nature of *Harry Potter,* Pattinson says he wanted to try something more intimate and was cast in the stage play *The Woman Before,* playing at the Royal Court Theatre. It was not the best of experiences. A review written during previews was scathing is its assessment.

"The Court has been somewhat obsessed of late with murder-mysteries which play radical games with time," said reviewer Kate Bassett. "Alas, Roland Schimmelpfennig's contribution to this genre proves a deadly evening of the keel-over-yawning variety." Although she referred to Pattinson as an "excellent newcomer," the director apparently disagreed. Robert was fired shortly before opening night and replaced with another actor.[36]

It was a minor setback. After *Goblet of Fire* was released, Pattinson turned his attention back to film and flew to Los Angeles to try and cash in on his *Potter* role by taking meetings with producers. "I like meetings there a lot," he said at the time.

"You go in, no one cares if you're a nice person or not." He also learned American culture had quite different sensibilities. "In England if you want to look rough, you go out and get really drunk and come in looking really hung-over. But if you do that in America, it's like, *Have you got a drinking problem?*"[37]

His performance in *Goblet of Fire* had British critics dubbing him the next Jude Law. *The Times* named him 2005's British Star of Tomorrow. The honor prompted an outpouring of praise, even from his old educators, who seemed to engage in some revisionist history. Caroline Booth, Tower School secretary, told the *Evening Standard* newspaper that Robert "was an absolutely lovely boy, everyone adored him. We have lots of lovely boys here but he was something special. He was very pretty, beautiful and blond." She acknowledged that "he wasn't a particularly academic child but he always loved drama . . . I wouldn't say he was a star but he was very keen on our drama club, I do remember that. We're all so pleased that he's found something he really shines at."[38]

Harry Potter was Pattinson's first big break and over the next two and a half years he appeared in six films, including *Little Ashes,* playing the young Salvador Dali. Pattinson was enjoying the work and happily single. "If somebody asks me out on a date, I go out with them! But I never get asked. And I never know how to ask other people. I'm not good at the whole 'dinner' thing. I'm a bit of a loner . . . I'm boring. I stay home, watch TV and eat a lot of fast food."[39] He also comments that, "The stuff I find attractive in women, I always regret finding attractive. I always like a kind of madness in a woman, and when they are really, really strong. And they're the worst—mental, strong women!" He laughs. "But I like it when they hate me right from the beginning."[40]

After his next film role, that would not be an issue—which became an issue unto itself for Pattinson.

RELUCTANT IDOL

Before getting the script for *Twilight,* Pattinson had not read the book trilogy. After spending the weekend reading them, he knew he was completely wrong for the role and claims he was embarrassed walking into the room. "I had no idea how to play Edward at all," he says. "I thought that even going into the audition was completely pointless, because they were just going to cast a model or something. I felt it was kind of arrogant of me to even go in. I was almost having a full-on panic attack before I went to the screen test."[41] Pattinson did not see himself as the perfect being Edward is described being, witty and beautiful.

His confidence didn't improve after being hired opposite Kristen Stewart because fans of the book were appalled at his casting. He recalls how 75,000 people signed a petition against him, using a still photograph from *Sword of Xanten* to emphasize their point. "I looked like somebody beat me in the face," he says. "I was wearing this disgusting wig, and they were like, *This is Edward* . . . that was my welcome into Twilight."[42]

Pattinson spent two months preparing for the role by obsessing over it and trying to find the essence of the character and his involvement with Bella. "It took me ages to think of it, but it ended up being really simple: if you are in love with someone, you can't see any flaw in the other person. So I finally figured out that I didn't have to play the most beautiful man on the planet, but just play a man in love."[43]

It worked. *Twilight* became an international hit, propelling Pattinson and costar Stewart into overnight stardom. Pattinson still isn't convinced he personally won over fans. "I still believe the initial reaction when I got cast was the true reaction," he says. "And now, everyone's like, *OK, I just love the book so much, I'll just let him go with it. . . . OK, he's beautiful!*" In fact, he'd prefer it if more fans still hates him. "You get little girls like, *I want to have your babies!* It's like, seriously— *I* don't even want to have my babies."[44]

Pattinson says that having gone through the *Harry Potter* experience helped him deal with the attention generated by *Twilight* by "having it being the hot thing for a few months and then it just going and no one giving a shit. It helps. It helps once you get used to it and know that no one will care. Once you're immune to failure it's like nothing matters."[45]

Unlike Kristen Stewart, Pattinson seems more affected by the loss of anonymity. He no longer plays music in public with friends because there's too much pressure not to mess up. He worries about his personal safety from unstable or overly enthusiastic fans and hired personal bodyguards to protect him while filming *Remember Me* in New York during June 2009. He also frets over how fame is affecting those around him. "I'm always really worried about ruining their lives," he admits, "especially with people that aren't famous. It's such a massive change. I'm kind of a paranoid wreck."[46]

ROBERT PATTINSON'S MUSIC

Starring in *Twilight* not only put his acting career into hyperdrive, it gave Pattinson a chance to show the world his musical skills. He sings two songs on the official soundtrack: "Let Me Sign," and "Never Think," which Robert cowrote with his longtime friend Sam Bradley, who he says taught him to play guitar. But the actor insists none of it was his idea. He says an unknown person gave the film's director, Catherine Hardwicke, a CD of him singing the songs. Pattinson was shocked when he saw a cut of the film and heard his music. "They're old songs, but one of them specifically . . . this little song with acoustic guitar . . . really made the scene better. It was like it was supposed to be there," instead of the orchestral film climax originally planned. "I'm singing it, maybe that makes it different, but it's kind of overwhelming. I hope it's overwhelming."[47]

Pattinson was worried people would think he was trying to cash in on his *Twilight* association to launch a second career. While music may remain plan B should his acting career tank, he says for the time being, "I'm not going to be doing any music videos or anything." But, he admits, the best part was that getting the songs into the movie "helped my friends."[48]

STEWART'S DREAM JOB

After finishing *New Moon* Kristen started filming what she has called her dream job—portraying Joan Jett in *The Runaways*. The movie tells the story of the famed group through the eyes of Jett and lead singer Cherie Currie (played by Dakota Fanning), beginning with their overnight success as teenagers to the band's breakup. Jett is on board as executive producer.

Prior to the start of filming, Stewart admitted portraying the iconic rocker was a bit stressful. "It's one of the most immense responsibilities to play a real person. Her story's important. It's an incredibly triumphant feminist story really."[49] Kristen first met Jett during the Christmas holidays in 2008 and the two became friends. Jett is also on the set every day.

"Thank God," explains Kristen. "It's not about seeking approval. It's just having her energy . . . This was the most important time of her life . . . She says the most ridiculous things to me, like, *Yeah, well, that's what it feels like to peak at 16.* I'm like, *You think you peaked at 16?* But in her mind that just tells me how important this part of her life was and how important the band was."[50]

For the part, Kristen dyed her hair black and cut it into a 1970s style mullet. "I'm trying to just make myself aware of the time period and what [Joan] was going through," she says. "I'm listening to her music all the time." Jett has also tutored Kristen on her vocal and guitar skills. "She sounded great and played well," Jett said of Stewart's guitar skills. "She has the passion for it, which you can't really be taught."[51]

Pattinson is stressed at having to continually deny there is or was a romance between him and Stewart, saying that the intensity of their roles has made them exceptionally close, which is being misinterpreted. He says that despite what any paper has written, he's not seriously involved with anyone.

As for his future, he's not looking too far ahead. He finished filming the first *Twilight* sequel, *New Moon* in early 2009, with the third film scheduled for a 2010 release. Pattinson notes that it's necessary to shoot the movies quickly "because I already look about three years older than I did then. So they can't wait too long, unless they recast me."[52]

The success of *Twilight* has given Pattinson the financial freedom to work on movie projects of his choice, or to leave it all behind and reinvent himself. One gets the sense that Pattison is still adjusting to the turn his life has taken and still feels like an observer watching what has happened to him from a distance. "Luck is what got me here," he says, "nothing else."[53]

NOTES

1. "Long-Lost Photos: Kristen Stewart's Rising Star!" http://www.radaronline.com/exclusives/2009/07/long-lost-photos-kristen-stewarts-rising-star.

2. Sheila Roberts. "Kristen Stewart Interview: The Messengers." *Movies Online,* http://www.moviesonline.ca/movienews_11136.html.

3. "Kristen Stewart: A Rising Star," *Portrait Magazine,* http://www.portraitmagazine. net/archives/kristenstewart.html.

4. Stephen Whitty. "At 19, Kristen Stewart Keeps Growing into Bigger Roles," *The Star-Ledger,* April 2, 2009.

5. "She Totally Missed the Twilight Frenzy," http://www.hollywood.com/feature/ Interview_Twilight_Kristen_Stewart/5350008.

6. "Kristen Stewart Isn't Famous in Los Angeles," December 18, 2008, reprint from CelebrityMania.com. http://www.zimbio.com/Kristen+Stewart/articles/29/Kristen+Stewart +Isn+t+Famous+Los+Angeles.

7. Whitty, "At 19, Kristen Stewart."

8. Ibid.

9. Anthony Breznican. "Kristen Stewart: Some People Think They Know Her, but . . ." *USA Today,* March 31, 2009, http://www.usatoday.com/life/movies/news/2009-03-31-kris ten-stewart_N.htm.

10. "Kristen Stewart."

11. Roberts, "Kristen Stewart Interview."

12. Whitty, "At 19, Kristen Stewart."

13. Kristen Stewart Profile. April 2, 2009, http://www.bebo.com/Profile.jsp?Mem berId=7609313666.

14. Whitty, "At 19, Kristen Stewart."

15. Paul Fischer. "Kristen Stewart Twilight Saga New Moon Interview," Girl.com.au, http://www.girl.com.au/kristen-stewart-twilight-new-moon-interview.htm.

16 "Kristen Stewart: 'Twilight' Is a 'Psychotic Situation'," *Celebuzz,* February 23, 2009, http://www.celebuzz.com/kristen-stewart-twilight-psychotic-situation-s88251/.

17. "Kristen Stewart Delays College Dreams," November 25, 2008, http://www.celeb rity-mania.com/news/view/00007328.html.

18. "Kristen Stewart Isn't Famous."

19. "Kristen Stewart Denies Having Special Romance With Robert Pattinson," July 31, 2009, http://www.celebrity-mania.com/news/view/00009527.html.

20. Friendster (social network), http://profiles.friendster.com/109712601.

21. Ibid.

22. Kristen Stewart Biography. IMDB.com, http://www.imdb.com/name/nm0829 576/bio.

23. Talia Soghomonian. "New Moon's Kristen Stewart gets inside Bella's head," *Metro Canada,* June 11, 2009, http://www.metronews.ca/edmonton/entertainment/article/ 243937—new-moon-s-kristen-stewart-gets-inside-bella-s-head.

24. Jessica Brinton. "Fancy Man: Robert Pattinson," *The Sunday Times,* December 14, 2008, http://women.timesonline.co.uk/tol/life_and_style/women/celebrity/article5307734.ece.

25. "Rob Pattinson: 'I Like Crazy Women!" Closer, December 23, 2008, http://2. bp.blogspot.com/_sASGYLkBNCU/SUSoyfS6gII/AAAAAAAACRI/mWKQ8igUoKc/ s1600-h/ScanofCloser.jpg.

26. "Robert Pattinson Reveals His Classroom Hell," *Asian News International,* April 21, 2009. http://www.highbeam.com/doc/1G1-199275949.html.

27. Simon Cable. "Vampire Star Pattinson to Sink His Teeth into £10m a Film," *Daily Mail,* December 5, 2008, http://www.dailymail.co.uk/tvshowbiz/article-1092038/Vampire-star-Pattinson-sink-teeth-10m-film.html.

28. Marie Morreale. "Robert Pattinson as Cedric Diggory in Harry Potter and the Goblet of Fire," *Scholastic,* http://teacher.scholastic.com/scholasticnews/indepth/harry_potter_movie_iv/interviews/index.asp?article=pattinson&topic=1.

29. Ibid.

30. Brinton, "Fancy Man."

31. Morreale, "Robert Pattinson as Cedric."

32. Jessica Flint. "Twilight Mania," *Vanity Fair,* November 5, 2008, http://www.vanity fair.com/online/culture/2008/11/05/twilight-mania.html.

33. Morreale, "Robert Pattinson as Cedric."

34. Ibid.

35. Corrina J. Antrobus. "Robert Pattinson Interview," *Virgin Media,* http://www.vir ginmedia.com/movies/interviews/robertpattinson.php.

36. Kate Bassett. "Theatre: Murder without the Mystery," *The Independent on Sunday,* May 22, 2005, http://www.highbeam.com/doc/1P2-1942822.html.

37. Tom Shone. "Fresh from Charm School Robert Pattinson Steals the Show—and the Girl—as Harry Potter's Handsome Love Rival at Hogwarts," *The Sunday Telegraph London,* November 27, 2005, http://www.highbeam.com/doc/1P2-8939978.html.

38. Flora Stubbs. "The Real Story of Harry Potter Star Already Touted as the Next Jude Law." *The Evening Standard* (London, England), November 17, 2005, http://www.high beam.com/doc/1G1-138828227.html.

39. "Dragtastic: Robert Pattinson's Cross-Dressing Past," MSNBC, May 1, 2009, http://entertainment.msn.co.nz/blog.aspx?blogentryid=273879&showcomments=true.

40. "Rob Pattinson."

41. Flint, "Twilight Mania."

42. Anna Dimond. "Before the Spotlight, Twilight's Robert Pattinson Was Intimidated by 'Perfect' Role," *TVGuide.com,* November 21, 2008, http://movies.tvguide.com/Movie-News/Twilight-Robert-Pattinson-1000071.aspx.

43. Flint, "Twilight Mania."

44. Dimond, "Before the Spotlight."

45. Steve Weintraub. "Robert Pattinson Interview TWILIGHT," November 9, 2008, http://www.collider.com/entertainment/article.asp/aid/9788/cid/13/tcid/1.

46. "Robert Pattinson Speaks Up About Rumors of Him Dating Kristen Stewart," April 24, 2009, http://www.aceshowbiz.com/news/view/00023755.html.

47. "Robert Pattinson on His 'Twilight' Songs," *Los Angeles Times,* October 9, 2008, http://latimesblogs.latimes.com/herocomplex/2008/10/robert-pattin-1.html.

48. Hillary Atkin. "Exclusive Interview: Robert Pattinson," *Fandango,* November 16, 2008, http://www.fandango.com/commentator_exclusiveinterview:robertpattin son_203.

49. "Joan Jett Gives Kristen Stewart a Hard Time," StarPulse.com, June 30, 2009, http://www.starpulse.com/news/index.php/2009/06/30/joan_jett_gives_kristen_stewart_a_hard_t.

50. Fischer, "Kristen Stewart Twilight Saga."

51. "Twilight Actress Kristen Stewart Meets Joan Jett for Biopic," NME, June 17, 2009, http://www.nme.com/news/joan-jett/45422.

52. Rebecca Murray. "Interview with 'Twilight' Star Robert Pattinson," About.com Guide, http://movies.about.com/od/twilight/a/rob-pattinson.htm.

53. Brinton, "Fancy Man."

FURTHER READING

Brinton, Jessica. "Fancy man: Robert Pattinson," *The Sunday Times,* December 14, 2008. http://women.timesonline.co.uk/tol/life_and_style/women/celebrity/article5307 734.ece.

"Rob Pattinson: 'I Like Crazy Women'!" Closer, December 23, 2008. http://2.bp.blogspot. com/_sASGYLkBNCU/SUSoyfS6gII/AAAAAAAACRI/mWKQ8igUoKc/s1600-h/ ScanofCloser.jpg.

In gymnastics, few athletes compete in more than one Olympics because of the physical demands of the sport. But golden girls Shawn Johnson and Nastia Liukin decided to test that trend and decided to compete to make the 2012 Olympics gymnastics team.

4 SHAWN JOHNSON AND NASTIA LIUKIN

She's barely tall enough for her feet to reach the floor when she sits at the dinner table. But as her competitors will attest, Shawn Johnson has the heart of a giant. Whether it's a romp on *Dancing with the Stars* or in the world's most important athletic event, Johnson performs to win and in the process proved that small stature and accomplishment are not mutually exclusive.

Nastia Liukin brings artistic grace to the sport, using each apparatus as a personal palette to showcase her fluid, seemingly effortless, routines. She is the yin to Shawn's yang. Although coming from vastly different backgrounds with dissimilar personalities, they became both competitors and unlikely friends who together became America's golden girls at the Beijing Olympics.

A BUNDLE OF ENERGY

Shawn Machel Johnson was born on January 19, 1992, in Des Moines, Iowa. An only child, her parents, Dough and Teri, met and fell in love during junior high school when they met at a roller rink. Neither were especially athletically inclined—Shawn's dad is a carpenter and her mom works as an accounting clerk—so the thought they may have brought a world-class athlete into the world never occurred to them. All the Johnsons knew was that their petite daughter was a bundle of nonstop kinetic energy.

"She walked at nine months," Teri recalls, "and pretty soon she was barreling into everything in the house." According to family lore Shawn began doing pull-ups while still in her crib. So even before she was out of diapers, her parents enrolled her in a recreational class for dance when she was three years old but it didn't suit her personality. "She needed a lot of movement," Teri says. "She used to stack furniture up and jump off of it. She gets that adrenaline rush from her dad. He wrestled, played hockey and a lot of other things. He broke a lot of bones."[1]

Finally, they put her in a recreational gymnastics class and discovered the activity was a perfect fit for their fearless child. After a couple of years Teri decided it was time to find a different class and visited a newly opened facility called Chow's Gymnastics and Dance. The gym was owned and operated by Liang Qiao—he anglicized his last name to *Chow*—and his wife Liwen Zhuang. Chow and Zhuang had been teammates in the Chinese national gymnastics team in the late 1980s. Chow immigrated to America in 1991, and moved to Iowa. He learned English as an assistant coach to the University of Iowa's gymnastics team. He quit after seven years. He and Liwen settled in West Des Moines and opened a gym. They wanted to work with young gymnasts who were training. Chow felt he had spent most of his time at the collegiate level trying to get the students to unlearn improper form and other bad habits. Working with youngsters gave them the opportunity to teach proper form and techniques from the very beginning.

They opened Chow's Gymnastics and Dance Institute in 1998. The gym had been open less than two months when Teri and Shawn showed up. Chow and his wife were impressed by Shawn's enthusiasm for the sport. While her energy level may have been a headache at home, for Chow it was a window into her competitor's heart.

"She and her mom walked in and there was this six-year-old, toothless little girl with a big smiling face," he recalls. "You could just tell, that kid loves gymnastics."[2]

Likewise, Teri sensed her daughter was in good hands and was immediately comfortable with Chow and his wife. "I couldn't have hand-picked anybody better," she says. "They are just incredible people."[3]

Shawn calls them her other parents. "I definitely think something happened when I met Chow and Li," she says. "They saw something special in me. I never started gymnastics thinking I wanted to become an Olympian. It was always just my passion and my love."[4]

What appealed to both Teri and Shawn is that Chow and Zhuang guide; they don't push. "They are always making sure this is what I want to do and make sure it's me making the final decision to push myself to the next level, rather than being pushed by them or someone else."[5]

Under their tutelage Shawn's skills improved dramatically and it wasn't long before she was ready for competition. Her parents were supportive, as long as she kept a balanced life. Shawn never obsessed about her weight and did not follow any particular diet. Instead she just made a point to eat healthfully. Breakfast was yogurt and scrambled eggs, lunch was a wrap or salad with fruit, and dinner some lean meat or fish and fresh veggies.

Chow felt strongly about not overworking his students. Most elite gymnasts will be in at least 40 hours per week training. But Shawn only spent around 26—four hours on weekdays; six on Saturdays. It is probably one of the reasons she has been so injury free. It also gave her time to have a relatively normal life and school experience.

MARY LOU RETTON

It was a vault for the ages.

At the 1984 summer Olympics in Los Angeles, 16-year-old Mary Lou Retton became the nation's official sweetheart when she scored a perfect 10 on the final apparatus to become the first American woman to win a gold medal in gymnastics and the then-only American to ever win the Olympic all-around title. It would take 20 years before Retton's golden achievement was matched by another American.

Retton was born on January 24, 1968, in Fairmont, West Virginia. After watching Romanian gymnast Nadia Comăneci on television, Retton was inspired to take up gymnastics. She eventually moved to Houston to train with Bela Karolyi, who had defected from Romania. In 1983, she placed second in the U.S. Nationals but hurt her wrist and missed the World Championships. The following year she won both the Nationals and the Olympic Trials.

But six weeks before the Olympics were to start, Retton hurt her knee and underwent arthroscopic surgery. The procedure was a success and Mary Lou was able to begin training the following week. By the time the Olympics began, she was fully recovered.

The 1984 Summer Games were in Los Angeles. That year, the Soviet Union boycotted the competition, along with most of its Eastern Bloc neighbors. Romania was the notable exception and many within the gymnastic community assumed Ecaterina Szabó would take the all-around gold medal. Athletic and solid, the tomboyish Retton looked almost muscular compared to the waifish Romanians.

At the time, gymnastics used a 10-point scoring system in which 10 was a perfect score. Throughout the competition Retton and Szabó were within fractions of each others' scores. After the uneven bars and high beam, Szabó was ahead. Retton scored a perfect 10 on the floor exercise to inch that much closer. Finally, it came down to the vault. She needed to land a 10 to win the gold medal. And she did it. To prove it was no fluke, she took the second vault—and scored another perfect 10. Retton won the gold.

In the competition, which was boycotted by the Soviet Bloc nations except for Romania, Retton engaged in a close battle with Ecaterina Szabó of Romania for the all-around title, to the delight of the patriotic audience. Trailing Szabó (after bars and beam) with two events to go, Retton scored perfect 10s on floor exercise and vault to win the all-around title by just 0.05 points.

She was the first American, and the first female gymnast outside Eastern Europe, to win the Olympic all-around title. Retton also took home two silver and two bronze medals won in the individual and team competitions. Her five medals were the most won by any athlete at the 1984 Summer Games.

After the Olympics, Retton's exuberant personality made her the advertising industry's darling. She was signed to endorse a number of products and predictably became a Wheaties cover girl. She retired from competitive gymnastics in 1985 after winning her third American Cup title. But no other female gymnast has managed to capture the imagination of Americans the way Retton did. But she is ready to pass the torch.

"I don't want to be 80 years old, in my walker and having people come up and call me America's Sweetheart," she quips. "I don't think anyone wants that."[6]

"I never told her parents she will be a world champion," Chow says. "I never promised anything. Honestly, I don't think anybody can see that from 6 years old, you can say, O.K., you will be a world champion. You will be an Olympian," Chow said. "If someone says that, it's not the truth. You're supposed to have a real life. It's only a little kid you are dealing with." All he told her parents was: "She has great potential . . . she can fly real high."[7]

Chow was impressed enough to send a video of Shawn to Martha Karolyi who coordinates the U.S. women's national team. He argued that Shawn was talented enough to attend the training camp run by Martha and her husband Bela. The Karolyis are credited with training star gymnast Nadia Comăneci while they lived in Romania, and Mary Lou Retton after they defected to the United States.

Martha says the tape gave glimpses of Shawn's potential; enough for the Karolyis to invite Shawn to Houston to perform for them in person.

"That immediately made up my opinion that the coach was right: This little girl probably will continue to have success," Martha says. "It's not only the physical things that you see, but the ability to focus and concentrate, control yourself and perform under pressure. All the components, I could immediately see."[8]

Bela agreed. "I'll never forget that first training camp," he says Karolyi said. "There was a very, very lovely incident. She just spoke up: *I've been here for over an hour and I haven't seen Bela yet!* Her personality jumped in my eye. Her physical abilities are very good, but her greatest trait is her personality. She has a lovely, confident smile on her face. She is disciplined and relates to everyone."[9]

Both Karolyis believed Shawn had what it took to be a champion. It was now up to Shawn to prove them right.

A FORCE OF NATURE

Shawn's junior career began in 2005 at the U.S. Junior National Championships, where she came in 10th place. A year later, she won the event in St. Paul, Minnesota, taking home gold in four of the five events and a silver in the uneven bars. As if the day wasn't memorable enough, 1984 Olympic Champion Mary Lou Retton presented Shawn with the all-around gold medal.

"I've wanted to meet her for a long time, and to have her be the person giving me the gold was amazing," Johnson said. "This is all happening very fast."[10]

Shawn's meteoric rise to the top was a stunning turn of events and made her a four feet six, 85-pound overnight gymnastics sensation. She was also grateful—she had her name written in Chinese characters on her competition leotard in honor of her coaches. But most of all, she was America's emerging Olympic favorite. Certainly Martha Karolyi thought so.

"If you watch her floor routine, she's not breathing heavily," she says. "She turns around, and I say, *Breathe,* but she's already gone. That means she is well-prepared, and her endurance is excellent."[11]

After watching Shawn's performance, Kim Zmeskal, America's first world all-around champion in 1991 and Shawn's idol, called her "a super-fierce competitor . . . It's been really fun to watch her. It almost made me cry [when she won the

Junior Nationals]. If she stays on the same path that she is on right now, she has a super chance [to make the 2008 Olympic team.]"

Mary Lou Retton also gave Shawn her stamp of approval. "She's a little spitfire. She reminded me of 20 years ago. She's a little image of me. She's got the full package—powerful and energetic. She has that smile and everybody loves her. She's definitely going to be in Beijing."[12]

Even though Shawn trained fewer hours than an average elite gymnast, it still took up a big chunk of her time. Training also meant less time with friends at Valley Southwoods High in West Des Moines, where she was a freshman. Teri Johnson admitted she missed her daughter, "because even when she's in town, she's training." Shawn acknowledged it was hard giving up social time with friends and family. "But it's only two years until the Olympics. After that, I can have all the time I want."[13]

Her senior gymnastics career began at the 2007 U.S. National Championship in San Jose, California. Martha Karolyi predicted a strong showing for Shawn. "She is a gymnast with high skill level routines, and a gymnast who is very determined and very much able to compete at her best in any situation," Karolyi said during a pre-match interview.[14]

Despite her success as a junior, Shawn would not have necessarily been the favorite going into the competition. But two of America's best gymnasts were struggling physically. Chellsie Memmel, a former world champion, had been slow to recover from an ankle injury and had seen limited competition. Nastia Liukin, winner of the last two national titles, had also been hampered by an ankle injury. Even though her injury had dramatically cut back on her training time and she was admittedly not at 100 percent, Nastia chose to participate as an all-around competitor at the 2007 U.S. National Championships, setting up her first head-to-head competition with Shawn.

Nastia earned the highest score of the entire meet on the uneven bars and won that event for the third year in a row. She was also placed second on the balance beam. But her lack of training showed itself in the vault—traditionally her weakest event—and the floor exercise. She came in third in the all-around competition. Shawn won the U.S. all-around championship along with titles for floor routine and balance beam.

Shawn's performance couldn't have come at a better time for her. The Olympics were only a year away and the upcoming World Championships in Stuttgart, Germany would be the qualifier for the Olympics—the top two women would automatically get a spot in the national team going to Beijing.

"When I started getting into the higher levels and we talked about going elite, I started thinking I maybe could work hard enough to get there and see myself in the Olympics," Shawn said after the Nationals. "It makes me really nervous and really excited. Scared I won't be ready, but excited because I know that I could be ready and I might be going."[15]

When she wasn't training for the World Championships, Johnson spent whatever time she could spare enjoying a normal teenage life—attending Friday night football games, going to movies, and volunteering at a local animal shelter.

Gymnastics was simply one of many things she enjoyed in life. So as she prepared to compete in Stuttgart, Shawn was excited but not stressed. And it showed in her performance. She won the all-around title, along with the floor exercise gold, to secure her spot as America's leading gymnast. She became just the fourth American women to win the world title, along with Kim Zmeskal, Shannon Miller, and Chellsie Memmel.

Shawn says the enormity of her achievement didn't really hit her until she found her parents after the meet for a group hug. "They just said, 'I'm so proud of you', and, 'Enjoy every moment of it because it's real'," Shawn recalls. "I just broke down. I started crying. I couldn't stop."[16]

The Beijing Olympics were less than a year away. And while Shawn was clearly on top of her game, she would be pushed to improve even more by teammate Nastia Liukin. Their gymnastic styles could not have been more different says Bela Karolyi, who calls Shawn the "dynamic one. She is explosive, charming, and athletic." Liukin is like watching poetry. "The artistry she can create is just amazing," he says.[17]

But their personalities melded easily and the two young athletes would forge a bond of friendship and competitiveness that would follow them all the way to China.

NASTIA LIUKIN'S OLYMPIC HERITAGE

Anastasia Liukin literally has athleticism her blood. Born in Moscow on October 30, 1989, her parents were both international competitors. Her dad, Valeri, won two gold medals in gymnastics at the 1988 Olympic Summer Games in Seoul, South Korea. Her mother, Anna Kochneva, was the 1987 rhythmic gymnastics world champion. When Nastia was two and a half, her parents moved to the United States where they opened a gym.

Initially, Nastia's parents did not want their daughter to pursue gymnastics because of the physical toll such training took on the body. But as young parents they could not afford to hire a babysitter so they brought their daughter to the gym while they worked. She would sit off to the side and watch. By the time she was four years old, Nastia began imitating the gymnasts' moves. Her talent was obvious even at that age so Anna and Valeri relented and started her in formal training. She entered her first competition when she was six and from that moment her life revolved around gymnastics.

In 2002, Nastia won a silver medal in the balance beam, a bronze medal in the all-around competition, and was placed in the top five in floor exercise and uneven bars. Her performance earned Nastia an invitation to the USA Championships and, later, a spot in the junior national team. During her junior career she was the U.S. national champion twice and was undefeated in junior all-around competition for two years, from January 2003 to January 2005.

Her senior career was equally impressive. At the 2005 World Championships in Melbourne she won gold on the uneven bars and balance beam and a silver medal in the all-around competition. She won more medals than any other gymnast and secured her reputation as one of America's brightest future stars. Her accomplishments in Melbourne were especially sweet for Nastia's parents—that was the city where they first met while preparing for the 1988 Olympics.

Success in gymnastics gave Nastia the opportunity to experience life outside the training gym. She and other gymnasts, including Carly Patterson and Bart Conner, appeared in the movie *Stick It,* about a gymnast looking for personal and professional redemption. She was only on the film set a few days but it left a lasting impression and Nastia admitted that after her competition days are over she'd like to pursue acting as a full-time career. But that was a dream for the future. Gymnastics remained her focus.

In 2006, she won her fourth consecutive National Championships. She was named USAG Co-Athlete of the Year, sharing the honor with Chellsie Memmel. Her dad was named Coach of the Year.

The physical toll of training caught up to Nastia when she injured her ankle prior to the 2006 World Championships. She still competed and came in second on the uneven bars final behind Great Britain's Beth Tweddle, but the injury failed to heal; so shortly after her 17th birthday, she had surgery on her ankle and took the rest of the year off to recover. She resumed training in 2007 but suffered from ankle swelling, which limited her practice regimen. Even so, she returned to competition at the 2007 Pan American Games held in Rio de Janeiro during July, where she won silver medals for the uneven bars and balance beam.

Her uneven performances continued at the World Championships in Stuttgart, Germany. Her uneven bar scores for the team finals, a 16.375, were the highest of the entire meet. But she miscued on the balance beam dismount and opted for a safe landing with a lesser degree of difficulty. Despite this and other uncharacteristic errors by other team members, the U.S. women won the team gold with the Chinese coming in second.

In the all-around final, Liukin made another, more serious mistake, falling off the balance beam and came in fifth. In the event finals, she won a gold medal on the balance beam and silver for the uneven bars. Overall, it was a strong showing and most gymnasts would have been pleased. But Nastia held herself to a much higher standard because she had her eye on the ultimate competition: the 2008 Olympics. Since she was a little girl, her dad's Olympic medal had hung in her room so it was the first thing she saw every morning she woke up. Rather than feel intimidated or pressured, Nastia says the medal was a constant inspiration.

By early 2008 her ankle was fully healed and Nastia won the American Cup in New York City then won the all-around competition and balance beam at the Pacific Rim Championships. At the 2008 U.S. National Championships Nastia won the balance beam and, for the fourth consecutive year, the uneven bars, scoring a 17.1—the highest score ever recorded for an American gymnast since the new scoring system went into effect. No gymnast has a higher degree of difficulty in the uneven bars and Nastia's routine has a spectacular combination of changing handholds and releases. But it wasn't enough. Liukin placed second in the all-around competition behind Shawn. She also finished behind Shawn in June at the Olympic Trials but easily won a spot on the team.

With the Olympics just weeks away, Shawn Johnson had become the favorite to bring all-around gold home to America. Those closest to Nastia, though, knew better than to underestimate her competitive fire. Only one thing was sure—as friends and competitors, Nastia and Shawn would push each other to perform to the peak of their ability.

"If Shawn did not have Nastia there, and if Nastia didn't have Shawn there, neither one of them would have been so good," Karolyi said. "They also push the rest of the girls because they raise the bar so high."[18]

AMERICA'S GOLDEN GIRLS

In the months leading up to China, most of the media attention had been focused on Shawn, who exudes a more outgoing personality than the quieter Liukin. Plus, everything about Shawn screamed all-American girl next door. She never missed a chance to go shopping at the mall, was impatiently waiting to get her driver's license, and was the football team's ball girl. But to corporate America, she was the next major "brand" and companies such as Adidas and Coke were courting her.

For her 16th birthday Shawn was given a new Land Rover, donated by a local Cadillac dealer. She also filmed a commercial for Hy-Vee supermarkets.

Leave it to Teri Johnson to keep all the attention in perspective. "I'm not going to paint her to be a perfect kid," she says, "I think she's just a lover of life. She's a happy kid." Leave it to Shawn to take the pressure of being the world's best female gymnast in stride. She knew she had a bull's-eye on the back and accepted that the competition would be extra motivated to beat her. "I'm still out there to try to beat myself, basically. I'm still working to get even better. I've always loved the feeling of pressure and the nerves you get. I love the adrenaline rush," which she says helps her perform better. And when it's time to compete, Shawn says "I'm just doing it for myself."[19]

In addition to her regular training with Chow, once a month she and her trainer flew to Houston. There she took notes from Karolyi and worked alongside others hoping to make the Olympic team. Despite being competitors on the floor, the hopefuls all became friends, laying the foundation of the team bond they would need to compete on the Olympics' world stage.

Back in West Des Moines, Shawn tended to keep her gymnastics life separate from her high school life. "Public school has always been my fallback from gymnastics," she says. "I'm able to go to school during the day and have that place where I don't have to think about gymnastics all the time. It gives me another world that keeps me calm and grounded and normal. I basically have two separate lives."[20]

She also remained low key when at Chow's. Although she was the city's pride and joy, Shawn never played it up, preferring to blend in. The only time she turned it on was during competitions. And none was bigger than the Olympics.

The U.S. team, Liukin and Johnson, expected to get the most competition from the Chinese team. At the 2007 World Championships, the two teams together won 9 of 15 medals. The U.S. took the team title, beating China by 0.95 of a point.

The rivalry was ratcheted up more when before the opening ceremonies accusations surfaced that some of the Chinese gymnasts were under 14 and therefore ineligible to compete in the Olympics. The scandal simply added to the drama. The anticipated showdown was a hot ticket and every day of the women's gymnastics competition sold out immediately.

"I think we're the strongest team probably in history," Shawn said, "I don't think there'll be anyone that can beat us."[21]

For the Olympics, Shawn and Nastia were roommates. They decorated their room in Beijing together, filling it with candles and making it a cozy home away from home. At the venue, things were less comforting. Samantha Peszek was injured during warm-ups. It was evident that the turn of events rattled the Americans, who started with shaky performances but still managed to be in second place behind China after the qualification round. And that's where they would stay. The Chinese team took the gold, the United States the silver.

Then it was time for the all-around competition. During 2008, Nastia had trained twice a day to prepare. "I was physically and mentally more prepared than I have ever been in my life," she says. "I was so ready to be there and to have the best performance of my life."[22]

It was a tense, dramatic competition with Shawn, Nastia, and China's Yilin Yang battling for the gold. The first apparatus was the vault, one of Shawn's best events and Nastia's self-admitted weakest. And it held to form with Shawn scoring a scoring 15.875 while Liukin earned a 15.025.

Then the situation was reversed on the uneven bars, an event Liukin excelled in. She scored a 16.65 while Shawn's routine was given a 15.275, which dropped her to third place behind Nastia and Yang. Then on the high beam Nastia outscored her 16.125 to 16.05. The years in the gym, the training, and sacrifice all came down to the floor exercise.

Unlike the team qualifying round when she stepped out of bound during her floor routine, Liukin was controlled and scored a 15.525. Johnson needed a 16.25 to tie Liukin for the gold but it proved too high a mountain. She also scored a 15.525 to secure the silver medal. Nastia was the Olympic all-around champ. Yang took home the bronze.

If Shawn was disappointed, she hid it well. "I'm so happy seeing (Liukin) up there with the Olympic gold," she said. "It's inspiring. She deserved that medal, and she's been around a long time working for it." Shawn embraced the half full glass. "We worked our whole lives for this. To feel all the emotions we are feeling, it's been a long road. I wouldn't take anything back today." Shawn finally got a gold medal of her own a few days later when she won the balance beam, her favorite event, in the individual events.[23]

The media swarmed over the two golden girls, who once again displayed their different personalities. After a day of interviews Nastia flew back to Texas. Johnson stayed in China to shop and sightsee with her parents, attend some events, and march in the closing ceremonies. Even before the Beijing Olympics were over, Shawn confirmed her intention to try out for the 2012 Olympic team.

Liukin's plans included attending Southern Methodist University in Dallas and a post-Olympic gymnastics tour with Shawn. "I really hope that young kids will watch TV and say, *I want to be like Nastia,* or *I want to be like Shawn,* because gymnastics is such a unique sport," Nastia says. "It's a really fun sport."[24]

While Shawn never let fame go to her head, she did enjoy some of the perks. In February 2009, she was named a contestant on *Dancing with the Stars.* With partner Mark Ballas, Shawn was the youngest celebrity to appear on the show. In the closest finale in the show's history, Shawn emerged the winner.

Of course she did.

NOTES

1. Liz Clarke. "New Face of Gymnastics," *The Washington Post,* March 1, 2008, http://www.highbeam.com/doc/1P2-15425660.html.

2. Luke T. Johnson. "Buoyed by Chinese Know-how," *China Daily,* June 20, 2008, p. 14, http://www.chinadaily.com.cn/olympian/2008-06/20/content_6781099.htm.

3. Dave Krider. "Small Wonder," *Sports Illustrated,* September 6, 2006, http://sportsillustrated.cnn.com/2006/writers/dave_krider/09/06/hs.notebook/index.html.

4. Clay Latimer. "Shot of Gym Beam," *Rocky Mountain News,* August 11, 2008, http://www.highbeam.com/doc/1G1-182597350.html.

5. Johnson, "Buoyed by Chinese."

6. Diane Pucin. "Don't Call Mary Lou Retton *Sweetheart,*" *Los Angeles Times,* July 27, 2008, http://articles.latimes.com/2008/jul/27/sports/sp-olymarylou27

7. Juliet Macur. "Johnson Balances Life and Gymnastics," *New York Times,* August 4, 2008, http://www.nytimes.com/2008/08/04/sports/olympics/04johnson.html.

8. Clarke, "New Face of Gymnastics."

9. David Barron. "All Eyes on Johnson for '08," *Houston Chronicle,* August 20, 2006, Sports p. 14.

10. Rachel Blount. "U.S. Championships," *Star Tribune,* August 20, 2006, http://www.highbeam.com/doc/1G1-149864496.html.

11. Barron, "All Eyes on Johnson."

12. Krider, "Small Wonder."

13. Ibid.

14. Nancy Armour. "Des Moines Native Becomes Gymnastics' Next 'It' Girl," *Telegraph—Herald,* August 12, 2007, http://www.highbeam.com/doc/1P2-11237100.html.

15. Ibid.

16. "Johnson Snares All-Around Title," *Daily Breeze,* September 8, 2007, http://www.highbeam.com/doc/1P2-10959689.html.

17. Mark Sappenfield. "Russian Elite and America's Girl Next Door Power U.S. Gymnastics," *The Christian Science Monitor,* August 12, 2008, http://www.highbeam.com/doc/1G1-182626160.html.

18. Juliet Macur. "All-Around Appeal," *New York Times,* August 21, 2008, http://query.nytimes.com/gst/fullpage.html?res=9C05E1DF103AF932A1575BC0A96E9C8B63.

19. Clarke, "New Face of Gymnastics."

20. Latimer, "Shot of Gym Beam."

21. Ibid.

22. Nastia Liukin Website, www.nastialiukin.com.

23. Clay Latimer. "Showstopper," *Rocky Mountain News,* August 15, 2008, http://www.highbeam.com/doc/1G1-182966148.html.

24. Juliet Macur. "Liukin and Johnson Have Only Gold Medals in Common," *New York Times,* August 21, 2008, http://www.nytimes.com/2008/08/21/sports/olympics/21gymnastics.html?pagewanted=print.

The former *Wizards of Waverly Place* star once agreed to live on $1.50 a day for a week to support a United Nations Children's Fund (UNICEF) initiative to help feed children in Africa.

5 SELENA GOMEZ

Like Miley Cyrus, Selena Gomez found success as a Disney star; unlike Miley, Selena has suffered no scandals nor has she been criticized for behavior deemed inappropriate by the parents of some fans. However, although Selena openly promotes wholesomeness and is very public in her decision to wear a purity ring, she is now at the age where she is looking to make the transition to more mature teen roles and seems willing to be patient while her fans get used to seeing her in more mature roles.

Selena Marie Gomez was born in New York City on July 22, 1992. Her mom, Amanda "Mandy" Cornet, was only 16 when she gave birth. Five years later Mandy broke up with Selena's father, Ricardo Joel Gomez, and moved to Grand Prairie, Texas, outside of Dallas, to be close to her mom, who helped Mandy raise Selena.

Despite the help she got from her mom, life was a struggle for Mandy—there never seemed to be enough money and Selena remembers that they often lived paycheck to paycheck. But in the end, they always managed to be okay.

Selena says she inherited the love of acting from her mom, who was involved in community stage productions, "My mom did theater, and I loved memorizing her lines with her and watching her rehearse," she told *J-14*. "I told her that I wanted to do what she did but on television."[1]

After years of Selena's nudging, Mandy finally agreed to let her try. When Selena was 10—a very young-looking 10—a casting call went out for news kids to join the then-hugely popular PBS kids' show, *Barney & Friends,* which happened to film in the Dallas area. It seemed as if every young girl in the state showed up at the audition, making the naturally shy Selena that much more nervous.

"I remember we had to wait in this line with about 1400 other kids and I didn't know what I was doing," she told *People*. "But then when I got to the audition,

I realized it was just running lines, just like I always did with my mom. It was scary—and those situations are still scary for me—but it was fun at the same time."[2]

The producers liked Selena enough to call her back for a second audition. And then a third. Finally, she received word that she had been hired to play the character Gianna—and admits her first day of filming was like being in an alien world. She told *People*, "I didn't know what *camera right* was. I didn't know what blocking was. I learned everything from *Barney*."[3]

She also learned that not everyone would be happy about her success. "I'd miss a couple of weeks for *Barney* and then I'd go back to school and I'd deal with some jealousy," she recalled to *Discovery Girls*. "I wouldn't talk about the show unless somebody said, *How was your episode?* So not a lot of people were jealous; just this one group of girls who didn't like me."[4]

But those few girls caused Selena a lot of grief. She says they began spreading rumors about her, trying to give her a bad reputation. But rather than letting herself get drawn into the drama of it all, Selena chose to ignore it. "You can't get involved, fire back, or do anything," she explained to *J-14*. "If people say, *I heard you did this*, just say, *I'm sorry—that's not true*. At the end of the day I really ended up finding out who my true friends really were."[5]

After two years on *Barney*, producers felt Selena was getting a little too old to be romping with a big, purple dinosaur so her contract was not renewed. Or as Selena put it to *People*, "I got the boot."[6]

"A lot of people would be embarrassed to say they were on Barney," Selena commented during an *Early Show* appearance. "But I embrace the fact. I had such a wonderful time doing that show."[7]

Now that she had experienced performing, it was hard to go back to Danny Jones Middle School and leave acting behind. Although she enjoyed school, excelling in science, and playing basketball, her desire to act overshadowed everything.

While doing *Barney*, Selena began taking acting lessons at the EveryBody Fits studio that offered a variety of classes including dance, gymnastics, acting, and music. Her teacher Cathryn Sullivan is the mother of fellow kid-actor Cody Linley, so she was sensitive to Selena's ambitions. Cody and Selena became good friends and under Cathryn's tutelage, Selena was able to hone her natural performing gifts.

Selena appeared in several commercials, both local and national. In 2003, when she was 11, she was cast in her first film, playing the water park girl in *Spy Kids 3-D: Game Over*. She followed that with a role in a *Walker, Texas Ranger* made for TV movie and a TV show called *Brian Zapped*.

While she enjoyed every acting opportunity she got, Selena felt those opportunities were limited in Texas. Not long after being let go from *Barney*, Selena found out Disney Channel was hosting an open casting call in Dallas and begged her mom to take her. Once the audition was over, all Selena could do was wait.

She didn't have to wait long. Three weeks later, Disney contacted Mandy and invited Selena to Los Angeles for another audition. "They flew us out to California," Selena recalled in a *Variety* interview. "I was in this room full of executives and I was testing against girls who have done movies."[8]

Disney Channel President Gary Marsh later told *Entertainment Weekly* that while Selena's talent was still not fully developed, "she had that *It Factor.* We go into this thinking we are going to build a star; it's not thinking we are casting a role."[9]

Selena and Mandy put their faith in Disney and decided to relocate to Los Angeles—a move Selena did not take lightly. "It was hard," she admitted to *PBS Kids.* "It was a test of how badly I really wanted to pursue acting, which I did—there was no question in my mind that I wanted to come out here and do this. But it was really tough to leave my friends behind."[10]

It was around that time that her dad gave her a purity ring, no doubt a reminder not to succumb to the temptations that were sure to present themselves in Los Angeles.

Once settled, Disney had Selena appear on a number of their hit cable shows. She played Gwen on *The Suite Life of Zack and Cody'* and mean girl Mikayla on *Hannah Montana.*

While working on *The Suite Life,* Selena had to film her first onscreen—and real life—kiss with Dylan Sprouse, who plays Zack.

She recounted the awkward moment in *Twist.* "I actually leaned in to kiss him and I had my eyes closed a little too early and I ended up missing like half of his lips. So it ended up being the most awkward kiss in the world. But I was twelve, so it was okay and it was good. Thank goodness he is such an awesome guy!"[11]

For many young people, moving to a new city, especially one as large as Los Angeles, could be a lonely experience. But not only did Selena have her mom, it just so happened that her best friend Demi Lovato was also in Los Angeles working for Disney.

"We met in line at Barney," Selena told the *Miss O & Friends* website. "We sat right in line together, it was awesome."[12] Not only did they bond working on *Barney* together, but they also shared similar dreams about leaving Texas to follow their acting hearts.

DEMI

Demetria Devonne Lovato was born on August 20, 1992, in Dallas, Texas. Demi's mom Dianna was a Dallas Cowboys cheerleader in 1983. She also pursued a career as a country singer. Demi proudly says, "I get my voice from her."[13] Performing runs in the family. Demi's sister Dallas, who is five years older, is also a singer and an actress.

Dianna divorced Demi's dad, Patrick, in 1994. Afterward, Patrick moved to New Mexico so Demi rarely saw him as she was growing up. But Dianna remarried Eddie De La Garza in 1995. Demi is close to her stepfather and says they have a close-knit family, which now includes her younger sister Madison. She is proud to be multiethnic, with an Irish, Italian, and Hispanic heritage.

Demi's first performance was in kindergarten. "I knew from the second I stepped onstage. I was like, yep, this is what I want to do."[14]

Her first professional job was playing Angela on *Barney & Friends.* And while Demi enjoyed acting, music was her passion. "When I was around eight, my mom came to me with the idea of songwriting. So I always had it in the back of my head but it never came out of me until about the 7th grade."[15] But once she started, Demi said she couldn't stop.

"Since then I've written probably around like 200 to 300 songs. It's kind of like therapy for me. It is what I do in my spare time and I can't live without it. I have my mom to thank for that."[16]

Her musical talent would eventually make her a star. But first, Demi would suffer through some hard times. After leaving *Barney,* Demi's career stalled. Audition after audition ended in disappointment. Even worse, Demi started getting bullied at school. "I went through a really hard time," she admits. "I blamed it on myself at the time, but looking back I guess it was out of jealousy."[17]

The taunting caused Demi to lose her self-confidence. "I'd gone through so much rejection at that point with girls at school that I couldn't do acting anymore, where all I was doing was working hard and hearing *no.*"[18] Tired of the rejection, Demi decided to quit for a while. She also left the school and started home schooling.

But quitting performing for a while ended up being a blessing. "I started missing it." Demi was surprised to realize she missed acting just as much as singing. "I always thought that music was my No. 1 passion. But when I quit I realized that I have a true passion for acting, and that's when I picked it back up again."[19]

Once she started auditioning again, "things starting rolling. I think that's because there was a new drive in it, there was more passion than there was before."[20]

In 2006, Demi appeared in the FOX series *Prison Break* and on an episode of *Just Jordan* on Nickelodeon. Then in early 2007, she auditioned for a new Disney Channel series called *As the Bell Rings.* Demi admits the thought of being on the Disney Channel freaked her out. "I went to my acting coach, I was crying. I said, 'I'm not funny. I just can't do it'. I never thought that I would be funny enough to be on Disney Channel."[21]

She thought wrong. Demi was cast as Charlotte Adams. The series premiered on August 26, 2007. She only appeared in eight episodes but her talent caught the attention of Disney executives who signed Demi to a contract. Now both she and Selena were Disney girls.

WIZARDS

In 2006, Mandy married Brian Teefey. In an interview with the *Daily Mail* newspaper, Selena Gomez said that it is thanks to her parents that she is down-to-earth: "Living with my mom and Brian helps me to be down-to-earth and to keep things real. I consult them about everything I do, especially because my mom is my manager. She's someone who loves me and wants the best for me. So even though I'm living this life and have been given such wonderful opportunities, I still have my parents with me to tell me no."[22]

"There are a ton of yes-people in this town," Mandy explained to *People,* "so it is my place to say no and remind her she is not owed anything."[23]

In 2007, just as Demi's career with Disney was taking off, Selena was cast as Alex, a teenage tomboy witch on *Wizards of Waverly Place,* set in New York's Greenwich Village.

A show that was no doubt inspired by the popularity of *Harry Potter,* the live-action sitcom centers on the Italian-Mexican Russo family, which includes Alex and her brothers Justin and Max (David Henrie and Jake T. Austin). The three siblings are wizards-in-training and live with their father, a former wizard, and their mortal mom Theresa. Alex's best friend is Harper, played by Jennifer Stone, the only other mortal who knows the family secret—when the siblings become adults, there will be a wizard competition to decide who will become the family wizard of their generation. They winner keeps their powers forever while the other two will lose their powers and become mortal.

Being an only child, Selena immediately bonded with her TV siblings. "They basically *are* my brothers; they're my real family," she told *PBS Kids* in 2007. "My mom laughs at me all the time because we're constantly in touch with one another off the set, we're always calling. They're always there for me, and it is torture when I can't see them every day. We do fight like brothers and sisters sometimes, but mostly we play around and joke around."[24] David and Jake take their surrogate brother roles so seriously that they insist on approving who Selena dates.

Jake also taught Selena how to surf. She admits the ocean scared her initially but after riding her first wave, it became addictive.

In addition to giving Selena a place to showcase her comedic abilities, *Wizards* also gave her the chance to pursue her musical skills. She sang the show's theme song, "Everything Is Not What It Seems"; she also signed with Disney's Holly-wood Records label in 2008 and began contributing to several soundtrack albums. The appeal of music for Selena is that she says she can be more of herself and have more control over the finished product. Plus, in the recording studio she doesn't have to constantly worry about how she's looking on camera.

Her dream, though, isn't to be a solo artist. "I've always said that I wanted to be in a band, so hopefully when I start my music I'll be in a band, not just solo," she explained to PBS. "It's different from what any other Disney Channel star has done so far, and I like having people with me to lean on, and people to write with and have fun with."[25]

Demi, on the other hand, has dreamed of being a pop star since she was a kid and so it was fitting that in early 2008 Demi was cast as Mitchie Torres in *Camp Rock* because her costars were the Jonas Brothers. The movie premiered on June 28, 2008, and suddenly Demi was a star.

After the movie aired, Demi says her life became a whirlwind. "It actually started to change doing press for the movie. Right after that, I started working on my album. Right after *that,* I started touring."

She first went on a solo tour. When that ended, she joined the Jonas Brothers in their 2008 *Burning Up Tour.* "It's definitely been extremely intimidating to work with people who are as known as the Jonas Brothers," she admits. "But what I've learned is that the more people that you work with the more you realize they are just people."[26]

Demi, who plays guitar, piano, and drums, admits she was nervous the first time she performed in front of a huge crowd. "I was crying and scared. Selena was there with me and she was like, *You've got to pull it together.* So that was pretty funny."[27]

In September 2008, Demi released her first solo album, "Don't Forget." It sold almost 100,000 copies the first week. Looking to take advantage of both her rising popularity and her friendship with Selena, Disney cast them together in the 2009 Disney Channel movie, *Princess Protection Program.* In the movie, Gomez plays a tomboy whose family takes in Lovato's princess after a dictator invades her country. The two girls butt heads at first but eventually realize that they complement each other.

Gomez admitted to AP that while filming in Puerto Rico, Disney tried to separate the two friends putting them in different buildings. "They knew we would never get any work done because we'd spend the night and we'd stay up late and talk." The studio's plan failed miserably. "I ended up living in her room half the time."[28]

Although Selena was an older teen with a successful series, Mandy kept a close eye on her daughter. And life at home for Selena mirrored the home life of most teens. "She has to do her own laundry," Mandy reported to *People.* "If she cooks, I clean. If I cook, she cleans. She has to help feed the dogs. There are really no set chores. We just all pitch in when needed." Her curfew is 11:30 and "she never goes to movie premieres, wrap parties or anything related to the business without a parent—period," Mandy said. "That rule is not changing until she is 21!"[29]

On the other hand, Mandy trusts her daughter. "I was never really concerned about Selena. She is a very headstrong and driven girl. I really haven't changed any rules for her. If she wasn't allowed to do it in Texas, she's not allowed to do it here. Selena knows who she is, and I am around to make sure she doesn't change."[30]

DATING

On occasion, Selena's romantic life has overshadowed her professional accomplishments. She was involved with Nick Jonas and suffered through a very public breakup after he dumped her. Although she refuses to identify him by name, she has talked publicly about the experience and the lessons she learned, such as, never change for someone else.

"I wasn't myself for a year," she told *Seventeen.* "I think that was really damaging. I felt like it was me always trying to be perfect for him and I always tried to please everyone around him. I'd always go to his places and his favorite restaurants or whatever. And there was a point where I kind of lost myself completely. I didn't smile as much, I didn't laugh as much, I wasn't a goofball, I didn't get up and dance like I usually do. And when that one ended, it was just horrible because I didn't know where I was."[31]

She admits her friends tried to tell her she was making a mistake. "I didn't listen to them. I think a girl has to go through that, because now I'm the strongest I've ever been. I dare someone to try to change me again. I've gotten so strong about that. It would never happen."[32]

She says she got through it with a little help from her friends, especially Taylor Swift. "Every single problem I ever have is healable by Taylor Swift! If I ever I have an issue, Taylor has gone through it, because she's older than me, and she gives the most thought-out answers. And what I love about Taylor is that she does believe in the whole love story and Prince Charming and soul mates. Because of her, I haven't lost faith."[33]

Selena dated *Twilight*'s Taylor Lautner for a while but says they are now just good friends and maintains she is proudly single and in no rush for a serious relationship at present. However, she backtracks from once saying she'd never date an actor.

"I've also said that I wouldn't date rock stars. I've said a lot of things," she laughingly told *Seventeen*. "I'm going to say a lot of things now that I'm sure two years or even a year from now I'm not going to keep to. Of course, my passion for God and my family won't change, so hopefully I won't change who I am. But I can't say that I'll never date an actor."[34]

But she would date the most popular teen heartthrob in the world. In March 2011, Selena admitted she was romantically involved with Justin Bieber. Whereas Selena had grown up in the public eye, Justin was an overnight success, having found fame in the most unlikely of ways.

CANADIAN SENSATION

Justin Drew Bieber was born in London, Ontario, on March 1, 1994. His parents, Jeremy and Pattie, separated when he was two years old. His dad eventually moved to Winnipeg. Justin stayed with his mom and grew up in the town of Stratford, Ontario, located about an hour and a half east of Toronto.

Justin has always been musical and says he started playing the drums as a toddler. "My mom bought me my first drum kit when I was four, because I was banging on everything around the house, even couches."[35] He also taught himself to play guitar when he was six. For as much as he enjoyed music, as a young kid, Justin's ultimate dream was to be a professional hockey player.

But as time went on, music and sports became escapes from his unhappiness at school, where he was bullied, mostly because of his diminutive size. Not having many friends, he spent a lot of time playing sports or playing music.

Justin says he started getting interested in singing when he was 10, belting out everything from dance songs to ballads. His mom was a single parent so money was often tight. To help out, Justin started singing as a street performer to bring in extra money.

When Justin was 12, he entered a singing competition called Stratford Idol, performing the Matchbox Twenty song "3 A.M." He didn't win, but he came in second place.

"Some of my relatives who couldn't make it wanted to see how I did," he recalls. So Justin and his mom uploaded a video of him singing on YouTube.[36]

After a while Justin and his mom noticed that people other than his family were watching his video. "I was like, 'Well, I don't have a hundred people in my family'," Bieber says. "Then I was like, 'I don't have *500* people in my family'." But the number of views just kept going up.

Inspired, Justin made more home videos to post online. He sang songs by Usher, Ne-Yo, and Stevie Wonder. And each time he did, more and more people watched. After seven months, Justin had gotten more than 50 million views of his videos. He was a true YouTube sensation. One of the people who checked Justin out was Scott "Scooter" Braun, a former record executive turned talent manager.

Braun flew Justin and his mom to his office in Atlanta for a meeting—the first time Justin had ever been on an airplane. While in Atlanta, Braun introduced him to Usher and in October 2008 Justin signed a record deal with Usher and Island Def Jam.

Justin and his mom moved to Atlanta and he immediately began recording his first album. In May 2009, his first single, "One Time," was released. The song peaked at number 20 on Billboard's Hot 100 and the song's video was viewed more than 17 million times on YouTube.

Despite some homesickness, Justin adapted to his new life quickly and embraced the hectic life of a music star. After the release of his single, promoting his music took all his time. The worst part was appearing on radio shows located in office buildings because he is claustrophobic and scared of elevators.

Justin released three more singles on iTunes during the summer and autumn of 2009: "One Less Lonely Girl," "Love Me," and "Favorite Girl." He became the first solo artist to place four songs in Billboard's Top 40 before releasing an album. When his album, *My World,* was finally released on November 17, 2009, it debuted at number 7 on the Billboard 200 album chart.

Despite turning 15 in March 2009, Justin still looked much younger than his age. So his manager and Usher hired a special "swagger" coach to work with Justin. "He has helped me with my style and just putting different pieces together and being able to layer and stuff like that."

It obviously worked because everywhere Justin went mobs of screaming fans followed, prompting the media to dub it Bieber Fever. In early 2010, Justin said he was too busy for a girlfriend. "I've only had a couple girlfriends, and haven't gotten too serious, but I look for girls with a good personality who can make me laugh. And I like taking a girl out for dinner and buying her flowers."[37]

Or in the case of Selena Gomez, traveling the world and being photographed in the middle of endless public displays of affection. The young couple got together after Justin's manager called Selena's mom to set up a meet and greet between the two. Gomez has been mostly tightlipped about their relationship, although she admitted on the *David Letterman* show, "It's just nice to have someone that understands what you're going through."[38]

In May 2011, the couple spent a romantic vacation together on Maui, where they were photographed parasailing, jet skiing, and romping in the surf while exchanging kisses. Sparing no expense, they stayed in a $10,000 a night suite at the Four Seasons Hotel. They have also been photographed together out and about in Los Angeles and New York. Justin was also spotted accompanying Selena while she promoted the release of her 2011 movie *Monte Carlo.*

Her public relationship with Bieber and her decision to take more mature acting roles gives the perception that Selena is weaning herself away from being a "Disney kid." While appearing on *Fox & Friends* to promote her 2011 film *Monte Carlo,* Selena took issue with the suggestion she might be tarnishing her carefully constructed Disney image.

"I have a right to live my life and I feel I've done a very good job in the position I've been put in," she said. "I should be able to grow up. I have finished with Disney Channel but that doesn't mean I want to completely disown the fact I do have a younger generation looking up at me, I guess. But in a way I feel like I have done the best I can and that's how I am. If I make my family and fans proud, that's all that matters to me."[39]

Although she is surrounded by high-wattage friends, Selena says she has never felt envious of their accomplishments or competitive. "It's not normal for me to feel jealous. I'm competitive with myself more than anything. And anyway, all of my friends in the business are bigger than me! Most of them are musicians, and I think music takes them to a whole new level. For me, I'm going to try out music, but it will be more fun than anything else. I'm really trying my hardest to become a well-respected actress."[40]

After she ends her *Waverly Place* run in 2011, Selena's plan is to concentrate mostly on acting. "All I really want to do is movie after movie after movie. I love acting, and I want to create that so I can be around for a long time."[41]

The key to success, she told PBS, was to trust in yourself. "Self-confidence is a huge part of it. You can't think that you're not as good as anyone else. And I think it's important to be careful of what you do and say and who you hang out with. Represent yourself well."[42]

NOTES

1. "My Mom Had Me at Sixteen," *J-14,* December 2008, http://www.oceanup.com/2008/12/selena-gomez-my-mom-had-me-at-16.html.

2. Michelle Tan. "Is Selena Gomez . . . the Next Miley Cyrus?" People.com, http://www.people.com/people/archive/article/0,20203953,00.html.

3. Ibid.

4. "Selena Gomez Discovery Girls Interview," http://selenagomezwiki.wetpaint.com/page/Selena+Gomez+Discovery+Girls+Interview.

5. "My Mom Had Me at Sixteen."

6. Tan, "Is Selena Gomez."

7. "Selena Gomez: Proud of Start on *Barney,*" CBS *Early Morning,* February 11, 2009, http://www.cbsnews.com/stories/2008/10/23/earlyshow/main4541439.shtml.

8. Betsy Boyd. "Up Next: Selena Gomez," *Variety,* October 4, 2007, http://www.variety.com/article/VR1117973330?refCatId=2721&query=%22selena+Gomez%22+AND+Barney.

9. Jennifer Armstrong. "The Making of a Kid Star," *Entertainment Weekly,* July 13, 2007, http://www.ew.com/ew/article/0,20044989,00.html.

10. "It's My Life," PBS, http://pbskids.org/itsmylife/celebs/interviews/selena.html.

11. "Video: Selena Gomez Opens Up about Her Weirdest Kiss," *Twist,* http://www.aceshowbiz.com/news/view/00021359.html.

12. "Selena Gomez interview on Miss O & Friends," http://www.missoandfriends.com/interviews/selena-gomez-interview.php.

13. Demi Lovato interview by author during Winter Press Tour, January 16, 2009.

14. Ibid.

15. Ibid.

16. Ibid.

17. Ibid.

18. Ibid.

19. Judy Coleman. "At Sweet 16, Lovato's Ready for Her Close-Up," *Boston Globe,* September 23, 2008, p. 8SID.

20. Laura Yao. "Disney Demi-Goddess—'Camp Rock' Likely to Catapult Teen into Stardom," *Washington Post,* June 21, 2008, p. C1.

21. *Sonny with a Chance* production material from Disney.

22. Disney Dreaming, "Selena Gomez Says Her Parents Help Her Be Down-To-Earth," http://www.disneydreaming.com/2010/05/30/selena-gomez-says-her-parents-help-her-be-down-to-earth/.

23. Tan, "Is Selena Gomez."

24. "It's My Life."

25. Ibid.

26. Demi Lovato interview.

27. Ibid.

28. "Selena Gomez Says Demi Lovato Is a Bigger Princess," *AP Online,* 2009. High-Beam Research, http://www.highbeam.com/doc/1A1-D98S03BG0.html.

29. Tan, "Is Selena Gomez."

30. Ibid.

31. Carissa Rosenberg. "Selena Gomez," *Seventeen,* http://www.seventeen.com/entertainment/features/selena-gomez-interview.

32. Ibid.

33. Ibid.

34. Ibid.

35. "Justin Bieber's World Centers on Young Love," *Billboard,* http://www.billboard.com/#/news/justin-bieber-s-world-centers-on-young-love-1004041759.story.

36. Ibid.

37. "GL's Crushin' on . . . Justin Bieber," *Girl's Life,* December 1, 2009, http://www.highbeam.com/doc/1G1-213527994.html.

38. "Justin Bieber Understands What I'm Going Through," *US Magazine,* March 16, 2011, http://www.usmagazine.com/moviestvmusic/news/selena-gomez-justin-bieber-understands-what-im-going-through-2011163.

39. *Fox & Friends,* June 30, 2011.

40. Rosenberg, "Selena Gomez."

41. Ibid.

42. "It's My Life."

FURTHER READING

Heller, Corinne. "Selena Gomez 'Freaking Out' over First Big Film *Ramona and Beezus,* which Opens on Friday," OTRC, November 11, 2010. http://www.ontheredcarpet.com/2010/07/selena-gomez-freaking-out-over-first-big-film-ramona-and-beezus-which-opens-on-friday.html.

McGrath, Kristin. "The 'World' Is Already Teen Heartthrob's Oyster," *USA Today,* December 21, 2009. 6D.

Selena Gomez Interview. Facebook. http://www.facebook.com/topic.php?uid=7686420994&topic=3826&post=11593.

Times of the Internet. "Selena Gomez Loves Her Parents," April 2009. http://www.timesoftheinternet.com/66600.html.

Not content to be an international singing star, Rihanna has branched out into acting. In 2012's *Battleship*, she plays a tough Navy Seal.

6 RIHANNA

It was supposed to be a night of shared celebration for R&B's golden couple. They were scheduled to attend the Grammy Awards together and perform their nominated songs. But instead of participating in the music industry's biggest night, Rihanna was being treated for injuries and Chris Brown was in police custody being interrogated for allegedly physically assaulting Rihanna. It was the beginning of an ugly scandal that would rip their relationship apart and make Rihanna the reluctant poster girl for dating abuse. It was a stunning turn of events for the vibrant young woman who had taken the music world by storm as a fresh-faced teenager just a few years earlier.

YOUTHFUL LESSONS

Robyn Rihanna Fenty was born on February 20, 1988, on the Caribbean island of Barbados. Her father, Ronald, is also a native Barbadian and her mom, Monica, is from Guyana. Rihanna grew up in the city of Waterford in St. Michael parish— the equivalent of a county—along with her two younger brothers, Rorrey and Rajad. From the outside, the Fentys seemed like an average middle-class family. Ronald worked as a store supervisor and Monica was an accountant. But behind closed doors the Fentys were struggling with a debilitating illness—Ronald was an alcoholic and a crack cocaine addict.

As a child, Rihanna didn't understand what was happening to her dad. "He would go into the bathroom all the time. I didn't know what it was. I knew that my mom and dad would argue when there was foil paper with an ashtray."[1]

Even when she started to understand, Rihanna says she looked up to her dad so much that, "I couldn't put him and this negative thing together. At the time there was no way I could help him out of it." She clung to good memories, such as playing with him on the beach and catching crabs together. Rihanna describes her dad as a product of the 1960s generation; a hippy with a "big Afro, bell-bottoms—a real party dude who took drugs as a matter of course. But his partying got way out of hand, spiraled out of control."[2]

Ronald spent everything he earned on drugs, so there was never much money. He finally left when Rihanna was nine. Monica supported the kids on her own so there was never much money. While her mom was at work, Rihanna often looked after her brothers, a responsibility she didn't see as a burden. "It was just reality."[3]

But that reality took an emotional toll, made worse because she kept her feelings bottled up. When she was eight, Rihanna began suffering from migraine-like headaches. At one point, doctors suspected a brain tumor, but CAT scans ruled out any physical cause and her doctors remained mystified for years. After years of separations, Rihanna's parents finally divorced when she was 14—and the headaches abruptly stopped. She began to acknowledge her resentment of her father's life choices and the suffering it caused their family. "I started to get angry at him, maybe even hated him. Because I started to realize that no child should have to experience what I'd been through."[4]

School was another sore spot. She attended Combermere High School, which was established in 1695 and is the oldest high school in Barbados. But Rihanna says she hated school because the teachers gave her a hard time and the other girls bullied her. "People hated me because I'm fair in complexion. I had to develop a thick skin because they would call me white."[5] So she found some solace in . . . guns!

When she was 13, Rihanna joined the cadets, similar to what we would call the ROTC. Like real soldiers, Rihanna and her fellow cadets dressed in fatigues and combat boots, participating in drills, going on weekend expeditions, and learning to shoot. Interestingly, the singer Shontelle was a cadet at the same time as Rihanna—and was her drill sergeant.

"Picture me and Rihanna in combat boots and fatigues crawling through mud and things like that," she says, laughing at the memory of ordering Rihanna around.

BARBADOS

Barbados is located in the West Indies, approximately 200 miles north of the coast of South America. The island was originally settled around 1623 BC by Amerindians who came from Venezuela in canoes. In 1200 BC, the Arawaks were conquered by another Amerindian tribe, the cannibalistic Caribs. Taller and physically stronger than the Arawaks, the Caribs were a bellicose people skilled with bows and arrows dipped in a paralyzing poison. The island got its name from Portuguese explorers who passed through on their way to Brazil, calling it *Los Barbados*, which means bearded ones. It's believed the name refers to the fig trees that flourish on the island, the fronds having a "beardy" appearance.

"That's what drill sergeants do—we boss cadets around, we make them do push-ups . . . especially when they show up on the parade square late."[6]

Rihanna remembers the discipline involved. "Uniforms had to be spick and span, our boots had to shine like diamonds and we'd often need to cook for the entire camp." The best part for Rihanna was learning to shoot pistols. "I was a good shot, although I couldn't kill a fly from a hundred paces."[7]

Music was also an escape, and a passion. "Growing up, I always sang. No one was pushing me to do it. It was something that I wanted to do. So I developed a passion for it, fell in love with music and developed my own style."[8]

Rihanna formed her first band when she was 14 with a couple fellow class-mates. It was around that time that she went through her teenage rebellion phase. She admits she'd go out and drink with friends, something that is culturally ac-cepted in Barbados. Rihanna stresses, though, that she never got out of control, the memory of her father's alcohol abuse keeping her in check.

"I knew my limits when I was a kid and I still do," she stresses, saying she goes out to have fun, "to dance and laugh at people fighting or dressed like whores," not to get drunk. "I might have a few drinks . . . but I don't ever get to the point where I want to throw up, can't stand up straight or say things I'm likely to regret in the morning."[9]

Rihanna credits her mother for instilling responsibility and common sense. "My mom raised me to be a child and know my place but also to think like a woman. She never held back from me in terms of being too young to know certain things, so I am very mature for my age."[10]

And very determined. She took her first tentative step toward a music career in high school when she performed at the Colors of Combermere School talent show, singing Mariah Carey's "Hero." She won the competition. She also learned a painful lesson. After winning the talent show and the Miss Combermere Beauty Pageant, Rihanna says she lost a lot of people she thought were her friends. "Even the person who I thought was my best friend stopped speaking to me, but the people who are real have stuck around." She explains some of it is cultural. "In Barbados we have this pride thing, people hate to give up compli-ments," she says. "It physically hurts them to say congratulations—they find it easier to be mean."[11]

But Rihanna was about to learn that success really is the best revenge.

WHIRLWIND

In late 2003, music producer Evan Rogers was vacationing in Barbados with his wife, who was born on the island. While there he agreed to meet with the girl group Rihanna belonged to, which they called Contrast. The girls gave Rogers an im-promptu performance in the lobby of his hotel but his sole focus was on Rihanna. Evan says the minute she walked into the room, "it was like the other two girls didn't exist. She carried herself like a star even when she was 15. But the killer was when she opened her mouth to sing. She was a little rough around the edges, but she had this edge to her voice."[12]

Rogers was impressed enough to introduce Rihanna to his business partner, Carl Sturken. They invited Rihanna to visit their Manhattan studio during her spring break and over the next year they worked on recording her demo, with Rihanna and her mom commuting between Barbados and America, staying at Roger's home in Connecticut. After she turned 16, Rihanna moved to America full time and finished her high school education with a tutor.

"When I left Barbados, I didn't look back," she says. "I wanted to do what I had to do [to succeed], even if it meant moving to America."[13]

Finally, in 2005, the four-song demo was ready. Rihanna left to go back to Barbados and Evans sent it to Def Jam CEO Shawn Carter, better known as Jay-Z. After listening to the demo, he immediately arranged a meeting with Rihanna, Evans, and Sturken. The demo was sent in on Wednesday, Def Jam called back Thursday, and Rihanna flew back for a Friday meeting. Once there, the nervous teenager was required to sing a capella in front of Jay-Z, her two producers, her lawyer, and some label executives.

"I was so terrified that my make-up would run because I could barely sleep the night before. My throat was dry and I was trying so hard to act like this was normal for me."[14]

This time she sang the ballad "The Last Time," Whitney Houston's "For the Love of You," and "Pon de Replay." Rihanna recalls that she stayed until 3:00 in the morning because Jay-Z wouldn't let her leave until she signed with his record label Def Jam.

Her first album, *Music of the Sun,* was released in August 2005, which contained her first hit, "Pon de Replay." The album reached number 2 on Billboard's Hot 100. To promote the album, which ultimately sold more than 2 million copies worldwide, she toured with Gwen Stefani. *Rolling Stone* called *Music of the Sun* "a seductive mix of big-voiced R&B and souped-up island riddims—what Beyoncé might have sounded like if she had grown up in the West Indies and skipped the whole Destiny's Child thing."[15]

The following spring *A Girl Like Me* came out, which spawned the hits "SOS" and "Unfaithful." It earned Rihanna four Billboard Music Awards, including Female Artist of the Year. But her nonstop work schedule concerned Jay-Z. Too make sure she didn't burn out, he encouraged Rihanna to take a break and go back to Barbados to recoup. But it was a short vacation because Rihanna was eager to get back into the recording studio. "That has a lot to do with my youth," she explains. "Younger people are usually very restless and can't keep quiet. But I am also very passionate about what I do."[16]

By March 2007, Rihanna was a grown woman of 19 and her third album, *Good Girl Gone Bad,* reflected her personal and creative maturity. The innocence of her first two albums was replaced by an edgier sound and Rihanna herself projected a noticeably sexier persona, as seen in the "Umbrella" music video. At the time, the singer admitted she felt she was being forced to assume an innocent image and wanted to break away from that pigeonhole. She called *Good Girl Gone Bad* "an expression of where I am at this point in my life, where I am in my career. It just represents my rebelliousness."[17]

It also showed her expanding musical palette. Growing up, she says she listened primarily to reggae music, which has been a primary influence on her music highly, as have R&B artists like Mariah Carey, Whitney Houston, and Destiny's Child. "I try to fuse songs together." On "SOS," for example, she samples the song "Tainted Love," even though she didn't really know about the group Soft Cell until she moved to America. Once she did, Rihanna says, "I put that in my music, I fused that with pop and R&B and made a new song. That's art, yeah, I like to be creative."[18]

For Rihanna, 2007 was her big break-out year. She moved out of Rogers's house and into her own New York apartment. She was voted one of *People* magazine's Most Beautiful People, ranked number 8 on Maxim's Hot 100, and was included in *Entertainment Weekly's* 100 Stars We Love. In addition, the "Umbrella" video was honored as Video of the Year and Monster Single of the Year at the 2007 MTV Awards. In 2008, her hot streak continued. She performed "Umbrella" and "Don't Stop the Music" at the 2008 Grammy Awards and won her first Grammy for Best Rap/Sung Collaboration with Jay-Z for her hit "Umbrella."

With her career skyrocketing, there was little time for anything else. She admitted in 2007 that "there's no balance: it's 99 percent to one percent, 99 percent being my career, there's one percent of my life which is personal. And even in that 1 percent, my career always seems to find its way in there somewhere. But it's great, that's how passionate I am about what I do."[19]

Jay-Z supported Rihanna's bid for personal and creative independence. "That's the best thing for any label—to have an artist step in and take control of their own career." He also, though, offered her perspective based on long experience. "The biggest advice I can give her is to keep her circle tight . . . She can't control people's opinion of her records or what's being said on the blogs . . . But if she has the proper friends, she won't get caught up in the wild-child lifestyle. They will bring her back and be like, *You might wanna pull your skirt down.*"[20]

Rihanna says she has always been mindful of not crossing the line from fashionable to tarty, explaining that she doesn't like wearing outfits that are too revealing. "If I do shorts on the bottom, then it's gotta be something very conservative at the top. If it's skimpy at the top, it's gotta be long jeans or something. I like to balance it out."[21] She uses Alicia Keys as her personal role model. "She became so successful off of just her music. She was really conservative about her style at first."

She's mindful of her wardrobe because she has experience firsthand the pressure put on young performers to be role models. She recalls the time she went to the beach wearing jeans and a bikini top. Paparazzi photos made it look like she was wearing an overly revealing top, not a bathing suit. "There were call-in [radio] programs about it. It was a big deal for, like, three weeks straight, talking about I'm not setting a good example."[22]

Prior to leaving Barbados, Rihanna says she was painfully shy and retiring. But success gave her the confidence to become more outgoing, to let her true personality shine through. Add that to look and talent and you have one of the music industry's most eligible bachelorettes. It wasn't long before Rihanna was being linked in gossip columns to various love interests including Shia LaBeouf, Josh Hartnett, basketball player Andrew Bynum, and even Jay-Z. While she neither confirmed nor denied most reports, she did vehemently shoot down rumors of a relationship with Jay-Z, who at the time was Beyoncé's longtime boyfriend (and is now her husband).

Press speculation aside, Rihanna explains that she would not want to go public with a possible romance until she was sure it was more than just hanging out. "It's tough because you want to be able to talk about it and be proud, but you have to be sure of that person first." The kind of guy who attracts her attention is humble and individualistic. "If a guy is hot and he knows it—forget it. I hate arrogance." On the other hand she likes "facial hair and a guy who dresses rugged."[23]

Rihanna says she gets relationship advice from her friends, which includes three girls and about 20 guys. (She admits she gets along much better with guys as friends than other females, believing men are more loyal and less jealous.)

"I love listening to guy talk because I learn a lot. Here's the key: You can't lower your standards for a guy because he won't respect you . . . You always have to stick up for yourself and speak your mind."[24]

Rihanna had no idea the price she would pay for following that advice.

BATTERED

Initially, the police did not release the name of the woman Chris Brown was accused of battering. But Rihanna's abrupt absence from the 2009 Grammys left little doubt as to the victim's identity. After turning himself in, Chris Brown was eventually charged with felony assault and criminal threats. Then, just three weeks after the assault, reports surfaced that Rihanna and Brown spent time together at Sean Combs's Miami house. The idea that she would reconcile had experts, peers, and fans alike dismayed, especially at the message it sent to young girls in similar abusive relationships. Oprah Winfrey felt so strongly that she discussed the turn of events on her show, speaking directly to Rihanna.

> If a man hits you once, he will hit you again. He will hit you again. It makes me so sad. Love doesn't hurt. Both Chris Brown and Rihanna: if I were your friend, I would call you up and say give it some time. Get yourself some counseling. Take care of yourself. Heal yourself first.[25]

Whether because of the outpouring of concern and criticism or her own second thoughts, the reconciliation—if there had actually been one—was short lived. By early April it was clear the former couple had gone their separate ways. The Los Angeles District Attorney's office confirmed that Rihanna agreed to testify against Brown should it go to trial, where he faced a possible nine-year sentence if convicted on the filed charges. He chose not to take that gamble.

On June 22, he pled guilty to assault charges. On August 25, he was sentenced to five years of formal felony probation, 180 days of community hard labor, fined $2,960, and ordered to complete a 52-week domestic-violence counseling program. The Los Angeles judge agreed to let Brown fulfill his sentence in Virginia, where he lives. In addition, the judge kept in place a protective order preventing Brown from contacting Rihanna or getting closer than 100 yards from her. The only exception was if they were at the same industry event; then Brown had to stay 10 yards away. Should Brown break any terms of his probation, he faced four years in prison.

Once the sentencing was done, court documents were released, describing what could only be deemed a savage attack. According to the file, the alleged assault began after Rihanna discovered a lengthy text message from another woman on Brown's cell phone, he became enraged. He pulled the car they were driving in over and tried to push her out of the car, but Rihanna was wearing a seat belt. So he smashed her head against the passenger window. He hit her face, causing blood to splatter in the car and on her clothes. He also allegedly threatened her, yelling: "I'm going to beat the s*** out of you when we get home! You wait and see!"[26]

Rihanna tried to call her personal assistant. Even though she didn't answer, Rihanna pretended to talk to her, saying she was on her way home and for the assistant to call the police to meet her there. She later told detectives that she did it "because she did not want to get beat anymore." But all the ruse did was infuriate Brown even more, who according to the court documents told her, "You just did the stupidest thing ever! Now I'm really going to kill you."[27]

Brown began punching her again. To protect her face, Rihanna covered her head with her arms. She tried to get out of the car but Brown began driving so she couldn't. He put her in a headlock and bit her ear. When he stopped the car again, Rihanna took the keys out of the ignition while Brown allegedly continued to punch her face and arms. He grabbed her around the neck again and squeezed tightly enough so that she started losing consciousness. He bit her fingers then let go. When she tried breaking the window with her high-heel shoe, the beating allegedly continued. He finally stopped hitting her and got out of the car to look for his keys. When he couldn't find them, he set off on foot. By that time, neighbors had called 911 to report a woman screaming. Photos released later showed the extent of Rihanna's injuries and the viciousness of the attack.

According to the Probation Officer's report, Brown stated he was "ashamed and embarrassed of his actions," and claimed he wanted to plead guilty to the charges, but that his attorney insisted he plead not guilty. The report also states Brown apologized to Rihanna several times after the incident and that he wants to take "responsibility for my mistake."[28]

Since his sentencing, Chris Brown continued his attempts to make amends, apologizing publicly and saying what happened that night in February was not a true representation of who he is as a person. He told talk host Larry King: "I wish I could have changed that night. I just need to prove to people I can be a role model. That's not who I am as a person, and that's not who I promise I want to be." He also claimed to still be in love with Rihanna. "I definitely would be affected if she decided to date someone else, but at the end of the day, I mean, we're not together, so, if she's happy, I'm cool."[29]

After staying under the radar for much of 2009, Rihanna began getting back into the public eye after Brown's sentencing officially closed the criminal case. She appeared in a provocative fashion shoot for Italian *Vogue*, performed on the

DRIZZY DRAKE

Although Drizzy Drake is being touted as America's next hip-hop star, he grew up as Aubrey Graham in the well-heeled, upper-middle-class Forest Hill neighborhood in Toronto, where he was born on October 24, 1986. His dad, Dennis, is an African American Catholic, his mom a Caucasian Canadian Jew. Aubrey attended high school at Forest Hill Collegiate Institute, and says it was difficult being one of the only minorities. "When you're young and unaware that the world is made up of different people, it is tough growing up. But me being different from everyone else just made me a lot stronger."[30]

Music has always been part of Aubrey's life and is literally in his blood. His uncle Larry Graham played bass for Prince; another uncle, guitarist Mabon "Teene" Hodges, was also a songwriter who collaborated on "Let's Stay Together" and "Love & Happiness" with Al Green; and his father drummed for Jerry Lee Lewis. His parents divorced when he was five years old and he grew up spending summers in Memphis, where his father lived. Aubrey says it gave him the chance to immerse himself in the local music scene.

"Growing up around all the hip hop: Three Six Mafia, Kingpin Skinny Pimp, early Yo Gotti . . . shit like that was kinda what really influenced me."[31]

But while in high school, Aubrey developed an interest in acting. The father of a classmate was an agent who offered to represent him. One of his first jobs was the television movie *Convicted*, opposite Omar Epps. Shortly after, he was cast in the role of Jimmy on *Degrassi: The Next Generation*. The series became phenomenally successful and made Aubrey a star in Canada. While acting gave him notoriety, music remained his passion. He says he became interested in rap when he was 16 during the time his father was in jail. "He shared a cell with this dude who didn't really have anyone to speak to . . . and he would always rap to me over the phone." Aubrey started writing his own rhymes and would perform them for the cellmate. "Eventually I learned from meeting people who were into music, too, the art of making a song and I accepted the fact that I wanted to be in music."[32]

He didn't give music a full court press until he was released from *Degrassi* and decided to use his middle name as his nom de music. "I just really loved the name and I embraced it my whole life," he says. "I use Aubrey more for the acting, which is how I separate myself . . . I find that in this industry you have to have dual personalities . . . It's not that I'm pretending to be somebody else but it's just that the people that I act with, the Directors, Producers and Agents, can't really relate to what I talk about . . . Drake is who I am and Aubrey is more of a separate, sort of proper individual."[33]

But Drake distances himself from any gangsta posturing. "I'll be honest," he says, "I'm an actor. I'm not a thug who decided to be in a movie and play himself. I'm not reppin' a 'hood', I'm not claiming a set, no street shit. I try and keep my lyrics triumphant."[34]

24. Ibid.

25. "He WILL Hit You Again," *Daily Mail,* March 9, 2009, http://www.dailymail. co.uk/tvshowbiz/article-1160652/He-WILL-hit-Oprah-issues-warning-Rihanna-reconc iliation-Chris-Brown.html.

26. Information on Brown's attack, court documents.

27. Ibid.

28. "Court Documents Reveal History of Violence between Chris Brown & Rihanna," *The Insider,* August 26, 2009, http://www.theinsider.com/news/2761686_Court_Documents_ Reveal_History_of_Violence_Between_Chris_Brown_Rihanna.

29. "Chris Brown in Love with Rihanna," September 1, 2009, http://www.femalefirst. co.uk/celebrity/Chris+Brown-28266.html.

30. Jordan Harrison. "Degrassi Actor Says Being Different Made Him Stronger," *The Canadian Jewish News,* December 21, 2006, http://www.interfaithfamily.com/arts_and_ entertainment/movies_theater_tv_and_music/Degrassi_Actor_Says_Being_Different_ Made_Him_Stronger.shtml?rd=1.

31. Charlie Brown. "Drake Interview," *Complex Magazine,* February 19, 2009, http:// www.welivethis.com/newsfeed/2009/02/19/drake-interview-complex-magazine/.

32. Ibid.

33. Safra Ducreay. "Interview with Drake." HipHopCanada.com, July 12, 2006, http:// www.hiphopcanada.com/_site/entertainment/interviews/ent_int314.php.

34. Shanel Odum. "Google Me: Drake," *Vibe,* December 8, 2008, http://www.vibe. com/music/next/2008/12/drake_google_me/.

35. Taylor, "Move over, Beyoncé."

Miley has been known to make some controversial decisions but takes the criticism in stride. "I don't want to be perfect, but I do want to be a role model. My mom always tells me that imperfections equal beauty. All of us are imperfect."

7 MILEY CYRUS

It's got to be the oldest cliché in entertainment, but the fact is Miley Cyrus *was* born to perform. Being the daughter of country star Billy Ray Cyrus means it's literally in her blood. But her passion for entertaining goes beyond family ties.

"She was born with a song," Billy Ray says. "From the day she could talk she said she was going to be on stage. She was going to be a movie star, a singer, songwriter, entertainer. And she would write this down. Like, she would write down her goals. Musically, she is the real deal. The songs that come from inside of her . . . You know the saying she's got an old soul? Well, she's got an old soul, and her old soul's got a lot of soul."[1]

Miley remembers the thrill of watching her dad on stage. "When I first started going to my dad's concerts, I started watching to see the crowd just go wild for the music and see the reactions. Then I really knew that's what I wanted to do because I love being entertained. I love having an audience. I love everything about it. And I love just the reaction that you can get through music."[2]

Miley was born on November 23, 1992, at the height of the "Achy Breaky Heart" craze. Billy Ray's *Some Gave All* became the first debut album by a country artist to enter the pop charts at number 1; it also topped the country charts as well, fueled by the popularity of the breakout single "Achy Breaky Heart."

As if suspecting the daughter born amidst his new found fame would also be a force of nature, Billy Ray and his wife Leticia named her Destiny Hope Cyrus. According to Miley, Billy Ray gave her the nickname Smiley. Over time, it morphed into Miley. The only family member who still calls her Destiny is Miley's grandmother.

Miley grew up on a 500-acre ranch outside of Nashville, where Billy Ray and Leticia were married in 1993. The middle-born among five children, Miley has three older half-siblings from her mom's previous relationships—Christopher Cody,

Trace, and Brandi—and two younger siblings, brother Braison and sister Noah. Trace belongs to the band Metro Station and Noah is an actress and has appeared in multiple episodes of *Doc* and *Hannah Montana*. Although they lived just outside of Nashville, the Cyrus ranch was a little corner of down-home country, home to horses, chickens, cows, dogs, and cats.

Despite her parents' efforts to give their children a stable home life, Miley's life has always been informed by the lure of performing. She sang on stage with Billy Ray when she was two years old and was just as theatrical at home. "I would sing 'Hound Dog' and silly songs for the fun of it," she recalls.[3] "We had these showers that are completely glass, and I would lock people in them and make them stay in there and watch me perform. I'd make them watch."[4]

Miley even found a way to combine athletics and performing by joining a competitive cheerleading squad called the Premier Tennessee All Stars when she was six years old. "It wasn't like rah-rah, like school cheerleading," she explains. "It's competition cheerleading so it was really hard. But just like acting or anything that you really set your mind to, once you're up on the stage doing your routine or you see your show for the first time, all the hard work pays off."[5] Miley appeared in meets all around the country with her award-winning squad, earning a mantel full of trophies.

But being a cheerleader didn't mean Miley was the most popular student at Heritage Middle School. In fact, she says she was the victim of relentless bullying by a particular group of girls. "The girls took it beyond normal bullying," Miley wrote in her autobiography, *Miles to Go*. "These were big tough girls. I was scrawny and short. They were fully capable of doing me bodily harm." She recalls the time they locked her in the bathroom. "They shoved me in. I was trapped. I banged on the door until my fists hurt. Nobody came. . . . It seemed like Operation Make-Miley-Miserable was escalating to a new level. More like Operation Take-Miley-Down."[6]

It got to the point where they challenged Miley to a fist fight. "Three girls strutted up and stood towering over me. My stomach churned. I clutched my grilled cheese sandwich like it was the hand of my best friend. It pretty much was my best friend those days. I was done for. They started cussing me and telling me to get up. I sat there, frozen. I didn't know what to do."[7]

Tired of the abuse, Miley stood up for herself and the girls backed down. In a case of what doesn't kill you makes you stronger, the experience of being bullied made her that much more determined to succeed as a performer. While she might not be able to control whether or not other girls liked her, she could control being the best she could be. So her dedication to cheerleading gradually gave way to a passion for acting, especially when Bill Ray was in Toronto, Canada, shooting the series *Doc* for the now-defunct network PAX. The series aired in over 40 countries, making Billy Ray an international TV star. Miley appeared in two *Doc* episodes, including the pilot.

Her mother, Tish, and the kids stayed in Nashville but Miley spent time in Toronto with her dad and, while there, studied acting with some of the city's best coaches, working hard to develop her skills. Despite her dedication, and even though her dad was a well-known performer, breaking into acting was not easy.

Billy Ray remembers all the times Miley went to auditions only to come home disappointed when she didn't get the part. "This business has a lot of heartbreak ahead of it; there's a lot of ups and downs," which is why Billy Ray says he tried to talk her out of pursuing acting as a career. "It's always a roller coaster, and I would always tell her just be a kid and heck with the business. Just do school. But she never was that way. She set goals. She had a dream. And next thing I know, another audition would come up and she'd be right out there going at it."[8]

Billy Ray recalls how Thomas Edison once said the most important ingredient for success is failure. "Every time you fail you eliminate one way that won't work. Well, she kept getting knocked down, and she would dust herself back off and step back up to the plate and take another swing. That's why I'm the most proud of Miley, because she just kept persisting."[9]

Eventually, her persistence paid off. In 2003, Miley was cast in *Big Fish* and appeared in the music video for "If Heartaches Have Wings" by bluegrass singer Rhonda Vincent. That same year, Miley heard about a new Disney Channel series about a young girl who is keeping a huge secret; at school, she is a normal, anonymous teenager. Only her family and closest friends know that she is living a double life as a famous pop singer. The show was called *Hannah Montana.*

After seeing Miley's audition tape, Disney Channel President Gary Marsh flew her in for an audition. Although they liked her presence, they thought she was physically too small for the role and too inexperienced to be the series lead. The producers kept auditioning young girls for the next six months but were unable to find the combination of qualities they were looking for. So Marsh asked Miley, now 12, to come in for a second audition.

"She walked into a conference room full of executives. She stood in front of us and knocked us out," he says.[10]

Executive producer Steven Peterman said Miley's age quickly became a nonissue. "This is a tough process, and you've got kids from all over the country coming up to Disney. They're sitting out in the hall, looking at each other. Then they go into that room. And I was an actor a long time ago. I know what it's like to be in that hallway. You come into that room, and this girl, at 11 years old, came into that room and stood up there and not only performed, but also sang a capella for all of us and came back over and over again. At first, we thought, *Well, she's so young, you know, we're going to have to make her a little bit more insecure and shy of a character.* But as we got to know Miley, everything that Billy says about her is true. She is so strong and so focused and so beyond her years in so many ways . . . and yet still a kid."[11]

Despite impressing the executives, she still didn't get hired right away and had to endure a long, emotionally grueling process, repeatedly flying to Los Angeles for more auditions. Billy Ray saw the toll it was taking but says, "I couldn't stop her. I mean, this was her dream. So when this opportunity came, she laid into it."[12]

More unexpected was Billy Ray's participation. He admits that after finishing *Doc,* he swore he'd never do another TV series. "It was just really, really hard. We did 88 episodes and I really missed making music and being with the fans. We've got a very loyal fan base around the world, and I just really missed that live experience with the fans."[13]

With each audition, the producers narrowed the field until it was just Miley and two other girls. Billy says it was at that point the possibility of him auditioning for the role of Hannah's widower father came up. It was an intriguing possibility. For one thing, he thought the script was exceptionally well written. "A TV show is like a song," he says. "It all begins with what's on the page. And from the moment that we read the script, we knew that the writers knew what they were doing." Plus, the idea of working with Miley was another incentive. That said, Billy played it low key. "I had the common sense to know that she's worked really hard to get to this point, and I didn't want to get in the mix until they had hired Miley."[14]

Once Miley was hired, Billy Ray accepted an official offer to audition, which he said was nerve-wracking because "the last thing I wanted to do was mess up her show!" At the auditions they asked him to read some scenes from the script and sing. "We talked and sang a little bit and they hired me. The next week we did the pilot and now here I am doing a series."[15]

Executive producers Peterman and Michael Poryes admit that they originally saw Billy Ray as a courtesy, not expecting much—they had already decided to offer the role to another actor.

"So he came in, and he got it on his own," says Poryes. "He just blew us all away."[16]

Peterman explains that since Miley was so inexperienced, they originally thought it would be best to have a well-known sitcom actor play the role of her dad. Because of *Doc,* Billy was known as more a dramatic actor. "But what Billy had was an incredibly relaxed manner. What he also had was that unique relationship with his daughter that no other actor could duplicate. She teased him. She goofed around with him. She felt comfortable with him in a way that we looked at each other and said, you *cannot* duplicate that."[17]

Billy Ray is the first to admit he was never the family disciplinarian so his relationship with Miley is perhaps closer than most. "It's almost embarrassing to say this, but I've never spanked my kids—I never could do that. Timeout has probably been my strongest form of discipline." He says like his *Hannah Montana* character Robby, he parents by being a best friend. "That's what I've always tried to be to my kids. It's a real fine line, and thus far it's a line I've been able to walk. So I've been a great playmate for the kids."[18]

Miley says her dad gives her space and never gives her advice about acting unless she asks for it. "It's kinda weird. Me and my dad are best friends; we're like the same person." She also says she can tell her father anything, "When we come home, we forget that we even work together and just hang out."[19]

DISNEY'S NEWEST STAR

Hannah Montana began being filmed in 2005. To accommodate Miley's new job, the Cyrus clan relocated as a family to Los Angeles. The move was hard on Miley at first. She missed the farm and the animals. She missed her friends at school and being able to hang out with them. She especially missed the small-town feel of Nashville. So when looking for a house, Miley told her parents she wanted to live in a small neighborhood where she would know all her neighbors; where she could walk across the street and have friends. Miley says her family loves having people over. "We go out and throw barbecues and invite the whole neighborhood. We always do big family stuff like that. We never shut ourselves off."[20]

That was before *Hannah Montana* aired on March 24, 2006, becoming Disney Channel's most watched series debut. Miley says the producers came into her dressing room the next day saying they had good news and bad news. The good news: the first episode had been seen by over 5 million viewers. The bad news? "Your life is about to totally change."[21]

A month later, Miley got a clue of just how popular *Hannah Montana* was becoming when her six-year-old sister Noah admitted she had entered a contest on DisneyChannel.com to win backstage passes to a concert Miley was performing.

Miley says she used another Disney star, Hilary Duff, as a role model for navigating the road to Disney stardom and beyond. "She started out at about the same age. She hadn't done much before starting her series, either. She started with soundtracks, then did her own CD, the series, the movies—the exact same thing I'm doing. So I can model my career after hers, but with my own experiences."[22]

Although she missed her Tennessee friends, Miley quickly grew close to her *Hannah* costars Emily Osment and Mitchel Musso. She also became friends with fellow Disney stars Vanessa Hudgens, Zac Efron, Ashley Tisdale, and Brenda Song. But for as much as Miley enjoyed working on the series and being on the Tribune studio lot, there were two drawbacks. The first was the wig she had to wear when in the *Hannah* persona. "It's really itchy and hot." The second was doing schoolwork on the set for three hours a day, as required by law. Even though she has a tutor, Miley says it's difficult going back and forth between acting and studying. "I may act for 45 minutes, then do an hour of school and go back to acting. That makes it hard to concentrate on either acting or schooling. I hate math. I also hate history."[23]

While producers may have been uncertain about Miley's acting chops before hiring her, there was never a question about whether she could sing. And much of *Hannah's* appeal came from her rollicking performances. Just as they had done with Hilary Duff, Disney also groomed Miley for a recording career. Miley opened for the Cheetah Girls on the first 20 dates of their 2006 *The Party's Just Begun Tour* to promote the release of the first *Hannah Montana* soundtrack in October 2006 by Walt Disney Records. Miley also signed a four-album deal with Hollywood records for solo albums. At the time, she said she had written over 100 songs, both alone and with her dad, which she kept in a journal.

Miley's schedule left her little free time for sleep, much less hanging out, so she frequently combined the two. "My friends and I just do sleepovers and hang out and play guitar," she says. "I'm teaching all my friends to play different instruments and music, and they tell me what's going on with their friends. I don't go to school with them, but I can hear all the things that are going on at their high school and what's normal."[24]

The best part of the arrangement, Miley admits, is being able to hear about high school without having to actually attend. "I do still keep myself normal . . . but I'm

MILEY'S CO-STAR, JASON EARLES

Jason Earles, who plays Miley's brother Jackson on the series, says it was a little intimidating at first working with a real-life father and daughter.

"I was really nervous at first. When I found out that Miley was cast, I was like, *Oh, cool, Miley Cyrus. That's neat.* And then, like, two days later, I found out that Billy Ray was cast as the dad, *I'm like, Whoa. . . .there's, like, 13 years of history there. How am I going to fit into that?* But it took all of about three days, and they immediately kind of accepted me into their little clan. I felt like I was going to change my name to Jason Ray Cyrus. I adore the whole family, even all the little Cyruses that you don't see."[25]

Jason says Miley is always teasing her dad for being "a dork" but says he and co-star Mitchel Musso, who plays Oliver, "are in love with him. We think he's the coolest. We hang out in his dressing room every day trying to learn how to play guitar. We get him to play music for us [including] unreleased tracks. There's probably three or four that he shared with us"[26]

Jason says his relationship with Billy Ray has taken on a father-son aspect off-camera. "We pal around very father-son-like. We kind of enjoy the boy jokes—Miley is kind of disgusted by the whole thing."[27]

In the original *Hannah Montana* pilot script, Jason's character only spoke through a puppet named Fletcher. Jason said that network executives saw a run-through with him, Billy, and Miley; they opted to fire Fletcher.

"They decided, 'You know, we don't need the puppet. I think we'll just kind of turn these three loose on each other and see what happens'."[28]

over it. There is just so much going on I don't think I could handle high school. Because for high school you've gotta be so tough to be there because there's always some people who are a little crazy."[29]

As it was, her life was crazy enough. By the end of 2006, *Hannah Montana* was the most popular show for kids ages 6 to 14. In October, the *Hannah Montana* soundtrack album debuted at number 1 on the Billboard Top 200 and eventually went triple platinum. In June 2007, the double set, *Hannah Montana 2: Meet Miley Cyrus,* was released. The first disc was another series soundtrack; the second was Miley's solo debut album. She wrote 8 of the 10 songs on it and the single, "See You Again," was her first non-*Hannah* song to hit the Billboard Hot 100. But perhaps the most significant even of that year was Miley had fallen in love for the first time.

PRINCE CHARMING

In July 2007, the Internet began buzzing with rumors that Miley and Nick Jonas were dating. The biggest surprise was that the young couple had managed to keep it a secret for so long. Miley and Nick, the youngest of the musical trio Jonas Brothers, met in June 2006 at a benefit for the Elizabeth Glaser Pediatric AIDS Foundation. Before that night, Miley says she didn't know much about Nick but after Zac Efron introduced them, she admits she was instantly attracted to Nick.

When Miley got home after the benefit, she and Nick talked on the phone until four in the morning and by the time they hung up, she was in love. "It felt like the whole world stopped," she recalled in her biography." Nothing else mattered." She also says her family took her feelings seriously. "My family doesn't set rules around love; when you fall in love, that's it. No one called it puppy love, or made fun of me. My mom doesn't believe there's such thing as being too young or too naive to be in love."[30]

Nick lived on the East Coast, which prevented them from seeing each other as often as they wanted in the beginning of their relationship. But they kept in constant contact over the phone and by the time Nick bought a house in Los Angeles, they were best of friends as well as boyfriend-girlfriend. Nick lived only a few blocks away from Miley's so she could walk over to Nick's house and spend time with him before going to work at the studio. When she got home from work and on weekends they'd play basketball at Miley's house or she would go over to his house to have dinner with his family. Miley says it was a blissful time.

"I was so in love . . . The kind of love where the sun could shine or not shine all day long and you wouldn't care. The kind of love that makes you want to jump in the pool in December. The kind of love that makes you want to dance in the rain . . . This was the most magical journey of my life and it was a total rush."[31]

Being in love grounded Miley and inspired her songwriting. Many of the songs on *Meet Miley Cyrus* were written about Nick and their relationship. Ironically, by the time the relationship became public, it was already on the wane. There were arguments and tension and eventually they decided to take a time-out. But the next time they saw each other, Miley says her heart lurched in her chest and they were right back together—at least for a while. The relationship ended for good in December 2007 while Miley was on tour with the Jonas brothers. Miley calls it the hardest day in her life because the show had to go on.

"People were counting on me, but my heart was dizzy . . . When I love someone, I love them with everything in me. Deep down I knew we weren't being our best selves, and that was what I wanted, and I thought I deserved in a relationship—to be my best self and bring out the best in someone else."[32]

Cyrus wasn't single long. She was introduced to her next boyfriend, Justin Gaston, by her dad; Billy Ray met Justin while hosting *Nashville Star*—Justin was eliminated in the third week—and thought he was a "good kid; great heart. Justin's a good friend of the family. He lives for the light and he's very talented. He actually reminds me a lot of myself when I was 20 years old and I was living and searching for the dream."[33]

Even though Miley is five years younger than Justin, Billy Ray and her mom, Tish, approve. But they are very aware how easy it is for young stars to get into trouble and they keep a close eye on their daughter. "Everything is about keeping her grounded," says Tish. "It is so scary as a mom to see all these kids who are so whacked now. I don't want to be too much and have her rebel. Not that we think she's going to do that, but Miley does have a very explosive personality, which scares me a little." "She knows that if there was any time I felt like things were getting to be too much for her, we would just not do it."[34]

Miley, who legally changed her named from Destiny Hope to Miley Ray in March 2008, claims she has less freedom than any of her friends. "I probably have an earlier curfew than anyone just because my mom wants to keep me really safe. My mom loves Beyonce, and she brings me every article on her," Miley adds. "She's like, *Look, she's so humble, but she is still amazing.*"[35]

Miley has been called the anti-Britney and anti-Lindsay, insofar as she is not seen as self-destructive, or the poster child for out-of-control young stars. Miley has a more tolerant perspective. "I think most 21- to 25-year-olds go through this kind of thing," she says, acknowledging that she is friends with both Spears and Lohan. "I guess that's why I'm so adamant . . . I know those people and I know they have good hearts and they're struggling."[36]

Besides her parents, Miley credits her faith with guiding her priorities. She calls herself a hard-core Christian, is a regular churchgoer, and has repeatedly said she is a virgin and plans to remain so until she gets married. She is involved with several charities and in 2007 gave $1 from every *Hannah Montana* concert ticket sold to the City of Hope. She participated in the Just Stand Up benefit single with 15 other singers, such as Carrie Underwood, LeAnn Rimes, and Mariah Carey, and performed the song during the *Stand Up to Cancer* television special, which was aired simultaneously on ABC, NBC, and CBS on September 5, 2008.

For a while Miley's life seemed almost too charmed to be true—until she got a reality check.

GROWING UP IN THE SPOTLIGHT

No amount of fame or wealth can keep teenage angst at bay. Miley admits she frets constantly about her appearance. "I feel like I stare in the mirror 400 hours a day. I swear, I will be in that mirror saying, *I hate my hair. I hate my nose. I hate, hate, hate my teeth!* I look in the mirror and think, *This shirt is ugly. These pants are stupid.* It's a lot easier when I have someone to put my makeup on and fix my hair. People on TV have a lotta people pulling it together for us. It makes all the difference."[37]

But in one case, fashion put Miley in the hot seat with her fans and Disney. While doing a photo shoot for the June 2008 issue of *Vanity Fair*, Miley posed while draped in a sheet for one series of shots, taken by famed photographer Annie Leibovitz. Her back was exposed but she was otherwise covered and the photographer was famed. When news of the shot broke, Miley initially dismissed it as an artistic picture she was comfortable with. "I thought, *This looks pretty, and really natural.* I think it's really artsy."[38]

But after the incident grew into a firestorm of controversy—before the public had actually even seen the photos—Miley backtracked, apologizing to her fans and expressing her embarrassment. Disney accused the magazine of manipulating and exploiting a naïve teenager in order to sell more magazines.

Vanity Fair stood its ground, releasing a statement saying: "Miley's parents and/ or minders were on the set all day. Since the photo was taken digitally, they saw it on the shoot and everyone thought it was a beautiful and natural portrait of Miley."[39]

The controversy was a hard lesson learned. "It's hard growing up in the spotlight," Miley later said, "and I'm changing. I can't be the 12-year-old who just moved to LA forever. I'm having a great time doing what I do, but I'm also going to stumble and fall." Sometimes it felt to Miley that people were expecting her to self-implode. "People mention child performers who have gone off the rails, but there are also stable people like Jodie Foster. She was a child star and look where she is now. She called to give me advice which was great."[40]

Friends, Miley discovered, can never be over-appreciated. "A true friend is someone who is there for you. I have a song called "True Friend," and it says that you're supposed to be there through all the ups and downs. There have been a lot of ups, a lot of positive things in my life, but there are things that are not so fun to deal with. My friend hears about things from me, and a true friend is someone who listens to everything."[41]

However uncomfortable it was in the short term, the *Vanity Fair* scandal passed with little, if any, impact on her popularity. Her second solo album, *Breakout,* was released in July 2008, reaching number 1 on the Billboard 200. She was also named one of *Time* magazine's 100 Most Influential People in the World for 2008. Her song, "I Thought I'd Lost You," from the movie *Bolt* was nominated for a Golden Globe Best Original Song. She was also cast to star in *The Last Song*. But perhaps the most exciting, Miley was given a car for her 16th birthday, although "not the one I wanted. I took my mom's old car, which wasn't so bad because it was a Porsche . . . It was a pretty good hand me down."[42]

Miley maintained she was happy to take life as it came, in no hurry to grow up any faster than she is already was. She agreed to live at home until she was 20, in exchange for getting her own section of the house as a personal apartment of

HANNAH MONTANA: THE MOVIE

In *Hannah Montana: The Movie,* Miley Stewart is taken back to her country roots. Believing his daughter is on the verge of letting her celebrity as Hannah Montana take over her life, Robby Ray suggests she forego a professional engagement to spend a couple weeks in her home town, Crowley Corners, Tennessee, so she can attend her grandmother's birthday party. Miley, of course, objects; Robby Ray, of course, makes it happen anyway, and once there, Miley finds romance and perspective.

Prior to the start of the filming, Billy Ray Cyrus campaigned to have the movie shot on location in Tennessee, the Cyrus clan's home state and ultimately got his wish. Principal photography began in April 2008. Locations included Nashville, Franklin and Columbia in Tennessee, and Santa Monica, California.

The movie premiered on April 2, 2009, at Disney's El Capitan Theatre in Hollywood. It opened in general release on April 10, earning $17.4 million— the best opening-day gross for a live-action G-rated movie ever—making the week's number 1 film. It would go on to earn $87 million worldwide. The soundtrack reached number 1 on the Billboard charts and was certified 3x platinum.

sorts. And she was content with continuing as Hannah Montana, despite a swirl of rumors in late summer 2008 that she and Bill Ray were trying to get out of their contracts.

"I am fully committed to Hannah Montana. It's what gave me this amazing opportunity to reach out to so many people,"[43] Cyrus said, adding that reports of tension on the set were untrue. "It's a lot of craziness . . . We have an amazing cast that is so supportive. I'm really excited about our new season. We are making great new episodes that I can't wait for our fans to see."

Despite all she has gone through—the skyrocket success of *Hannah Montana,* the nonstop schedule, establishing herself as a top recording artist, public controversy—Miley has come through it with both feet still firmly on the ground. "That's just my personality. I'm very much like my dad. My dad's like this. I don't get shaken or stirred up over anything. I just don't let things faze me."[44]

NOTES

1. Ann Oldenburg. "Lifelong Work Pays Off, says Miley Cyrus, 13." *USA Today,* January 14, 2007, http://www.usatoday.com/life/television/news/2007-01-10-miley-cyrus_x.htm.

2. Spoken to the author at the Television Critics Association press tour, July 2006.

3. David Hiltbrand. "Newfound Fame on Disney Shouldn't Faze Miley Cyrus." *Philadelphia Inquirer,* May 17, 2006, http://www.highbeam.com/doc/1G1-145874063.html.

4. Oldenburg, "Lifelong Work Pays."

5. Spoken to the author at the Television Critics Association press tour, July 2006.

6. Miley Cyrus. *Miles to Go,* New York: Disney Hyperion, March 3, 2009.

7. Ibid.

8. Spoken to the author at the Television Critics Association press tour, July 2006.

9. Ibid.

10. Oldenburg, "Lifelong Work Pays."

11. Spoken to the author at the Television Critics Association press tour, July 2006.

12. Ibid.

13. Ibid.

14. Ibid.

15. Ibid.

16. Ibid.

17. Ibid.

18. Ibid.

19. Ken Beck. "Teen Miley Cyrus Leaves Tennessee Hills for Hollywood," *The Tennessean,* March 19, 2006, p. 10D.

20. Marina Khidekel. "My Oh Miley," *CosmoGirl!,* March 1, 2008, http://www.highbeam.com/doc/1G1-175075180.html.

21. Tom Dorsey. "Achy Breaky Daughter," *Courier-Journal,* May 12, 2006.

22. Spoken to the author at the Television Critics Association press tour, July 2006.

23. Beck, "Teen Miley Cyrus."

24. Beth Neil. "Your Life: Hannah Montana," *The Mirror,* May 6, 2008, http://www.highbeam.com/doc/1G1-178652121.html.

25. Spoken to the author at the Television Critics Association press tour, July 2006.

26. Ibid.

27. Ibid.

28. Ibid.

29. "Miley Cyrus Is Glad She Is Not in School," Disney Dreaming, http://www.disney dreaming.com/2009/04/03/miley-cyrus-is-glad-shes-not-in-school/.

30. Cyrus, *Miles to Go.*

31. Ibid.

32. Ibid.

33. "Billy Ray Cyrus Calls Miley's Boyfriend 'A Good Kid'," *People,* October 7, 2008, http://www.people.com/people/article/0,20231559,00.html.

34. Khidekel, "My Oh Miley."

35. Ibid.

36. Bruce Handy. "Miley Knows Best," *Vanity Fair,* June 2008, http://www.vanityfair.com/culture/features/2008/06/miley200806.

37. Jodi Bryson. "The Secret Life of Miley Cyrus," *Girls' Life,* December 1, 2006, http://www.highbeam.com/doc/1G1-154755948.html.

38. Handy, "Miley Knows Best."

39. The Associated Press, April 29, 2008, http://www.highbeam.com/doc/1G1-175075 180.html.

40. MSNBC, http://wonderwall.msn.com/music/miley-i-want-to-keep-my-virginity-until-i-marry—1514227.story.

41. Lina Das. "Me, Myself and Miley," *The Daily Mail,* May 1, 2009, http://www.dailymail.co.uk/tvshowbiz/article-1175848/Me-Miley-Cyrus-talks-frankly-stardom-virginity-Hannah-Montana-dazzling-screen-alter-ego.html.

42. *Extra!,* syndicated TV show, December 11, 2009.

43. Michelle Tan. "Miley Fully Committed," *People,* September 22, 2008, http://www.people.com/people/article/0,20227748,00.html.

44. Spoken to the author at the Television Critics Association press tour, July 2006.

FURTHER READING

Alexander, Lauren. *Mad for Miley: An Unauthorized Biography*, New York: Price Stern Sloan, 2007.

Kent, Brittany. *Miley Cyrus: This Is Her Life,* New York: Berkley Trade, 2008.

Miley Cyrus Official Website, www.mileycyrus.com.

MySpace, www.myspace.com/mileycyrus.

People.com, www.people.com/people/miley_cyrus.

Known for her love of fashion, Blake Lively was named to Victoria's Secret 2012 What's Sexy Now list for her summer styles.

8 BLAKE LIVELY

Sometimes when things seem as if they cannot get any better, life serves up a reality check. In October 2008, Blake Lively was enjoying the heady experience of new stardom. She was living in New York, starring in a hit television series, and enjoying a passionate romance with her costar Penn Badgley. She was the magazine world's new It Girl, her face appearing on over a dozen covers in less than a year, everything from *Vogue* to *Girl's Life*.

Then came the telephone call on October 13. Blake's father, actor-director-acting coach Ernie Lively, had been in a car accident. The initial press reports were grim: he had suffered a broken back and was in very serious condition. Blake immediately left New York and headed home to California to be with her family at Ernie's side.

But the family received good news from doctors at the hospital. Fortunately, the injuries turned out to be less grave than first feared. Blake's mom, Elaine Lively, told reporters. "It is far less serious than we thought. Yesterday it didn't look good. It was a horrific accident."[1]

The incident happened in the early morning hours as Ernie was on his way to the set of *Criminal Minds*. He swerved to avoid another car and lost control of the vehicle, which tumbled down an embankment.

"He's going to make a full recovery, thankfully, but we do not know when he will be out of hospital," Elaine said, confirming her husband was being treated for arm, back and lung injuries. "We are just happy he is going to be OK."[2]

Once she was assured he would recover, Blake returned to New York on a redeye flight so she could make a 5:00 a.m. call time on the set. But the sleep deprivation was worth being able to see her father. "It was very serious," she says, "and it's hard to be on the other side of the country from him. I'm so used to being within 10 minutes of my family."[3]

The Lively clan is nothing if not tight-knit, right down to their career choices. Ernie, Blake, and her four older siblings—Lori, Jason, Robyn, and Eric—are all actors. Mom Elaine is a talent agent. But as a child, Blake says she had no burning desire to act. "I never really went after it, just because it was already so much a part of my life." It may not have been her passion, but it was her destiny.[4]

THE FAMILY BUSINESS

Blake Christina Lively was born on August 25, 1987, in Tarzana, California. The dusty San Fernando Valley community was originally part of the San Fernando Mission, established by Spanish missionaries in 1797. A hundred years later it was part of a wheat farm. In 1915, Edgar Rice Burroughs, author of the *Tarzan* books bought a huge ranch in the area, which he named *Tarzana*. When the local area was incorporated in 1928, the residents voted to adopt *Tarzana* as the name for their town in honor of the author. By the time Blake was born, Tarzana was a sprawl of suburbia with mini malls on every corner.

After divorcing Ronnie Lively, with whom she had Lori, Jason, and Robyn, Elaine married Ernie. In a twist, Ernie, whose last name was Brown, took Elaine's last name and became Ernie Lively. Together they had Eric, born in 1981, and Blake, who was literally dragged into the family business. "My mom and dad always taught acting, so instead of getting me babysitters, they would just bring me to class," Lively recalls. "And I'm a naturally shy person, so it really helped. I would've just been hiding under the table, pulling on my mother's dress if I hadn't been in their classes. It forced me out of my shell."[5]

Where other families take home videos, Blake's dad made movies featuring his kids. Blake's first role was playing Trixie the tooth fairy in *Sandman,* a film Ernie directed in 1998 that was never released theatrically. The experience was not life changing and she maintained her ambivalence toward acting, something her brother Eric was not about to let go unchallenged. When he was 21, Eric took Blake, then 15, on a six-week European vacation. Once he had her as a captive audience, he urged her to think seriously about acting as her vocation.

"He was trying to get me to make life decisions at 15!" she says.[6]

The trip, though, was worth the lectures. Eric originally told their mom that he and Blake would only be gone for the two weeks of her winter break from school, they kept her out an additional four weeks. "That was the plan all along but he knew they wouldn't let me miss so much school. But he realized the trip was more important than me being in school. I got a much better education about world history in that month and a half than I did in the entirety of my high school life."[7]

Blake said they toured Cambridge, Rome, Cologne, Florence, Paris, and Brussels. Sometimes they stayed in fancy, five-star hotels; other times they bunked in Spartan youth hostels. The only downside was lunch, she says, "Because every single day he'd be like, *What are you going to do for a living?*"[8]

In the Lively family, such sibling involvement was not unusual, Blake says. "I am very close with all my family members and they all think they're my parents . . . Eric said he wanted me to be more cultured and see the world, and he'd go, *Look, you need to have a job that can help you experience everything there is in the world.*"[9]

But at the time, Blake was already experiencing a full life at Burbank High School where she was a cheerleader and top student. Instead of going out for the school play, she opted to join the Show Choir and belonged to six different clubs. "Each had different groups of people so I had a really big group of friends. And we were nothing alike, but we all had this common passion, so it was a really great bonding experience." A typical night on the town for Blake and her friends was going to the local Fuddruckers or attend school fund-raisers. "I was very involved in school—I was class president! And all of my friends were good; nobody was too wild."[10]

While her high school life certainly seemed charmed from the outside, Blake says she experienced her share of being the brunt of gossip and mean people. "It doesn't matter who you are, people will always talk about you, just because they're bored, insecure, or not happy for whatever reason." Her way of dealing with it was to get more involved to surround herself with others who all loved the same thing she did. "In my choir group, we were like family. That's one of the reasons I was in so many activities; I loved that feeling of belonging."[11]

"Your friendships are what get you through. That is what I'll remember, the people I've had a connection with and who know me inside and out will be lifelong friends."[12]

While some of her classmates went through phases of acting out, Blake said she never felt the need to go behind her parents' backs. She recalls going to parties where "there were people drinking or going off and doing drugs, but I would see how stupid they were after they got high or drunk—they seemed like they were just making fools of themselves."[13]

Blake has sympathy for the young Hollywood stars who have struggled with drug or alcohol issues or who have caused public spectacles of themselves because she believes it's not completely their fault. "When you don't have someone to model yourself after, you're going to make mistakes. There's no one there to tell them what's right or wrong or who is a positive example."[14]

Whatever downsides high school had, Blake was mostly content with her life and told Eric that her future plans included Stanford—not acting. Refusing to take no for an answer, Eric eventually asked his agent to represent Blake—much to Blake's surprise. "I was really busy at school," she recalls, "and I would have these agents calling and saying, *We have an appointment for you.* It was really hard to say no, because I didn't want to make my brother upset."[15]

To appease Eric, Blake agreed to have a headshot taken and go on some auditions. When Blake auditioned for *The Sisterhood of the Traveling Pants,* based on Ann Brashares's best-selling novel, all she had to give the producers was a picture of herself. She had no resume because she had no acting credits, save her turn as Trixie the tooth fairy. No matter, by the end of the audition she had secured her first credit. She'd been going out on auditions for less than two months.

Suddenly, Stanford was starting to look a little less certain.

SISTERHOOD

Sisterhood of the Traveling Pants is a coming-of-age story about four 16-year-old high school friends who go shopping one day and find a pair of magical jeans that fit each of them perfectly, even though they have very different body types. The girls agree to share the pants over their summer vacation, sending them back and forth to one another as they spend their summer apart from one another in different parts of the world.

Blake, who played tomboy Bridget, was the only unknown cast member in the movie. Also starring in the film were *Gilmore Girl* Alexis Bledel; America Ferrera, who was coming off her critically acclaimed role in *Real Women Have Curves*; and Amber Tamblyn, who had just finished two seasons in the TV series *Joan of Arcadia.*

Ferrera admitted that she ignored the script for quite a while, "That script just sat on my desk for months," and only read it at the insistence of her agent. Before she was halfway through, she was hooked on the project. "I wasn't expecting this story of teenagers to have such complexity, because what we're so used to seeing these days are such stereotyped, very petty problems. The movies reduce the teenage experience to something very materialistic and superficial. It becomes disheartening because we know that the experience of growing up is so much more complex than what's portrayed on screen most of the time."[16]

Blake says she initially found the title off-putting. "I was like, *There's no way I'm reading this stupid script,* even though I'd never done anything." But she read it, if for no other reason than "it was a good excuse for me not to cram script-reading in between cheer and choir practice." What excited her about the script was its portrayal of teenage girls as likable. "I can't remember the last time I saw a teen movie that didn't make young girls seem like these horrible, mean, back-stabbing, manipulative people."[17]

AUTHOR ANN BRASHARES

Ann Brashares was born in Alexandria, Virginia, the only girl of four siblings. She studied philosophy at Barnard College and after graduation took a job as an editor at 17th Street Productions. Her initial plan was to save up enough money to go to graduate school. But Brashares discovered she loved editing and never went back to college.

She began writing her first novel in 2000 and the following year *Sisterhood of the Traveling Pants* was published. Over the next five years, she wrote three sequels: *The Second Summer of the Sisterhood, Girls in Pants,* and *Forever in Blue,* the latter published in January 2007. That same year her first adult novel, *The Last Summer (of You and Me)* was released.

Ann says that she never writes with the idea of trying to teach any lessons. "I want to tell a story as truthfully and engagingly as I can, and then let the chips fall where they may."[18]

Sisterhood filmed on location in British Columbia during the summer between Blake's junior and senior year. She describes her character, the soccer-playing Bridget, as someone bursting with energy. Despite being the life of the party, Bridget harbors a dark side—her mother committed suicide and her relationship with her father is strained. Her way of coping is denial—she simply pretends none of the bad stuff ever happened. Blake says that she related to Bridget's energy. "I always have to be going, going and making things fun. Plus, I enjoy playing sports. I feel Bridget and I are the same in that way." The angst, not so much. "Bridget doesn't have any family at all, and I have a huge family that always supports me."[19]

Ironically, Blake was the only actual teenager among the four leads but she quickly bonded with her older cast mates. "We were crazy," she says. "It was actually difficult to work with us because we were in our own world and just talked all the time." They also choreographed dance routines to Vanilla Ice songs. "We had the same sense of humor and lots of inside jokes. So we were friends for real. If one of the four of us hadn't been as weird as we all are, it wouldn't have worked."[20]

In between the fun, Blake discovered making movies was hard work. She admits that before she got her first job, she mostly thought of the glamour factor. "Someone to drive you, do your hair and clothes, you act like someone else for a little while and go home!" The reality of 20-hour work schedule adjusted her view. "When we were shooting at night, we didn't see daylight at all for a while. You have to have as much energy 16 hours later as you did when you started."[21] Blake also had to undergo two months of rigorous athletic training for the film's soccer scenes.

In the end, though, all the hard work was worth it, both because Blake was proud of the film and because she had made three new lifelong friends. But she also missed her old friends. "Everybody was telling me, 'Oh, you can't go back to high school . . . You gotta keep doing movies now, get yourself out there.'"[22] But when Blake got back home from the movie, she found her other friends had moved on with their lives, too, and it took time to integrate back into her former life.

> Even though I was with my friends every single day throughout our entire high school career, when somebody's gone for that long, you can't sit at home by yourself, so my friends made other groups of friends. And then I came back after three months ready to go do what we used to do, and things change. People get older and there are inside jokes that you don't know about that have happened. And then the friends that they've replaced you with are a little territorial. So you feel a little lost for awhile.[23]

But not for too long—during her senior year in high school Blake got her first boyfriend, Kelly Blatz, who studied acting with Ernie Lively. Blake took Kelly with her to the premiere of *Sisterhood,* where she admitted she'd had a crush on him since second grade. Blake's prom was that same night so as soon as her obligations to the film's premiere were completed, she left to attend prom, where Blake says she danced the night away, "Ever since I was a little girl I wanted to dance to "At

Last" [by Etta James] at my senior prom," so she requested it, then after it was over, "They kicked us out."[24]

By the time Blake graduated, her plan to go to Stanford had been put on temporary hold. She decided to take a year off to act and see where it took her. She didn't imagine it would take her to the other end of the country and overnight television fame.

RISING STAR

In August 2006, Blake's second film, *Accepted,* was released. A sophomoric comedy about a high school senior who establishes a fake university so his parents won't find out he's been rejected by every college he applied to. Blake played the seemingly-out-of-his-league object of desire.

Her third film was *Elvis and Anabelle,* which never found a distributor and was only shown at a handful of film festivals. Billed as a unique love story, Blake played Anabelle, a beauty queen who dies of bulimia. After her death, Anabelle is taken to the local mortician, Elvis, where the love story ensues. Blake had to lose significant weight for the role, which she did by exercising and making chicken breasts on a George Foreman Grill, with sides of asparagus and broccoli. Even though she lost weight, Blake says she also got toned and felt the healthiest she's ever been.

There was no denying that her brother Eric had been right—Blake *did* love acting. She loved the process of making movies and the on-the-job training she was getting. So when the executive producer Josh Schwartz contacted Blake about his new TV series called *Gossip Girl,* she wasn't particularly enthusiastic. "I was loving films, so I thought, *No, I don't want to try TV.*"[25]

That was before Schwartz surprised Blake by revealing that he had actually written the part of Serena van der Woodsen specifically for her. He also told Blake that fans on message boards were clamoring for her to be cast as Serena after seeing the *Sisterhood* trailer. But Schwartz jokes that what sealed the deal was dangling a fashion carrot in front of Blake: Serena was an Upper East Side denizen with a fabulous wardrobe—and Schwartz let her know the producers might be amenable to letting Blake have some of that wardrobe. Whether it was the clothes and accessories or Blake's interest in possibly taking some classes at Columbia while shooting on location in New York, starring on *Gossip Girl* was an offer she couldn't refuse. And the producers made good on their fashion graft. "I probably have, like, 60 gorgeous bags," Blake says, adding, "The fashion is just unbelievable. You can watch our show on mute and be entertained."[26]

Blake says it's impossible not to absorb Serena's fashion sense just being in New York. "You put on skinny jeans and riding boots and a leather coat and handbag, and you take on that posture and character," Lively says. "It becomes very natural." Blake says that the *Gossip Girl* wardrobe people have also begun to incorporate her personal style in Serena's. "The more they work with me and see my style, and the more I learn about fashion, the more input I have," she says. "It's more collaborative now than it was in the beginning because then I had no idea what I was doing."[27]

So Blake's *Sisterhood* friends did not hesitate to give her advice. "They said, *Don't try to do anything. Don't try to clean your house. Don't try to get groceries. Just sleep and eat,* because I try to go to everything. I think I'm superwoman sometimes. So it really helps me to have such great genuine friends like that who have already been through this before, so they're definitely a good support group."[28]

Before she was hired, Blake had never read any of Cecily von Ziegesar's *Gossip Girl* novels, although she says, "My friends were obsessed." She remembers being in class taking a midterm and a friend sitting next to her was reading the book under her desk. "I thought it was silly," Blake says. But after getting the script, she went to the friend's house to borrow the books and admits, "Then I saw why they were all reading them!"[29]

Working on *Gossip Girl* meant leaving her family and her friends to live in New York. Blake says she still stays in touch with her high school friends, although it's more difficult on a TV show than it was on the films. "When you're on set, you can't have your cell phone ringing all day, so, of course, I e-mail and I text."[30]

The native Californian says teenagers who grow up amidst the wealth of the Upper East Side are a different species from the kids she grew up with. "They're definitely more cultured; much more worldly. And their money is old money. They've grown up in this, where a lot of kids in L.A., their father is some big producer or it is newfound fame and money, which is very different." She also thinks the elite of Manhattan take education more seriously. "It's very important to them, where kids in L.A. a lot of times just want to hang out at the beach, so I really like that about New York."[31]

Blake tries to bring her personal sensibility to Serena. "My character gets caught up in this universe. They're handed everything on a silver platter, and she's the center of her own world. What's important about her is that she realizes she needs to reform herself. I think that everybody has a good soul at the heart of it."[32]

Gossip Girl is known for its depiction of excess, be it money, sex, power, or gossip. While it's fun for viewers to watch, especially the steamy romantic encounters, it can be uncomfortable to portray. "It's *always* awkward," Blake says, recalling a scene in the first episode where she is sitting on the lap of costar Chace Crawford, who she had only met a couple weeks earlier. "Between takes, it was like, *So . . . did you like those cupcakes the other day?* Then we had to start kissing, and you kind of just go for it. It is not fun or sexy. Of course, everyone in the cast is gorgeous, but it's not this hot moment. It's not as romantic as people think it is."[33]

Blake also explains that it's not even real kissing; she says lips touch but nothing else . . . usually. "Some people are shady," she acknowledges. "They'll slip their tongue in. But nothing about kissing your costar is romantic, sexy, or appealing because you have 40 crew members watching you."[34]

Blake's shyness extends into her real life as well, which is partly the reason she didn't have a boyfriend until she was 17. "There were boys that I would find out later had a crush on me but I was too shy to them." Blake says she's a very trusting person—at first. "Then the second that they do something to break my trust, I just shut down. I get very guarded."[35]

Despite playing a character who spends her life out on the town, Blake is not a clubber. She says she doesn't see the point since she doesn't drink and clubs are so loud you can't carry on a conversation. She does like going to hear live jazz but her favorite pastime is playing *Guitar Hero* as her video game alter ego Pandora. She has participated in tournaments where she dons fake sailor tattoos and dresses like a rocker. "Everyone else dresses totally normally and must think I'm a complete freak!" she says.[36]

REAL LIFE GOSSIP GIRL

The success of *Gossip Girl* meant that Blake's personal life was no longer anonymous. And when the tabloids ran out of actual events to write about, they began speculating about her. Blake says the oddest thing she ever heard about herself was that she was the next Paris Hilton. "Since I have a dog and blonde hair, that must mean we're alike? . . . I don't like being compared to anyone by somebody who doesn't know me. I'm my own person. I don't go to clubs, I don't party, I don't dance on tables, and I don't like sex tapes."[37]

Although Blake and her costars work long hours that cut into sleep and social time, she says she's having more fun than she could have imagined because everyone in the cast is both funny and fun. She reveals that Leighton Meester entertains everyone with vocal impressions, Ed Westwick serenades the cast, and Penn Badgely shows off silly dance moves. Her description of on-set camaraderie is at odds with reports of tension between Blake and Leighton—accounts Blake takes issue with.

"There is always going to be drama on set," she says, "but it's just not true that Leighton and I dislike each other." Blake acknowledges she doesn't always get along with everyone she meets but, "if you pay attention to what everyone else thinks, you're going to be forever unhappy . . . All that really matters is that the people you care about think of you highly."[38]

Blake's romantic life was also the source of much speculation. She had begun dating Kelly Blatz in 2004 but by 2007, the relationship appeared to have run its course. Soon after rumors circulated that Blake and Penn Badgley were secretly dating. She denied it—repeatedly. Then in May 2008, the couple attended an after-party together for the Metropolitan Museum's Costume Institute Gala. Badgley told *People* "I think she's incredible. She's an amazing person and she's beautiful—there's not a lot to dislike."[39]

A week later, Blake and Penn were photographed cuddling and kissing in Cancun. The relationship was official. Even so, Blake was still reticent to discuss it publicly. "We put so much of ourselves out there all the time: there are very few things that we get to keep private," she explained while promoting *Sisterhood 2,* admitting the loss of privacy that came with success was hard. "You see these people who fall off the edge and it seems they have given the media all of themselves."[40]

Instead, Blake likes to keep her fun personal and says she happiest when she's home cooking and baking; when she's traveling Europe; when she's at Disneyland with friends; and when she goes shopping at Williams-Sonoma, a high-end cooking store.

Of all the *Gossip Girl* stars, Blake is emerging as the breakout star, the one who gets cast in the A-list films. In the spring of 2008, she filmed *The Private Lives of Pippa Lee,* written and directed by Rebecca Miller. The titular Pippa is a one-time drug user turned stay-at-home mom. Robin Wright Penn plays the 40-something Pippa; Blake portrays the youthful version. The movie also stars Alan Arkin, Julianne Moore, and Winona Ryder. Blake's been around the industry enough to know her good fortune but she's also careful not to revel in it at the expense of her *Gossip Girl* cast mates. It's all part of having the tools, and support, to stay grounded.

"I just think for too many people, it becomes a way of life instead of a job," Blake says. "My whole family is in this business, I grew up with that mindset. So I think that's the thing for me. It's just like at the end of the day, I want to go to dinner and watch a movie. I don't want to go to a club and . . . not wear panties!"[41]

Although acting may be her life's work, Blake can still imagine living a completely different life and being happy if her acting career ever fizzles—a life like Martha Stewart. "I love planning and throwing parties. I'm very detail-oriented and creative." Blake recalls the time she celebrated the release of a Harry Potter film by dressing up like Hermione for the midnight showing and making a tiered

KELLY BLATZ

Blake's ex-boyfriend Kelly Blatz has started to make his own in Hollywood as the star in the Disney XD TV series, *Aaron Stone.* In the action-adventure drama, Blatz plays Charlie Landers who excels at an online video game called "Hero Rising." He names his avatar for the game Aaron Stone. Charlie learns from a billionaire named Mr. Hall that the game isn't really a game; it's a re-creation of real-life events. It was also a recruitment exercise to find the person with the best potential to be a secret agent to help save the world from the evil Omega Defiance organization. Whether he likes it or not, Charlie must become a real-life Aaron Stone to help save the world.

Born and raised in Burbank, Kelly began acting as a kid, mostly appearing in commercials, but didn't like it very much and stopped for several years. Still interested in movies, he planned to attend film school after graduating from high school. But during his senior year he decided to give acting another try. He put off film school and started taking acting lessons instead—from Blake's father.

He made his film debut in *The Oakley Seven* and had small roles in the horror movies *Simon Says* and *Prom Night* before landing the lead role in *Aaron Stone.* In his spare time, Kelly is the lead singer of the alternative rock band Capra.

cake to look like a witch's hat. She also planned a Willie Wonka–themed 18th birthday party. "I don't want to have a party unless I can do everything I want to do. I'm just an all-or-nothing sort of girl."[42]

NOTES

1. "Blake Lively's Dad Hurt in Crash," UPI.com, October 14, 2008, http://www.upi.com/Entertainment_News/2008/10/14/Blake-Livelys-dad-hurt-in-crash/UPI-76091224033168/.

2. Ibid.

3. Dana Wood. "Levelheaded Blake Lively," *W,* December 2008, http://www.wmagazine.com/celebrities/2008/12/blake_lively.

4. *Today Show,* NBC, May 31, 2005.

5. "My Mom and Dad," Blake Livey Facebook Page, www.facebook.com/pages/Blake-Lively/109031362586?sk=info.

6. Wood, "Levelheaded Blake Lively."

7. Blake Lively Interview, Marie Claire UK, http://community.livejournal.com/ohnotheydidnt/32665719.html.

8. Ibid.

9. Ibid.

10. Carissa Rosenberg. "Blake Lively: This Year Going to be Amazing!" *Seventeen,* Hearst Magazines, A Division of the Hearst Corporation, 2008. http://www.highbeam.com.

11. Spoken to the author at the Television Critics Association press tour, July 2007.

12. Nell Minow. "One Size Fits All," *Chicago Tribune,* June 1, 2005, Tempo, p. 1.

13. Kristen Sardis. "3 Minutes with Blake Lively; A Couple of Things about Blake Lively: She Hates Shaving Her Legs and Is a Popcorn Freak. Read On for More Secrets!(cg! insider: q & a)." *CosmoGirl!,* Hearst Magazines, A Division of the Hearst Corporation, 2006. http://www.highbeam.com.

14. Ibid.

15. Wood, "Levelheaded Blake Lively."

16. "An Afternoon of Serious Shopping Helped Film's Actresses Get the 'Sisterhood' Message," McClatchy-Tribune Information Services, 2005. http://www.highbeam.com.

17. Bob Strauss. "It's More Than Pants," *Daily News,* May 29, 2005, http://docs.newsbank.com/s/InfoWeb/aggdocs/NewsBank/10A86080955188A3/1083311554222450.

18. "Sisterhood Central," Random House, http://www.randomhouse.com/teens/sisterhoodcentral/author.html.

19. "Little Sister: Meet Blake Lively, the Youngest Member of the 'Sisterhood' (One-on-One Interview)." Know Your World Extra. Weekly Reader Corp., 2005. http://www.highbeam.com.

20. "Sisterhood' Stars Talk Proms and Premieres," Associated Press, June 1, 2005, http://www.msnbc.msn.com/id/8061775/page/2/.

21. Minow, "One Size Fits All."

22. Erin Carlson. "Blake Lively Talks about 'Gossip Girl' Stardom, Playing 'Guitar Hero'," *Gwinnett Daily Post,* December 8, 2007, Family & Spirit, p. 1.

23. Spoken to the author at the Television Critics Association press tour, July 2007.

24. Associated Press, "Sisterhood' Stars Talk."

25. Wood, "Levelheaded Blake Lively."

26. Ibid.

27. Alessandra Stanley. "East Side Story," Vogue.com, February 2009, http://www.style.com/vogue/feature/2009_Feb_Blake_Lively/.

28. Spoken to the author at the Television Critics Association press tour, July 2007.

29. Lori Berger. "Blake Lively Has Some Gossip!" *CosmoGirl!,* Hearst Magazines, A Division of the Hearst Corporation, 2007. http://www.highbeam.com.

30. Spoken to the author at the Television Critics Association press tour, July 2007.

31. Ibid.

32. Ibid.

33. Sardis, "3 Minutes with Blake."

34. Rosenberg, "Blake Lively."

35. Blake Lively Interview, Marie Claire UK, http://community.livejournal.com/ohno theydidnt/32665719.html.

36. Rosenberg, "Blake Lively."

37. Ibid.

38. Blake Lively Does Teen Vogue, http://thebosh.com/archives/2008/01/blake_lively_does_teen_vogue.php.

39. "Having a Ball," *People,* http://www.people.com/people/gallery/0,20198154_20452581,00.html.

40. Prairie Miller. "The Blake Lively Sisterhood of the Traveling Pants Interview," August 6, 2008, http://newsblaze.com/story/20080806055412mill.nb/topstory.html.

41. Ibid.

42. Sardis, "3 Minutes with Blake."

FURTHER READING

E! Online, www.eonline.com/uberblog/celebbios/makeCelebUrl.jsp?uuid=f79a6381-4aa3-4dcb-b714-09de56020324.

Gossip Girl, www.cwtv.com/shows/gossip-girl/cast/blake-lively.

Robin, Emily. *Blake Lively: Traveling to the Top,* New York: Scholastic, 2009.

TV.com, "Blake Lively Trivia & Quotes," www.tv.com/blake-lively/person/278281/trivia.html.

In a case of life imitating art, Lea Michele and costar Cory Monteith started a romance in February 2012, during *Glee*'s third season.

9   LEA MICHELE

Nothing much seems to rain on the parade of this Broadway baby. Like her character Rachel Berry on *Glee,* as a teenager Lea pursued acting with single-minded purpose. Unlike Rachel, Lea has already achieved stardom on stage and small screen and some think she may prove to be the Barbra Streisand of her generation.

AN ONLY CHILD

Lea Michele Sarfati was born on August 29, 1986, in the Bronx borough of New York. When Lea was young, her mom, Edith, a nurse, and her dad, a deli owner, decided it would be best for her education to move to New Jersey. She attended elementary school in Tenafly, New Jersey, which is right over the George Washington Bridge.

Lea never gave much thought to performing until she was eight years old. "My best friend at the time would take me to see musicals with her," she recalls. "We went to see *Camelot* and I think that I fell asleep, and then we went to see *Cats* and I was scared. Finally, we went to go see *Phantom of the Opera,* and I think that was the first time that I really saw the beauty of theatre and I instantly fell in love with it."[1]

As it happened, a couple of days later they were having an open call for the part of young Cosette in *Les Miserables* and Lea's friend wanted to go for auditions; but her father became ill, so Lea and her mom accompanied the friend. "And for whatever reason I decided that I wanted to audition as well," Lea told *Broadway World.* "I had been listening to the soundtrack of Phantom non-stop and had memorized 'Angel of Music.' I went in and sang it a cappella at the open call. Literally, I had never sung before."[2]

The casting agent called Lea's mother into the room and told her they were going to call her back for another audition. Edith told her daughter not to get her hopes up. But at the callback they told Lea that she had been cast. Looking back, Lea says that being a young Cosette was a great way of stepping in to the business "because you learn so much so quickly. The size of the role, the amount of work that they put on me was just enough," she told writer Robert Diamond. "I basically came into this with nothing, knowing actually nothing about theatre or acting or anything."[3]

She stayed with the show for a year and a half until she outgrew the role.

Lea left the show in early August and after coming back from a week's vacation with her parents, auditioned for *Ragtime.* She got the part and says she and her mom were on a plane to Canada by the 30th of August. "We packed up our bags, my mother and I, and we left for Toronto. It was literally one thing right into the next."[4]

She spent a year in Toronto with the original cast and then stayed with the show another year after it moved to Broadway. She says being in *Les Miserables* and *Ragtime* was the best education possible because it was hands-on experience in the company of stage veterans. Her education continued when she was cast in *Spring Awakening,* a rock musical adaptation of a late-19th-century play by German playwright Frank Wedekind. The story follows the lives of teenagers discovering their sexuality against a repressive background. Lea was cast as the female lead, Wendla. Her costar was Jonathan Groff—who would later play her *Glee* love interest Jesse.

The play went through several rewrites and workshops, which worked out in Lea's favor. "While I did workshops of Spring Awakening during my freshman, sophomore and junior year of high school I wasn't really auditioning very much because I wanted to give myself time to focus on school and . . . have a normal high school life for a little while," she told *Broadway World.*[5]

"I tried to dabble in a bunch of different things, and I had lots of different kinds of friends. I had a really great high school experience."[6]

Her break from acting ended the summer before her senior year at Tenafly High School, when she was cast in a revival of *Fiddler on the Roof.* It was at that point that Lea realized she was at a crossroads. She was about to graduate from high school and had just been accepted into the Tisch School of Art at New York University. "So it was a real deciding factor for me," she recalled to writer Robert Diamond. "Which way is your life going to go—the college route and act a little bit on the side and major in law or something or are you just going to really give yourself to this? And that's what I decided to do. When I graduated I got an apartment in the city and I decided to not go to NYU and I've been working from then on."[7]

After she left the production of *Fiddler* she was cast in *The Diary of Anne Frank* for a short run, all the while continuing to do workshops of *Spring Awakening,* which finally premiered off Broadway on May 19, 2006, for a three-month run at the Atlantic Theatre Company. It moved to Broadway and opened on December 10, 2006, at the Eugene O'Neill Theatre. It ran for over two years and closed on January 18, 2009. The original cast recording won a Grammy award in 2008 for best Musical Show Album.

Lea, who left the production with costar Groff in May 2008, acknowledged to *Village Voice* that her experience with *Spring Awakening* had been unique. "It's a rare thing that starting at such a young age, someone would continue in a project for so long. Generally, kids will outgrow the part, or they'll want to try someone new. But I really grew into this role; my voice grew a lot." Plus she grew into the content. "It's a very dark play. As I got older, I could deal with those issues, and I think they felt more comfortable as the years went on in taking it a bit further. Obviously, when I started, scenes such as the hayloft scene, which is the famous sex scene, weren't as intense when I was 14 as it was when I was 20."[8]

One of the many people who came to see *Spring Awakening* was TV writer Ryan Murphy, creator of *Nip/Tuck*. "I met Ryan and we just had a great night talking about Barbra Streisand and our shared love for her, and musical theatre and what not—and I never saw him ever again," she said during a press conference.[9]

Not long after finishing *Spring Awakening,* Lea was cast to play Eponine in a four-week engagement at the Hollywood Bowl. "I figured I'd come out and try L.A. for a month or two after that, try out for some pilots or some guest spots for TV shows."[10]

Glee was one of the first auditions she went for. "Ryan was there, and I went, *Do you remember me?* and he was like, *Of course I remember you.*"[11]

What Lea didn't know was that the role of Rachel Berry had been written with her in mind. "It was written for her," Murphy confirmed to the *Daily News*. "We had the prototype, which was a Reese Witherspoon Election-esque Broadway baby that was a mix of Barbra Streisand and Patti LuPone. I really believed in Lea's talent because her talent was once in a lifetime."[12]

Not surprisingly, Murphy cast her as Rachel, the Ohio girl with Broadway dreams. "Rachel is very much like me when I was about 10 to 12, working in theater, very driven," Lea commented to the *New York Daily News*. "I was similar in the sense that I didn't conform to what people thought was cool. It was important to do what I believed in . . . I saw the real world when I was eight, and I knew Tenafly High School was not the real world. It was OK to be different shapes, sizes, whatever."[13]

"I grew up in a high school where if you didn't have a nose job and money and if you weren't thin, you weren't cool, popular, beautiful. I was always told that I wasn't pretty enough to be on television. I was never pretty enough to be the pretty girl and I was never quirky enough to be the quirky girl. Boys didn't look at me in high school and think I was the pretty girl. So I get Rachel."[14]

SINGULAR SENSATION

Not since *Buffy, the Vampire Slayer* has the essence of high school been depicted with such dead-on, creative accuracy. Where Joss Whedon used the brilliant metaphor of the Hell Mouth, *Glee* ingeniously uses music to explore teen angst and the emotional roller coaster of adolescence—but not in the *gee-whiz, High School Musical* kind of way. Where *High School Musical* was basically an updated incarnation of the old Mickey Rooney and Judy Garland musicals, where characters burst into song, *Glee* is a dramedy that uses music as an accompaniment to the characters' lives. Slyly sophisticated and laugh-out-loud funny, *Glee* artfully balances poignancy and farce in creating a series universe that shows how the insecurities, challenges, failures, and painful lessons that are a daily part of high school life can be channeled into something ultimately joyous and uplifting.

The cast was filled with young performers mostly unknown to TV audiences but the response from viewers after FOX aired the pilot in the spring of 2009 was so strong that fans adopted a name for themselves: Gleeks. *Glee* singlehandedly gave those kids who know Sondheim from Soundgarden a new respectability and cache.

Although known for her dramatic skills, Lea was excited at the prospect of doing comedy. "I really wanted it," she told *Village Voice*. "Every night [*Spring Awakening* co-star] Jonathan Groff and I would come off stage; I'd be covered in his sweat because he sweats profusely on stage. Tears and sweat from these intense scenes. And I'd say, *Next thing for us, I want to do a comedy*. And now I'm in *Glee* and I get to have Slushees and fettuccine alfredo thrown in my face, so I got what I asked for."[15]

Because *Glee* is such a labor-intensive show—when they are not acting in scenes, the actors are learning songs or choreography—the cast was initially largely insulated from the show's rampant popularity because they hadn't had a chance to be out in public much.

"We've been in this little *Glee* bubble of finishing the 13 episodes and working really hard," Lea said at a press conference in 2009. "So we were just really thankful to get to see the reaction especially when we went to Comic-Con. That was so great. And we're also just about to go on a 10-city tour in a couple of days, and hopefully we'll get to meet people that have seen the pilot and that are excited for the show. We are really excited about that. You're going to have all of us kids on a plane going to tons of cities, all of us together. So it's going to be great."[16]

The downside was that the show's popularity meant Lea was going to be in Los Angeles for the foreseeable future and away from boyfriend Theo Stockman, a Broadway actor who appeared in *Hair* and *American Idiot*. Whenever she has three or more days off, Lea flies to New York to be with Stockman.

"He lets me be who I am," she told *Glamour* magazine. "I'm a relationship girl. I would rather be long distance with him than not have a relationship at all."[17]

She admits relocating from east to west coast was difficult beyond leaving a boyfriend behind. "It was a very uncomfortable transition at first," Michele told writer Donna Freydkin. "My roots are in New York. I tried to create a new life [in Los Angeles], but then I realized that my life was in New York. So Los Angeles is my work base. I'm very comfortable out there and have a safe group of people that I trust. And then I come home. This is where I breathe. I work, work, work out there and then I come here. I see shows and hang out with my family and I recharge. And there I go full-throttle."[18]

When in Los Angeles, she keeps a low profile, says best friend Groff. "She lives a very quiet life. She doesn't party," he told *USA Today*. "She doesn't go out. When we're done with work, we rent a movie. Her life is very simple, and she likes it that way. It's her choice." Despite being low key, Groff says Lea isn't dull. "She's very silly and she doesn't take herself too seriously. She loves to laugh and to make jokes, and I'm telling you, I've never laughed harder than with her. She's a trip. One day on set, we were seeing who could do a better impression of her cats."[19]

Rather than go out to clubs and be paparazzi bait, Lea says she prefers to stay out of the spotlight. "I never did drugs. I wasn't that girl. I don't go out to clubs. You'll never see me on a table at a bar, jumping up and down."[20]

She says she and Groff love working out together. They do yoga at home together, go on hikes, and go to the gym. She hangs out with her cast a lot. "Everyone comes over to my house, and we like to do stuff together as much as we can. They are my family, honestly."[21]

Lea dismisses out of hand rumors of rivalries and points to her relationship with Amber Riley. "We're both big personalities, and you definitely would think we'd bump heads," she commented to *New York Daily News*. "But she has taught me more about myself than anyone. She inspires me, she protects me, she makes me laugh, she tells me not to take myself so seriously. She's my Mama Amber."[22]

After a work day, Lea says she unwinds by getting "the most delicious vegan food I can find, generally from Real Food Daily. I get kale, black beans, brown rice and tofu, with lime cilantro dressing and hot sauce. I'll pour myself a glass of organic wine. I'll watch the crappiest reality television, maybe take a bath or a shower, give myself a nice little face mask and go to bed."[23]

Nor has Lea, who became a vegan two years ago, been tempted to join the ranks of anorexic-looking starlets. "I love being healthy," she told *Glamour.* "I get a lot of sleep. I'm a girl who eats. I'll have a big Italian dinner, and I don't give a crap because it makes me happy," she says. "And I feel beautiful no matter how I look. I have my family to thank for that."[24]

She is also thankful for the opportunities *Glee* has provided. "Every now and then, I have blissful moments of thanking God for all the amazing things that are happening," she told Freydkin. "When I leave the White House after just meeting Obama or when I see my face on the cover of Rolling Stone or when I meet someone who tells me that their daughter is inspired by me, those are moments that are incredibly joyful."[25]

She is using her celebrity to promote some causes close to her heart, such as working with People for the Ethical Treatment of Animals to promote spaying and neutering, and voicing her opposition to carriage horses in Central Park. But mostly, Lea is just working hard to prepare for whatever the future might bring.

"I think it's good I'm still able to play very young right now," the *Daily Record* reported. "When there is a time for me to come back to theater, I'm hoping people will see me as playing that lead role. But there's no rush."[26]

When asked if there was any role in particular she'd like to tackle, Lea doesn't hesitate. "I want to be in *Funny Girl* and I want Ryan Murphy to direct it. I would do it in a basement in Brooklyn, if somebody would let me do it! It's the best role ever –any Jewish girl would want to play Fanny Brice!"[27]

NOTES

1. Press conference interview with the author, July 2009.

2. Robert Diamond. "Spring Awakening Fever: An Interview with Lea Michele," *Broadway World,* January 23, 2007, http://broadwayworld.com/article/Spring_Awakening_Fever_An_Interview_with_Lea_Michele_ 20070123.

3. Ibid.

4. Ibid.

5. Michael Gilboe. "Tony Nominee John Gallagher, Jr. with Lea Michele," *Broadway World,* May 16, 2007, http://broadwayworld.com/article/Tony_Nominee_John_Gallagher_Jr_with_Lea_Michele _20070516.

6. Press conference interview with the author, July 2009.

7. Diamond, "Spring Awakening Fever."

8. Michael Ayers. "Interview: Glee star Lea Michele," *Village Voice,* http://blogs.villagevoice.com/music/2009/09/interview_glee.php.

9. Press conference interview with the author, July 2009.

10. Ibid.

11. Ibid.

12. Richard Huff. "Glee Is the Word," *New York Daily News,* August 30, 2009, http://docs.newsbank.com/s/InfoWeb/aggdocs/NewsBank/12A6CB2C5CDBDCF8/1083311554222450?p_multi=NYDB&s_lang=en-US.

13. Ibid.

14. Ibid.

15. Ayers, "Interview."

16. Press conference interview with the author, July 2009.

17. "Glee's Lea Michele Is Back in the Arms of Her Real-life Leading Man after UK Tour," *Daily Mail,* July 10, 2011 (reprint), http://www.dailymail.co.uk/tvshowbiz/article-2012254/Glees-Lea-Michele-arms-real-life-leading-man-UK-tour.html.

18. Donna Freydkin. "Lea Michele Never Stopped Believing," *USA Today,* May 10, 2010, http://docs.newsbank.com/s/InfoWeb/aggdocs/NewsBank/12FA1BDFF4BD7318/1083311554222450?p_multi=USTB&s_lang=en-US.

19. Ibid.

20. Ibid.

21. Ibid.

22. Huff, "Glee Is the Word."

23. Freydkin, "Lea Michele Never."

24. "'I'm a Girl Who Eats': Glee Star Lea Michele Refuses to Follow the Super-Skinny Hollywood Trend," *Daily Mail,* September 2, 2010 (reprint), http://www.dailymail.co.uk/tvshowbiz/article-1308104/Glee-star-Lea-Michele-refuses-follow-super-skinny-Hollywood-trend.html.

25. Freydkin, "Lea Michele Never."

26. Ibid.

27. Taryn Mungo and Annie Cheng. "Talking with Lea Michele," *Newsday,* April 15, 1998, http://docs.newsbank.com/s/InfoWeb/aggdocs/NewsBank/109DDC9A1D3B8294/1083311554222450?p_multi=NWD1&s_lang=en-US.

When he's not acting, Shia LaBeouf writes graphic novels. In April 2012, he surprised fans by showing up at a comic book convention in Chicago to autograph copies.

10 SHIA LABEOUF

He's not movie-star handsome. He didn't attend prestigious acting schools or spend years honing his craft in theatre. His emotional insight came from a hard-scrabble childhood, his ambition sharpened by simple necessity. Despite his blue-collar pedigree, Shia LaBeouf has emerged as his generation's answer to Steve McQueen—the scrappy, average dude next door who rises to the cinematic occasion.

Shia grew up in the Echo Park neighborhood of Los Angeles, a working class, mostly Hispanic community. He admits being one of the few whites made him a bit of a target but he wasn't cowed by it. Nor did he feel poor, even though his family scraped by on minimal earnings, because it was the only life he knew.

Shia Saide was born on June 11, 1986, to Jeffrey LaBeouf, a six feet four Louisiana Cajun, and Shayna Saide, a New York–born Jew. His first name is reflective of his parent's disparate backgrounds. Shia means *gift* from God in Hebrew and LaBeouf is a French variant for *beef*. So my name means "thank God for beef."

He describes his parents as hippies. "My dad was a wandering dude recovering from the war in Vietnam," Shia says. "And my mom, before she met him, had a head shop in Brooklyn. Bob Dylan used to come in and smoke weed. All her furniture hung upside-down from the ceiling. She was out of her mind. It was the 1970s."[1]

Shia boasts that he comes from five generations of performers. In her youth, Shayna was a ballerina but was forced to give dance up after hurting her knee. His maternal grandfather, a Polish Holocaust survivor, was a comic and his paternal grandmother, a beatnik poet, who in the 1950s "used to run around with Allen Ginsberg. She hated her family because they wouldn't accept her as a lesbian.

It was a different time, obviously, and so she moved to Venice, California and changed her name."[2] His grandmother's mother played piano on Lucky Luciano's gambling boat.

Shia's dad, who he calls "tough as nails and a different breed of man," drifted through a number of jobs. "He did a lot of things," Shia says. "He was a clown. He sold snow cones. He did stand-up comedy. He even went on tour with the Doobie Brothers as their opening act. He was an artist, an explorer of life—just an adventurer."[3]

While in the circus, he was apparently also a chicken trainer. "He devoted his whole life to a chicken named Henrietta. I swear," Shia laughs. "He used to run around and light himself or rings on fire and the chicken would run through it. Or he'd put the chicken on his head and do a flip and the chicken would run from his head to his ass. It was pretty funny."[4]

THE BEAT GENERATION

"Beatniks" is a term to describe members of the beat generation of the 1950s that rejected the conventional, conservative values of the post–World War II Eisenhower generation in favor of a more liberal, alternative lifestyle noted for hallucinogenic drug experimentation, sexual promiscuity, and an embrace of Eastern spirituality. The beat culture was both immortalized and inspired by a group of poets and writers who came to prominence in the late 1950s, with iconic work including Allen Ginsberg's *Howl,* William S. Burroughs's *Naked Lunch,* and Jack Kerouac's *On the Road.* Kerouac coined the term beat generation in 1948 to describe a post-war generation that was beaten down, but also upbeat.

Beyond their cultural significance, the beat writers pushed the legal envelope. Allen Ginsberg's *Howl and Other Poems* was published in 1956 by a small publishing house owned by fellow beat writer Lawrence Ferlinghetti, who was subsequently charged with obscenity. Likewise, Grove Press, publisher of *Naked Lunch,* was also charged with obscenity. The resulting court cases, which ruled neither work was obscene, expanded the First Amendment creative freedom and eased restrictions on what could be published in the United States.

The original beat writers met in New York but most ended up living in the San Francisco area where they mingled with members of the so-called San Francisco Renaissance who were initially known for avant-garde poetry. The Renaissance later also encompassed visual and performing arts. It was this blend of creative minds that eventually morphed into the more politically active 1960s counterculture identified with hippies and anti–Vietnam War protesters.

The influence of the beat writers is still evident in San Francisco. Ferlinghetti founded the legendary bookstore City Lights, which is now a cultural landmark. Several streets near City Lights are named after beat poets to honor and commemorate their lasting contribution to the city's social and cultural environment.

After getting discharged from the military, Jeffrey spent time in Hawaii dealing marijuana. "[My dad] was in Vietnam long enough to come back and be a disaster . . . He was selling things to the Hawaiian mafia, and then they would give it to their cab drivers to sell when they picked people up from airports."[5] According to family lore, Jeffrey LaBeouf was responsible for introducing Thai stick, a particularly potent type of marijuana, to Hawaii.

When Shia was a toddler, Jeffrey developed a new money-making venture: he stole a maid's cart from a local hotel and made it into a vender's pushcart. He'd work the local park by their apartment dressed as a clown selling hot dogs and shaved ice. He also put Shia in clown makeup to help drum up business.

"I hated selling hot dogs. I hated dressing up in clown," LaBeouf says. "But the minute somebody would buy into my thing and buy a hot dog from my family because of my shtick, my parents would look at me like, 'All right, man'. Besides performing, I've never had that validation from anything else I've ever done in my life."[6]

Shia calls the clown shtick as "a hustle," bur says he was never embarrassed by it, in part because when they were working the streets, his parents couldn't fight. "There had to be some peaceful time for us, or we weren't going to make it through the week financially."[7] It was a constant struggle to put food on the table. "None of my friends were ever as broke as I was," Shia says without rancor. "My uncle was going to adopt me at one point because my parents couldn't afford to have me anymore. They had too much pride to go on welfare or food stamps."[8]

Shia says he and his parents lived in a run-down pink building and shared the one-bedroom, one-bathroom apartment with another family. He slept in the back room with another kid and his parents camped out in the living room. "They had a factory in the kitchen where my mom made jewelry she sold on the streets," Shia recalls. "My dad was working as a clown at the time, so clown makeup and clown outfits were all over the place. There was a chicken living in the apartment . . . My parents were strange people with a very strange relationship. We definitely weren't driving a station wagon and going to soccer practice."[9]

The unconventional was Shia's status quo. "I come from the kind of family that when I got home from school, my father would say: *Forget the homework; let's watch a Steve McQueen movie.*"[10] His dad would take him to Rolling Stones concerts and, later, AA meetings.

Jeffrey also let Shia try marijuana when he was just 10 years old. "It's just my family was raised differently," he says, explaining drugs were never a taboo or done in secret. "It was always out in the open and it was always explained to me. I'm so grateful for that . . . because I never had a curiosity. It's why I never tried anything beyond marijuana or drinking. I know that I can't do any of it. And so I don't."[11]

The same can't be said of smoking. "I still have that one bad habit," LaBeouf admits. "But my childhood never hindered me, and it never crippled me. They were pretty weird people, but they loved me and I loved them." But living with a heroin addict was an exercise in uncertainty and occasional fear—Jeffrey once pointed a gun at Shia while having a drug-induced flashback to being in Vietnam.

His father could also be moody and emotionally distant. "But I must give him credit because he always told me that he didn't want me to be like him."[12]

Despite his parents' eccentricities, Shia preferred it to the alternative. "Normal is boring," he says. "Instead of going to Chuck E. Cheese, my mom would take me and my friends to her ashram . . . I had the freedom to do whatever the f*** I wanted, and when you're a kid, that seems cool. It was anything goes."[13]

While the upside of such an upbringing may have been precocious independence, the downside was that Shia carried that attitude to school, after school, after school. He claims to have been expelled from every school he went to. "I was kicked out of Pinewood Elementary for stealing the tetherball and taking it home. I was always a smart-mouthed kid. At 32nd Street Middle School I was expelled for cursing."[14]

Jeffrey's drug use may have strained the marriage but Shia says money pressures proved too much and led to his parents' divorce in 1992. "Finance drove my family apart because they were co-owners in a fashion company that fell apart. And my mother blamed my dad for it . . . blamed him for wrecking it all. And vice-versa. It may not be the sole reason for the split, but it is the superficial reason. It's the surface reason that you can point at and go, *That's the reason.*"[15]

Shia lived with his mother but maintained a relationship with his dad, who continued to struggle with addiction. "When you're 10 years old and watch your father going through heroin withdrawals, you grow up real fast. You become the parent in the relationship."[16]

CLOWNING FOR MONEY

Money was constantly scarce for Shia's family. His mom sold fabrics and brooches but earned barely enough for them to survive. But neither of his parents was made to be entrepreneurs. "They're artists who just didn't have enough bureaucrat in them to get it all wrapped up in a nice little package to be able to feed to the American public." So money, he believed, "was a solution to whatever the hell was going on in my household. With money, I and my family would have had more options. So I went after a job that I thought I could make the most money for a 10-year-old or an 11-year-old boy."[17]

That job was stand-up comedy. He performed at a the HBO Theatre in Hollywood, then bulled his way into the Ice House in Pasadena, and the Baked Potato near Universal Studios. His humor was R-rated and Shia says was based on his eccentric upbringing, "from seeing my parents have sex, smoke weed, my mom being naked." His mom's friends would come over and hang around the apartment naked while they traced each others' auras with sticks of incense, "just weird hippie stuff. And I'd get up there in my OshKosh B'Gosh outfit and my bowl haircut—a little kid with a Lenny Bruce mouth."[18]

The audiences didn't quite know what to make of the foul-mouthed tyke who favored insult comedy. Some nights, he killed. More nights, he bombed—listening to a 10-year-old crack jokes about a heroin-addicted father and cash-strapped family was more cringe-worthy than humorous. Plus, liquor-serving clubs could not sell drinks during Shia's set, which did not help improve the audience's festive mood. Rough crowds aside, Shia decided that there simply was not good enough money to be made by a child stand-up.

He thought about one of his surfing buddies who seemed to have it all—or at least, everything Shia coveted. "He always had the coolest stuff. His mom drove a nice car. He had a nice watch and nice clothing. He always had a nice surfboard." His friend was an actor and after seeing him appear one night in *Dr. Quinn Medicine Woman,* Shia realized that clowning around in the right venue could be very profitable. "Initially, it was financial," he said. "I wanted opulence."[19]

Determined to pursue his new career choice, Shia looked in the Yellow Pages and looked up agents. He called Teresa Dahlquist and pretended to be the manager for a rising young actor named Shia LaBeouf. Impressed by his audacity, she took him on as a client—and also became a guardian of sorts. Dahlquist paid for Shia's headshots, drove him to auditions, and would, at times, pay his rent. "She became one of the few pillars in my life," Shia says. "She lifted me up and cared for me. She said, *Hey, kid, see that mountain? Go move it!*"[20]

The mountain budged almost immediately. A short time after getting his agent, Shia was cast in an Oreo commercial followed by a series of guest spots, including *Caroline in the City, The X-Files, Touched by an Angel, Jesse,* and *Suddenly Susan.* Then he got the role that set the course of his life. In 1999, he beat out hundreds of other hopefuls and was cast as Louis Stevens in the Disney Channel sitcom *Even Stevens,* which followed the life of a middle-class family living in Sacramento. Louis, the 14-year-old youngest of three siblings, lived in the shadow of his overachieving older brother and sister. Partial to practical jokes and money-making schemes, Louis's plans often backfire and land him in hot water.

"I grew up on that show and it was the best thing that had ever happened to me," Shia says. "Took me out of my house, it was real dramatic at that time. My dad was in a rehab facility. My mom was trying to hold down the fort and that wasn't working. So when the show came along it was a savior. It saved my life, my family's life."[21] California labor laws require all minors to have a guardian on the set. Shia's mom needed to work; so when his dad got out of rehab Disney paid him $800 a week to be on the set. For the first time in Shia's life, his family didn't have to worry about paying the rent or buying food.

The change in family fortunes didn't change Shia—adjusting to the world of family entertainment was a challenge for a kid used to swearing at will. "Especially because Even Stevens required a ton of ad-libbing, so the f***s would fly after a few takes," he admits. "Disney was such a wholesome place. It was full of clean-cut young people, all these kids from musical-theater backgrounds who wanted to be straight-up song-and-dance performers . . . so I'm instantly the doesn't-fit-in-here guy."[22] Shia also instinctively rebelled against the squeaky clean image promoted by Disney for its teen stars. "That All-American Disney role model, I'm not that," he says. "I'm still trying to figure out my own [stuff], so there's no way I can be the guy other people look to for answers."[23]

That search for self did not overtly include religion. "I come from a hippy lifestyle . . . so it was like, *What do you believe in? I don't know; what do you believe in? Alright, cool.*" Shia was bar mitzvahed when he was 13 to please his sick grandmother. "But like any Jew in Los Angeles," he says, "after your Bar Mitzvah is over you stop being Jewish. So that was the extent of my religion."[24]

But not necessarily the extent of his spirituality. In 2004, Shia contributed an essay to *I Am Jewish,* a book inspired by the last words of *Wall Street Journal* journalist Daniel Pearl, who was kidnapped and beheaded by Islamic terrorists because he was a Jew. In his essay Shia wrote:

> First off, let me make clear that I am in no way a Jew who attends Shabbat every Friday . . . I have a personal relationship with God that happens to work within the confines of Judaism, which to me is the name of the telephone in my heart that allows me to speak to God.[25]

> Really, I feel cocky when I say I am Jewish . . . because what I am really saying is that I am one of the few chosen ones out there. I made it; God chose me and I take pride in that.[26]

Even Stevens lasted three seasons and filmed 66 episodes, the typical original broadcast run at that time for a Disney Channel series. In its last season, Shia won a Daytime Emmy for Outstanding Performer in a Children's Series. As expected, *Even Stevens* had been a hit with the tween set. Surprisingly though, it also became a popular show among older, college-age teens. That popularity was a factor in Shia being cast in Disney's 2003 feature film *Holes.*

The movie is based on the popular novel by Louis Sachar about a teenager (Shia) who is wrongfully convicted of a crime and sent to a work camp run by an evil family who use young offenders to dig for buried treasure in a dry lake bed. The movie was filmed on location in the desert that according to Shia "was hot enough to fry a latke on your face."[27] Besides being his big-screen debut, the movie introduced Shia to costar Jon Voight. "He became my mentor. He took me under his wing at the exact time that I needed some serious adult guidance."[28]

Voight saw himself in the brash, ambitious teen who was a willing student—and listener—about acting and about life. He was the first to open Shia to the possibility that acting could be and should be more than just about earning a big paycheck. "I'm extremely intrigued and I soak up stuff like a sponge," Shia says. "I'm always asking him questions—which can get annoying—but it's sort of like a psychiatrist type of thing for him. He likes to talk. And not a lot of people honestly want to listen. It's a relationship I really cherish."[29]

The same year that *Holes* was released, in 2003, Shia also appeared in *Dumb and Dumber: When Harry Met Lloyd* and *Charlie's Angels: Full Throttle.* He describes the set of *Charlie's Angels* as a playground. "When I wasn't laughing hysterically, I was learning how to pickpocket from Cameron Diaz," he says, adding, that Lucy Liu was very nice to him. "You hear rumors that she was mean and all that stuff. She was so not mean."[30]

Maintaining his concentration around his leading ladies was a challenge. "They knew they were all my fantasy girls," Shia told *Playboy* in 2009. "Drew Barrymore was the first crush I ever had. I was deep in puberty at this point; having her around was too much for me." He admits he stole Polaroids of Drew from the wardrobe people. "And then I'd go into my trailer for a while. I had a lot of time with myself on that set."[31]

Even though he was no longer a Disney star, Shia was aware the label would be hard to shake. So he selected his next project for its image-makeover potential. *The Battle for Shaker Heights* was developed via *Project Greenlight,* a reality series/contest produced by Ben Affleck, Matt Damon, and Chris Moore that sought out would-be filmmakers.

Shia says the point of the show, "beyond the movie, beyond the show—was an opportunity for me to curse as much as possible, to talk about smoking cigarettes, for me to age myself publicly. That was my goal." While deeply appreciating the opportunity afforded him by the Disney Channel, he believed at the time, it was an obstacle. "It's just one tone, and as an actor, that's crippling." He admits, though, that Disney has morphed into a springboard. "Where it's at now are just two different worlds. If you were to have a show on Disney now, you can really have a whole popped-out career," he says, pointing to Miley Cyrus and *High School Musical* performer Zac Efron.[32]

By the time he turned 18, the days of poverty and sharing apartments were over. Acting provided a comfortable life for Shia and his family. He had moved into his own place in 2000 when he was 16; his mom settled in Tujunga and his father relocated to Montana where he lived in a teepee. Until then Shia had gotten by on affability, a baby face, and instinct. He credits his experience on *The Greatest Game Ever Played,* directed by fellow actor Bill Paxton, with introducing him to the *craft* of acting. Shia says he tended to act with a lot of mannerisms. "I love movement; movement makes me feel like I am someone else." But Paxton worked to break the habit. "He said, *No, no. This is how we are going to play it—don't do too much. Let the audience do it for you.* [Learning to have quiet moments] was a big deal for me."[33]

While Shia acknowledges he does have a career plan, it's more emotional than linear based on, "What have you not done yet? What are you scared to do?" He believes that if he's not stretching himself, "there's no point to be doing this at all." *Disturbia* offered Shia the chance to challenge himself and he admits being fearful of making a suspense thriller, "where it's primarily me for most of the film. It's a lot of pressure."[34]

In the film, Shia played Kale, a troubled 17-year-old who lands under house arrest for three months for assaulting a teacher. To pass time, he starts watching his neighbors and suspects one of them is a serial killer. Director D. J. Caruso already had a different actor in mind for the role until Shia auditioned. "[He] came in and completely won me over in the very first scene," Caruso says. "He was so dynamic and his eyes are so expressive. I thought . . . the guys are going to like him and the girls are going to like him because he's the kind of guy you are going to root for."[35]

Disturbia was a DreamWorks production. After Shia was cast in that film, Steven Spielberg, one of the principal owners of DreamWorks, cast him in the big action-adventure summer film, *Transformers*. Spielberg had first noticed Shia when he saw *Holes* with his children, thinking he would be a good casting choice to play Tom Hanks's son, should such a need ever arise. It didn't. But three years later, Spielberg remembered Shia for *Transformers.*

"Shia is within everyone's reach," says Spielberg. "He's every mother's son, every father's spitting image, every young kid's best pal and every girl's possible dream." He says that was the reason DreamWorks cast him in two larger-than-life films. "We felt those films needed a realistic human anchor."[36]

In *Transformers,* Shia plays Sam Witwicky, who discovers his car is a robotic alien. "Sam is just a normal kid," director Michael Bay says. "I didn't want him to be the stud or the geek, just a normal Joe. He's the type of guy who finds his edge through humor. He's a little awkward, but you immediately like him." Certainly his costar Megan Fox did, calling him one of the funniest people she's ever met. "Sometimes it was hard to get through scenes with him."[37]

The film was a hit and Shia signed on for two more sequels. That set the stage for the role that would catapult him into the rarified air of an adult-action star.

GROWING PAINS

In April 2007, Steven Spielberg requested Shia to come to his office. Once there, the director asked if he'd ever seen an Indiana Jones movie. Shia said of course. Spielberg announced they were making another one and wanted Shia to costar in it with Harrison Ford, playing his son. "My heart went nuts," he recalls. "I've had anxiety attacks before, but I've never felt that—where you can't breathe and your stomach tenses."[38]

Indiana Jones and the Kingdom of the Crystal Skull marked Shia's coming of age. Now a lean six feet one, his days of playing shaggy-haired teens were over. And with maturity came more scrutiny and temptation.

"I know what happens to young successful people in Hollywood," he said in 2007, shortly after turning 21. "These people get lost. They start believing their own press. They don't realize that the party scene isn't real. It's one long dream sequence, and I have no intention of getting lost in a dream." Shia acknowledged actors could not take their careers for granted. "If you're not careful, the next day you could be a train conductor."[39]

Despite being introduced to marijuana at a young age and being exposed to harder drugs when his dad battled addiction, Shia says drugs hold no allure, but notes, "The stress, anxiety, fear [that comes with fame and success] probably kills me just as fast as doing drugs. I don't know how you can get a grip on this." He admits the emotional cost of stardom is high. "Your life becomes secondary to your work."[40]

From 2004 to 2007 Shia was romantically involved with model China Brezner, who he called his best friend and his love. He's given somewhat conflicting reasons for their breakup. In April 2007, he said their timing was off. "There's only so far you can take a relationship before you got to get into things that are too serious or over the top. I'm 20 years old . . . Where do you go after three years? Then you've got to start thinking about other things, and I'm too young to think about those things."[41]

In June, he pointed the finger at his career. "My focus became so work-related that I couldn't devote any time to a relationship." He says the breakup was devastating and that the emotional aftermath "was like rebuilding after a tornado."[42]

Shia occasionally dates casually since but seems content to ride his wave of success and leave personal priorities on the backburner while this roll continues. His goal is to work until he's 70 and he seems willing to make the sacrifices to make it happen. But as with many carefully laid plans, life keeps presenting unanticipated obstacles. In late 2007, Shia was arrested at a drug store in Chicago for criminal trespassing after ignoring a security guard's order to leave the store. Shia admits he was drunk and acted like an idiot, explaining he just wanted to buy cigarettes. But he found the incident more amusing than mortifying. Then in February 2008, he received a ticket for smoking on public property in Burbank, California, a minor infraction. It turned into an arrest warrant when Shia failed to appear in court to deal with the ticket. After the initial media coverage, neither incident resulted in any lasting consequence. That would change dramatically in the early morning hours of July 27.

Around 2:45 a.m., Shia's pickup truck collided with another vehicle at a West Hollywood intersection. The truck rolled, seriously injuring his hand. "My hand got jammed under the car, and a slice of the finger came off," he explains. "So when people ask why I refused to take the Breathalyzer, it's that I wasn't exactly in a conversing kind of mode. No time to sit there and play detective, guys. The firemen were like, *Get this dude to a hospital.*" Police followed and arrested Shia for DUI before he underwent surgery on his left hand.[43]

He underwent surgery to repair the hand enough for him to return to work on the *Transformers* sequel. Once filming ended, he underwent more surgery but Shia says he'll never have full recovery. "I'll never be back to 100 percent." But he accepts it as a karmic life lesson and wake-up call. "This accident is what I needed in my life—it's coming to terms with my urges and limitations."[44]

Shia notes that being a celebrity means all his growing pains and learning curves play out in public. Because of that, he believes he has no room for more error. "I have to shut down the chaos completely or I'll be f***ed."[45] He stresses, though, that drinking is not his primary problem. "Being uncomfortable is my problem. Insecurities are my problem. Fear is my problem. The hardest thing in the world is being comfortable with myself."

NOTES

1. Rebecca Winters Keegan. "The Kid Gets the Picture," *Time,* July 5, 2007, http://www.Time.com/Time/magazine/article/0,9171,1640381,00.html.

2. "Oh Boy Shia LaBeouf," *Gurl.com,* http://www.gurl.com/showoff/spotlight/articles/0,648254_711127-2,00.html.

3. Barry Koltnow. "Watching the Moves," *The Orange County Register,* April 13, 2007, http://www.ocregister.com/ocregister/entertainment/abox/article_1649698.php.

4. Bethany Shady. "Shia Labeouf, Tastes Like Chicken," *TastesLikeChicken.* http://www.tlchicken.com/view_story.php?ARTid=91.

5. Dotson Rader. "Shia LaBeouf: I'm Proud of Growing Up Poor," *Parade,* May 29, 2009, http://www.Parade.com/celebrity/2009/06/shia-labeouf-growing-up-poor.html.

6. Keegan, "The Kid Gets the Picture."

7. Rader, "Shia LaBeouf."

8. Peter Rubin. "Shia LaBeouf's Arrested Development," *Details,* July 30, 2008, http://men.style.com/details/blogs/thegadabout/2008/07/shia-labeouf.html#more.html.

9. "Shia LaBeouf," *Playboy,* June 2009, http://www.playboy.com/articles/playboy-interview-shia-labeouf/index.html.

10. Koltnow, "Watching the Moves."

11. Rubin, "Shia LaBeouf's Arrested Development."

12. Koltnow, "Watching the Moves."

13. "Shia LaBeouf," *Playboy.*

14. Ibid.

15. Rader, "Shia LaBeouf."

16. Koltnow, "Watching the Moves."

17. Rader, "Shia LaBeouf."

18. Keegan, "The Kid Gets the Picture."

19. Susan King. "Disturbia," *Los Angeles Times,* April 12, 2007, E6.

20. Dotson Rader. "The Mixed-Up Life of Shia LaBeouf," *Parade,* June 14, 2009, http://www.Parade.com/export/sites/default/celebrity/2009/06/shia-labeouf-mixed-up-life.html.

21. Nate Bloom. "Interfaith Celebrities: Shia the Mensch," http://www.interfaithfamily.com/arts_and_entertainment/popular_culture/Interfaith_Celebrities_Shia_the_Mensch.shtml?rd=2.

22. "Shia LaBeouf," *Playboy.*

23. Jeffrey Ressner. "The Next Tom Hanks?" *USA Today Weekend,* July 1, 2007, http://www.usaweekend.com/07_issues/070701/070701shia_labeouf.html.

24. Paul Fischer. "Interview: Shia LaBeouf for *Constantine,*" http://www.darkhorizons.com/interviews/231/shia-labeouf-for-constantine-

25. Judea and Ruth Pearl. *I Am Jewish.* Woodstock, VT: Jewish Lights, 2004, http://www.fanpop.com/spots/shia-labeouf.

26. Bloom, "Interfaith Celebrities."

27. Karen Thomas. "*Holes* May Mean a Real Opening for Shia LaBeouf," *USA Today,* April 29, 2003, http://www.usatoday.com/life/2003-04-17-labeouf_x.htm.

28. Koltnow, "Watching the Moves."

29. "*Transformers'* Shia LaBeouf," Comics Continuum, http://www.comicscontinuum.com/stories/0707/02/shialabeouf.htm.

30. Thomas, "*Holes* May Mean."

31. "Shia LaBeouf," *Playboy.*

32. Molly Woulf. "All Grown Up, Shia Spouts Off on *Disturbia,*" *Northwest Indiana Times,* April 13, 2007, http://nwi*Times*.com/entertainment/article_2eb81129-cb1e-56d9-837d-0611fe351d85.html.

33. King, "Disturbia."

34. Woulf, "All Grown Up."

35. King, "Disturbia."

36. Keegan, "The Kid Gets the Picture."

37. "*Transformers'* Shia LaBeouf," Comics Continuum.

38. Keegan, "The Kid Gets the Picture."

39. Ressner, "The Next Tom Hanks?"

40. Rader, "The Mixed-Up Life."

41. Aaron Parsley. "Shia LaBeouf: How I'm Getting Buff for Indiana Jones," *People,* April 23, 2007, http://www.people.com/people/article/0,20036458,00.html.

42. Aaron Parsley. "Shia LaBeouf on Dating: 'I'm Not That Smooth,'" *People,* July 3, 2007, http://www.people.com/people/article/0,20044517,00.html.

43. "Shia LaBeouf," *Playboy.*

44. Ibid.

45. Keegan, "The Kid Gets the Picture."

To keep her starlet body in shape, Vanessa works out religiously by going to the gym and taking yoga classes.

11 VANESSA HUDGENS

LET'S PUT ON A SHOW!

The cast of *High School Musical* felt as if they were on the best kind of carnival ride. The last six weeks had been a head-spinning whirlwind of performing, recording, and traveling. Zac Efron, Corbin Bleu, Lucas Grabeel, Monique Coleman, Ashley Tisdale, and Vanessa Hudgens had been so busy—and having so much fun—they hadn't had time to really think about what it all meant. All they knew was that *High School Musical* was like no other acting job any of them ever had.

It all began with the most grueling auditions the young actors had ever experienced for a TV show. For most callback auditions, the actor goes in, reads a scene or two from the script, and maybe chats with the director and producers. Usually, they spent no more than a half hour before going home. But some of the final auditions for *High School Musical* would last almost eight hours.

Over 600 young actors originally showed up hoping to be cast as one of the six leads. Eventually, it had been narrowed down to 15 actors competing for each role. The final audition would decide who made it and who would be sent home disappointed. As it happened, Vanessa Hudgens was paired with another hopeful, Zac Efron. They were both nervous but Vanessa says she and Zac felt comfortable with one another right away.

Efron agreed. "From the start, we were always paired together in the auditions. I think we were the only pair from the mass of kids that was never separated," he recalls. "We always read together over and over. I wish I could put my finger on what makes our chemistry work onscreen. But I can tell you that she's easy to talk to, very kind, sweet and she has a great sense of humor. When you combine that with an amazing voice and her beauty, you're going to have a star. She's amazing to work with."[1]

As the day wore on, the number of actors remaining dwindled as the movie's director narrowed the finalists down to a handful. They would tap people on the shoulder and send them home, saying they were no longer needed until it was narrowed down to a handful of performers. A week and a half later, the cast was announced and the young performers were about to become part of a true international phenomenon.

That cast was whisked off to Utah, where they were put through a performing boot camp for two weeks. The training schedule was intense, beginning at nine every morning when the actors would sing and dance for hours. Exhausted, everyone would crash early and then start all over the next day.

Immediately after the two-week rehearsal was over, filming began on location at East High School in Salt Lake City. By then, the cast had become good friends and spent all their offset time together. They are dinner together and on days off, hung out together. Even after filming ended, all the actors stayed in touch. As the premiere date of *High School Musical* neared, they expected the movie would be popular with kids and teenagers; they were completely unprepared for the reaction it generated among adults.

Within a day of *High School Musical's* premiere on January 20, 2006, over a half million people visited the movie's website. The soundtrack ended up the biggest-selling CD in 2006. The single "Breaking Free" went platinum, selling over 1 million copies sold, and five other singles from the show were certified gold, having sold a half million each.

In July 2006, the Television Critics Association voted *High School Musical* the outstanding children's show of the year. A month later, it earned six Emmy nominations and would go on to win two: for Outstanding Choreography and for Outstanding Children's Program. Zac Efron won a Teen Choice award for breakout star.

Local stage productions of the film appeared in schools and communities all across America and it was just as big a hit in Europe and Australia. And the cast, minus Efron, went on a sold-out, 42-date concert tour. It was a genuine phenomenon.

The film's director, choreographer extraordinaire Kenny Ortega, praised the young actors. "In the old days, it took six weeks just to film the dance number. Now you get six weeks to do the entire film," Ortega, best known for his work on the movie *Dirty Dancing*, pointed out. "There was tremendous pressure. I've always said that *High School Musical* owes a lot to the cast, which was really focused and able to accomplish more than we should have been allowed to do in the time we were given."[2]

The *High School Musical* franchise made stars out of leads Zac Efron and Vanessa Hudgens. But while Efron's film career enjoyed a steady climb into adult film roles, Hudgens suffered through a series of personal and professional missteps. She learned firsthand that being a teen icon can be a hard image to overcome and to live up to, both personally and professionally.

CHIP OFF THE BLOCK

Vanessa Anne Hudgens was born in Salinas, California, on December 14, 1988. She's a true "melting pot" American. Her dad Gregory is Irish and Native American; her mom, Gina Guangco, grew up in the Philippines. Vanessa says she is proud of her mixed heritage.

> I love being a Filipina. She grew up in Manila and told me several stories about where she used to live. She has a big family—eleven brothers and sisters. I love Filipino food—halo-halo, pancit and adobo. I am such a Filipino—I eat rice every day.[3]

Vanessa feels a special responsibility to represent her heritage. "There aren't very many Filipino girls in the industry. So being able to stand up and be that girl makes me proud. I'd love to make it over there sometime. Unfortunately, I have not had a chance to visit." Vanessa says her mom tried, unsuccessfully to teach her Tagalog. "I am not that great at languages. I really want to learn, though."[4]

Vanessa's early childhood was nomadic. Her parents did not have much money and moved several times, living in Oregon and Paso Robles, California, until settling in Vista, California, when she was around five. Her sister Stella, who is seven years younger, was born there. Vanessa says the family moved to California so she could take dance and piano lessons. She says she remembers dancing around the house when she was three, making up choreography to songs on the radio. She first sang in public in preschool while still living in Oregon. The performance was in the evening and it was snowing so hard they almost didn't go. But in the end they did. "My parents got to see me singing 'Away in a Manger'. I was Mother Mary and was holding little baby Jesus."[5]

Vanessa attended Crest View Elementary in Vista but academics were not her primary passion—music and acting were. A loner, Vanessa says her time there was often solitary. "All through elementary school I think I had, like, one girlfriend and my idea of fun was lying on the ground and looking at the clouds. That was my cup of tea. I didn't really have many friends."[6] Instead, she spent time listening to Celine Dion. "If it wasn't for her, I wouldn't be singing," Hudgens claims. "I stole my parents' CD of hers and was belting out 'The Power of Love' at like the age of 9."[7]

Part of the appeal of performing was taking on a new persona. "When I was young, I would not talk to anybody if I didn't know them," Vanessa recalls. "I'd hide behind my mom if she tried to introduce me to anyone . . . When I was on the stage, I felt like I was hiding behind a person, and I adored it."[8]

She began performing in theatre when she was eight years old, appearing in local productions of *Carousel, The Wizard of Oz, The King and I, The Music Man, Cinderella,* and others. She attended the Orange County High School of the Arts, which offers classes for seventh grade through senior year. But Vanessa left the school after seventh grade. Her parents agreed to let her be homeschooled so she never attended high school. She did, though, spend time in England studying drama and singing.

She got her start in television after one of her girlfriends couldn't make a commercial audition for a Travelodge Public Service Announcement for Travelodge and asked Vanessa if she wanted to go in her stead. Vanessa went and to her surprise was cast. "it was so random . . . dancing around with a little Travelodge bear."[9]

But it led to more commercials and to the family moving to Los Angeles in 2005, so Vanessa could pursue other acting opportunities. Their faith in her talent paid off and she guest starred in the TV series *Still Standing, Cover Me,* and *Robbery Homicide.* But for every job there were dozens of rejections. Her mom Gina admits Vanessa sometimes "struggled with her ethnicity . . . losing jobs to blue-eyed, blond girls 99% of the time."[10]

Vanessa was able to work through the rejections because even as a young teenager, Vanessa was confident as self-possessed. She was also starting to get attention from the opposite sex. "Once I turned 13, I was the guy magnet," she admits. "It took some getting used to. I remember walking down the street to the mall and there was a fireman driving a truck. He sticks his head out of the window, turns his head around, and is staring at me while he is driving the ginormous fire truck. I'm like, *Don't you want to keep your eyes on the road?* It was weird."[11]

Vanessa made her feature film debut as Noel in *Thirteen,* which starred Holly Hunter and Evan Rachel Wood. The movie was directed by Catherine Hardwicke, who is now best known for her film, *Twilight.* Her next film was the action-adventure *Thunderbirds,* which she considers her first big movie. They filmed on location in the Seychelles. "So I was basically on vacation for three weeks even though it was work," says Vanessa. It was her first time being anywhere tropical and she admits, "I got extremely spoiled."[12] The experience made her want to travel to other exotic places like Morocco, India, and South Africa.

Vanessa also continued to guest star on series including *The Brothers Garcia,* and *The Suite Life of Zack and Cody,* as Maddie and London's classmate Corrie, and as Drake's girlfriend Rebecca on *Drake & Josh.* But a true breakout role eluded her. By early 2005, Vanessa had fallen into a funk. She even considered trying out for *American Idol.* "The only way I thought that I would be able to get myself out there would be on *American Idol.* But I was 15 . . . and you had to be 16 to audition."[13]

But her plans to compete on *Idol* were derailed by the role that would change her life.

A MUSICAL PHENOMENON

Like most teen actors, Vanessa had auditioned many times for Disney. Even though she had been passed over for starring roles, she had been making an impression. "She gave smart, engaging readings," says Judy Taylor, Disney casting vice president.[14] But Taylor and others were not aware of Vanessa's musical abilities, until the *High School Musical* audition when she sang Robbie Williams's "Angels," deemed "glorious" by Taylor.

Vanessa thinks the actors Disney cast bonded quickly because they shared similar professional musical backgrounds. "We all started off really young. We all started out doing musical theater so we all had a knack for it. We grew up watching musicals, grew up doing them. And I think we all share a strong passion for acting, singing, and dancing. I think it was something we all just loved from the start."[15]

Vanessa says she enjoyed portraying Gabriella Montez, who she describes as the brainy girl who likes to cuddle up with a good book. "It's nice to show that the brainy girls can also be pretty," she says. "Gabriella and I both fight for what we want. But I would personally rather go to the movies and hang out with my friends, where she likes to stay home by the fire."[16]

High School Musical was a surprise international hit, making its cast overnight sensations. It was a turn of events Vanessa says she was not prepared for. "I always loved the project. I thought I was working with an amazing group. I had tons of fun and I felt accomplished with everything that happened. To know that this was going to be put on TV was something I was truly thrilled about. But once *High School Musical* started to blow up . . . I'm still really blown away with it."[17] She recalls appearing on *Good Morning America* and performing in the middle of Time Square. "It was the first time I'd ever been to New York, and I'm looking at my surroundings just realizing where I am. I'm very blessed and appreciative for it all."[18]

Hudgens and Efron won the Best Chemistry award at the 2006 Teen Choice ceremony, solidifying their status as the breakout performers of *Hugh School Musical.* Vanessa's singing—she contributed five songs to the movie's soundtrack CD—attracted the attention of several record labels. Deciding who to sign with was a difficult decision, she admits, but ultimately Vanessa went with Hollywood Records. "It was a learning experience, being in the studio and finding what kind of music suits my voice best," she says. "I tried different kinds of music. I did pop, R&B and rock. I threw it all together and had this collection of different music," which, she explains is why the CD is titled *V*—for *variety,* not for *Vanessa.*[19]

The CD was released in September 2006 and was certified gold on February 27, 2007. Vanessa gives her mom most of the credit for that achievement because Gina was always so supportive of her singing. After she recorded *V,* "I said, *Mom, thank you. I can finally say thank you for all that stuff that you did for me.* It finally paid off. She's an inspiration. She always tells me how proud she is of me. It's really touching."[20]

To promote her album, Vanessa performed as the opening act for the Cheetah girls the Party's Just Begun tour. She also participated in the *High School Musical* national concert tour in the fall of 2006. Vanessa thinks the reason why young fans loved *High School Musical* so much was in part, it was new and different for them. "I grew up doing musical theater. But most kids my age haven't seen too many musicals, and this one was hip."[21]

The success of *High School Musical* prompted Disney to immediately plan for a sequel to air the summer of 2007. That same year *V* was chosen by *Billboard* readers as the seventh-best album and Vanessa was named Female Breakout Singer at the 2007 Teen Choice Awards. She was enjoying more success that she had ever hoped for. But she was about to get a sobering, and embarrassing, reality check.

WHAT THE OTHER STARS SAY

LUCAS GRABEEL: Things change all the time in Hollywood, and *High School Musical* has definitely given us something that, not only the Hollywood lifestyle, the fantasy aspect of what you can get from it, but just being able to have the opportunity to do a lot more things that we didn't do before. We've traveled the world. We performed in front of 65,000 people in Sao Paulo, Brazil. Now, that's something I would never do if it weren't for *High School Musical*. That's just amazing. Things like that, you can mark off the "10 things to do before you die" list.

CORBIN BLEU: There's a magic to *High School Musical*. We went on tour all across the U.S., all over South America. Now all of our own careers separately are taking off, and we've been able to have so many different opportunities to just pursue our own careers. I think it's just an unexplainable connection. Music is just a universal language that everybody is able to connect to, especially kids. It gives them a wonderful message.

MONIQUE COLEMAN: *High School Musical*, this whole enterprise, was such an incredible opportunity that I think we are in a position to make really good choices and decide what kind of work we want to do now. I've been more involved with, like, charity kinds of things and with things that have to do with what I want to say as a person. I'm thinking in lines of, like, books and tapes and, like, all kinds of other things that aren't necessarily acting-related but that are sort of personal and important to me. While I do have this moment that people recognize my name and face, I want to sort of take advantage of that while I can, and then, hopefully, other work will come from that.

ASHLEY TISDALE: When I was in high school, I worked at clothing stores, anything to be able to do this. I've always loved to act. I've always loved to sing. And I have been doing it since I was three, and most of us have been doing it since we were really young. So it hasn't been an overnight success. It's been a long time coming, and it's just really cool to be able to be recognized for something big like this, and that's wholesome.

ZAC EFRON: I love where I'm at with my fans at the moment. So, of course, when I look at projects, I try and find things that can take that audience and bring them on new and fun and interesting adventures. I don't want to shy away from them at all. But selfishly, I'm just trying to find an exciting role that I would enjoy playing.[22]

GROWING PAINS

Being a teen icon can be a tricky existence. So when Vanessa started dating costar Zac Efron after meeting on *High School Musical*, the couple decided to keep their relationship private. But Vanessa's personal life became front page news in September 2007, a month after the premiere of *High School Musical 2* when a nude photo, along with two others of her in lingerie, showed up on the Internet. The photos were intended only for the eyes of Efron but had somehow been hijacked.

She first found out about the photos from her manager, who told her the story was going to be in the tabloids. A few days later, the pictures were released while she was in Australia on vacation. "Thank God, I wasn't home," she says. "It would have sucked if I was at home. So I got to be away from L.A. for about a millisecond. But when I came back, it got kind of crazy."[23]

Her mom, however, took it in stride. After Vanessa told her what had happened, Gina announced, "Well, everyone can be naked if they want to." While Hudgens acknowledges it was stupid to take the photos in the first place, she lamented the way the Internet makes privacy that much more difficult. "Everyone knows everything, and they can find out everything about you. You're not as safe as you think you are, and you have to be aware of the people you're around."[24]

Vanessa quickly issued a public *mea culpa*. "I want to apologize to my fans, whose support and trust means the world to me. I am embarrassed over this situation and regret having ever taken these photos. I am thankful for the support of my family and friends."[25]

Later, she admitted it was a traumatic, upsetting experience. "I hope all my fans can learn from my mistake and make smart decisions. But I wouldn't have been able to get through it if it wasn't for my family, friends, and fans, who supported me all along the way."[26]

As did Efron, who Vanessa now openly acknowledged she was dating. She described their relationship as easy. "If you really love someone, you shouldn't have to work at it—you finish each others' sentences and have the same sense of humor."[27] But she refrains from looking too far in the future.

"Only time will tell. I'm still young," she says, adding that it's important to keep relationships in balance by spending time with family and girlfriends as well as boyfriends. "I think girls can be sucked into the relationship and give too much. And you can't do that, because you get too infatuated—and then you lose contact with your friends. It happens to a lot of girls."[28]

She also strongly urges girls to think long and hard before becoming intimate. "You have to think it through, not just do something spur of the moment. So that after it happens you won't regret it. I think girls can be infatuated with their boyfriends and they have to remember that they come first."[29]

While some media experts predicted that Disney would fire Hudgens from the upcoming *High School Musical 3* feature film over the photo scandal, they didn't. The Walt Disney Company released a statement saying: "Vanessa has apologized for what was obviously a lapse in judgment. We hope she's learned a valuable lesson."[30]

Unfortunately, in the current age of digital media, past mistakes seldom stay buried. In August 2009, a new crop of nude photos circulated the Internet. It was widely reported that these topless photos of Hudgens were actually taken prior to the previously leaked photos. Vanessa's representatives would not confirm it but her lawyers worked to have them removed.

"We asked the blog sites to take them down because posting such photographs of a minor is illegal, improper and offensive, violates her privacy rights, and infringes other legal rights in and to the photos," said attorney Christopher Wong.[31]

While Vanessa refused to discuss the incident publicly, not everyone was as discrete. At the 2009 Teen Choice Awards, filmed on August 9, comic Dane Cook made Hudgens the butt of a joke, saying: "Girl, you got to keep your clothes on. Phones are for phone calls, girl!"[32] Many members of the audience booed Cook and producers cut the line before the program aired the following night. Cook remained unrepentant, saying he only planned the comments about 20 minutes before going on stage. "Mostly I just wanted it to be funny That's the best part about being a comic; I can say the thing that everybody is kind of feeling and nobody [is saying]—the elephant in the room moment. So, I'll take the hit. It's okay."[33]

Some cynical observers suggested Hudgens herself leaked the photos to help promote her new film *Bandslam,* which happened to be premiering on August 14. The movie is about a group of misfit high school teens who form a rock group to compete in a battle of the bands. After appearing in three incarnations of *High School Musical,* Vanessa wanted to graduate to a less Disneyesque role and Sa5m (the 5 is silent) fit the bill. But Hudgens was caught off guard at the audition when she was asked to sing, assuming they knew she could. "So they had a pile and I went through all of it and found 'Rehab' by Amy Winehouse and sang that," she laughs.[34]

Vanessa admits that the angst-filled Sa5m was a welcome departure from Gabriella and her own personality. "I just run around happy, bubbly," she says. "I'm known for laughing and for singing all of the time . . . which becomes annoying to some people. The best part about being an actor is playing different characters so when I heard that she was just deadpan, introverted, I was like, *I'm so in.*"[35]

She realizes that playing grittier characters may leave some of her younger fans behind but notes, "I do what I do for myself. The fact that kids look up to me and especially my character, Gabriella, is extremely flattering. But at the end of the day I want to do R-rated films; I want to do things that are little bit edgier. So maybe kids won't be able to see some of them, but I'll try to do 50/50."[36]

Not only was media scandal one of the pitfalls of success, Vanessa discovered that lawsuits also came with the territory, especially when contracts were involved. In September 2007, attorney Brian Schall sued Hudgens for alleged breach of contract. Schall claimed that he became Hudgens's lawyer in October 2005 and he helped negotiate recording and songwriting deals worth more than $5 million. He also said he advanced her money for expenses during that time. Schall said their contract guaranteed him a five percent commission on her gross, or pretax, earnings on the deals he brokered up to a year after the end of his representation. Hudgens tried to get the suit tossed by claiming she had been a minor only 16 years old when she signed with Schall. The judge ruled her age had no bearing on fulfilling the contract and allowed Schall to pursue his court case. Instead, Vanessa paid Schall the relatively modest $150,000 he said he was owed. Then in 2008, she was sued by her former manager Johnny Viera who sought $5 million as his share of Vanessa's salaries, royalties, and merchandising. The case was settled out of court for an undisclosed sum in May 2009.[37]

Despite all the setbacks and hard lessons learned, Vanessa's career has continued to thrive and grow. She is regularly named in various most beautiful lists and is one of the top-earning young actors in Hollywood. She waited until she was 19 to move out of her parents' home. But the house she bought is only 10 minutes away. "They helped me move. They helped me fix my house up. They know I'm growing up, and they're proud that I can actually have my own home."[38]

Vanessa has also adopted a philosophical attitude toward a life in the spotlight and the barbs that often come with it. "I'm a very laid back, go-with-the-flow person. At the same time I'm passionate about what I do, so I have strong feelings towards [the public's misconceptions of her] but, yeah, I'm totally chill."[39]

NOTES

1. In person interview at a Television Critics Association press conference, January 2006.

2. Susan Young. "Bay Area Native Kenny Ortega Sees Emmy Gold for 'High School Musical' Musical Man." *Alameda Times-Star,* August 24, 2006.

3. Ruben V. Nepales. "Vanessa Hudgens: 'I Love Being a Filipina'," *Philippine Daily Inquirer,* August 9, 2007, http://showbizandstyle.inquirer.net/entertainment/entertainment/view/20070809-81617/Vanessa_Hudgens%3A_%91I_love_being_a_Filipina_%92.

4. Ibid.

5. Ibid.

6. "Vanessa Hudgens," *Seventeen,* February 2008, http://www.flixster.com/news/2008/01/03/vanessa-hudgens-seventeen-magazine-february-2008

7. Stephen Schaefer. "Vanessa Hudgens Plays Rockin' Role in *Band,*" *Boston Herald,* August 9 2009, http://www.bostonherald.com/entertainment/movies/general/view.bg?articleid=1189956.

8. "Vanessa Hudgens," *Parade Magazine,* July 30, 2009, http://www.disneydreaming.com/2009/07/30/vanessa-hudgens-parade-magazine-interview/.

9. Mark Ellwood. "Celebrity Pop Quiz: Vanessa Hudgens," *Daily News,* Sunday, August 9, 2009, http://www.nydailynews.com/entertainment/movies/2009/08/09/2009-08-09_celebrity_pop_quiz_vanessa_hudgens.html#ixzz0OSsmC4X4.

10. Jerry Ross. "How Vanessa Hudgens Went to the Top of the Class," *USAToday Weekend,* January 28, 2007, http://www.usaweekend.com/07_issues/070128/070128vanessa_hudgens.html.

11. "Five Questions with Vanessa Anne Hudgens," *Cosmo Girl,* July 2007, http://www.cosmogirl.com/entertainment/celeb-qa/vanessa-anne-hudgens-july07.

12. "Vanessa Hudgens Interview," Moviefone, http://community.livejournal.com/ohnotheydidnt/38176311.html.

13. Christopher Rocchio. "Vanessa Hudgens' Original Plan Was to Audition for *American Idol,*" *Reality TV World,* November 29, 2007, http://www.realitytvworld.com/news/vanessa-hudgens-original-plan-was-audition-for-american-idol-6189.php.

14. Ross, "How Vanessa Hudgens."

15. Interview with the author, July 2007, at a Television Critics Association press tour.

16. Geri Miller. "Catching up with the Cast of High School Musical," *Scholastic News,* http://teacher.scholastic.com/scholasticnews/indepth/highschoolmusical2.asp.

17. Interview with the author, July 2007, at a Television Critics Association press conference.

18. Ibid.

19. Nepales, "Vanessa Hudgens."

20. Ibid.

21. Ross, "How Vanessa Hudgens."

22. In person interview at a Television Critics Association press conference, January 2006.

23. "Vanessa Hudgens," *Seventeen Magazine,* February 2008, http://tv.popcrunch.com/vanessa-hudgens-on-february-2008-seventeen-magazine/.

24. Ibid.

25. "Disney Backs Star after her Apology for Nude Photo," *Reuters,* September 7, 2007, http://www.reuters.com/article/televisionNews/idUSN0746838620070908.

26. "Vanessa Hudgens," *Seventeen Magazine.*

27. *Cosmo Girl,* July 2008, http://www.etonline.com/news/2008/06/62902/index.html.

28. "Vanessa Hudgens," *Seventeen Magazine.*

29. *Cosmo Girl,* July 2008.

30. "Disney Backs Star," *Reuters.*

31. Marc Malkin. "Hudgens: The Real Story on Latest Nude Pics," *E!Online,* August 5, 2009, http://www.eonline.com/uberblog/marc_malkin/b137908_hudgens_real_story_on_latest_nude_pics.html?utm_source=eonline&utm_medium=rssfeeds&utm_campaign=imdb_topstories.

32. Teen Choice Awards, author attended, August 9, 2009.

33. Laura Hinton. "Vanessa Hudgens Nude Photos Scandal Gets Defense from Bandslam Co-Star," *National Ledger,* August 14, 2009, http://www.nationalledger.com/ledgerpop/article_272627420.shtml.

34. "Hudgens Stunned by Casting Director's Request to Sing," August 5, 2009, Contactmusic.com. http://www.contactmusic.com/news.nsf/article/hudgens-stunned-by-casting-directors-request-to-sing_1111891.

35. Schaefer, "Vanessa Hudgens Plays."

36. Ibid.

37. Lawsuit Info links, http://www.ninjadude.com/index.php/vanessa-hudgens-settles-court-case-pays-lawyer; http://www.foxnews.com/story/0,2933,402085,00.html; http://www.msnbc.msn.com/id/20853530/; http://entertainment.oneindia.in/hollywood/top-stories/scoop/2009/vanessa-5m-lawsuit-040509.html; http://www.dose.ca/story.html?id=3d340fa5-deeb-4cd7-8f25-09f61218707c.

38. See http://www.disneydreaming.com/2009/07/30/vanessa-hudgens-parade-magazine-interview/Vanessa Hudgens Parade Magazine Interview (reprint).

39. Ibid.

Grimes considers herself a fashionista and enjoys trying out new clothing and accessory trends.

12   SHENAE GRIMES

It was a case of Hollywood déjà vu. Just as Shannen Doherty did in the early 1990s with *Beverly Hills 90210,* Shenae Grimes made tabloid headlines for her allegedly wild ways causing problems on the set of the *90210* remake. According to *The Star,* Grimes was showing up late to work and forgetting her lines because she was turning into a party girl. Her super-slender frame also raised speculation that she suffered from an eating disorder. *TV Guide* reported that her shrinking size prompted the show's producers to consider staging an intervention. One doctor estimated that Shenae, who is just five feet three, weighed only around 90 pounds.

The buzz became so insistent Shenae was forced to defend herself and complained that fans should not believe everything they read.

"Nobody has asked me about it," she said. "I really can't help what someone thinks of me because they are reading a paper and choosing to believe it." Shenae blames the misperceptions on the media. "It's so frustrating. These are stories that have been written about everybody. Of course we're the new girls on a hit show, so we're plopped into these little boxes. And people buy it. It makes me totally second guess anything I've ever read about anybody."[1]

Grimes claims she's always been slender but stresses that she's also always been very healthy. "Meet me in person, and you can't say anything. Just because people are calling you skinny doesn't mean I'm like, *Yay!*" she says. "No! You're telling me I don't look right. This is me, this is my body—I have accepted it."[2]

Shenae is learning that having your dreams come true often comes at a price and that she's not in Kansas—or in her case, Canada—anymore.

EARLY ASPIRATIONS

Shenae Sonya Grimes was born on October 24, 1989, in Toronto, Ontario, Canada. Her artistic aspirations developed early but initially she thought she'd pursue fashion design, singing, or dancing, but never acting.

"It's a funny story how I got into acting at all," she says. "It's because of Jake Goldsbie, who is on *Degrassi*," and who also attended Randolph Academy for the Performing Arts along with Grimes. "I was a huge fan the first season, and he was

DEGRASSI, A CANADIAN ICON

Shenae's springboard to Hollywood fame was *Degrassi*. But the series itself is a Canadian broadcast television icon that has been on the air in one incarnation or another since the early 1980s. The first series was called *The Kids of Degrassi Street*, a low-budget production created by former teacher Linda Schuyler and filmmaker Kit Hood, about the lives of a group of children living in Toronto, which evolved from a 1979 short film, *Ida Makes a Movie*. The youths hired were not professional actors and the producers chose to name the series after a real street to reinforce the intended realistic nature of the program. Twenty-six episodes were aired of *Kids* between 1979 and 1985. By the end, the kids in the program were preparing to enter junior high school.

In 1987, *Degrassi Junior High* premiered. Again, the show focused on the daily lives of teenagers, who all come from different ethnic and racial backgrounds and who experience a range of home-life situations. Some of the actors who appeared on *Degrassi Junior High* will reprise the characters in future *Degrassi* series, such as Amanda Stepto and Stefan Brogren who played Christine "Spike" Nelson and Archie "Snake" Simpson, respectively.

The popularity of the series prompted producers to create a reason for the teens to spend ninth grade at Degrassi instead of moving on to Borden High, the high school depicted from the start of the series as their next destination. Then in 1989, the cast of *Junior High* and some characters attending Borden transfer to the never-before-mentioned *Degrassi High*.

Degrassi High ran for three years, continuing the *Degrassi* tradition of presenting gritty, real-life situations. When it was time for the *Degrassi* teens to graduate, the series finale was a 1992 TV movie called *Degrassi: School's Out*. A six-part documentary called *Degrassi Talks* also aired in 1992, featuring the cast talking about the series.

Almost a decade later in 2001, *Degrassi* returned in its current form: *Degrassi: The Next Generation*. The lead character is 14-year-old Emma, daughter of Spike Nelson, again played by Stepto. Snake Simpson returns as a teacher at Degrassi. Shenae's character, Darcy Edwards, was introduced in 2004.

The current series is less gritty but still addresses wide ranging, often controversial topics facing modern teens, and is the most successful and long running of the various *Degrassi* series, having completed its eighth season in April 2009; 161 episodes have been aired. Nearly half the regular viewers are adults and it remains the most-watched domestic drama series in Canada. It airs on the N in the United States, where it has also earned a loyal following.

in an acting class of mine, so I asked him for his autograph, and he set me up with his agent."[3] Her first role was playing a young Shania Twain for an *A&E Biography* episode. But her career started in earnest when she was cast as Darcy Edwards on *Degrassi: The Next Generation* in 2004.

Grimes says it's an important training ground for young Canadian actors. "There's not a lot of great material at home, and the stuff that there is, it's cute, but you're always playing 14-year-olds," she says. "No one has roles that are hearty and challenging for young actors there. So *Degrassi* was really it—that's the show that everybody's trying to get on."[4]

Once she joined *Degrassi,* Shenae says, "I've been working my way up into a bigger role ever since."[5] Initially, Darcy was a recurring secondary character—a "good girl" who was openly religious and who was proud of her virginity. She belonged to *Degrassi*'s Christian group, Friendship Club, and was a member of the Spirit Squad. In 2006, Shenae was promoted and Darcy became one of *Degrassi's* main players.

"I had to work my way up the food chain, and it took me a few years to prove myself for my producers," Shenae admits. "But I finally did."[6] Darcy the good girl became Darcy the rebellious teen with a self-destructive bent, such as when she uploaded provocative pictures of herself on the Internet—something Shenae would never do. Grimes says she has little in common with her onscreen alter ego. "Definitely lots and lots of differences," she stresses. "She's extremely into religion, which I think is very, very cool. I have yet to find any one area that I've really stuck with all my life. I've been studying lots and lots of different religions, so that's definitely a major difference. I'm not exactly the cheerleading type either. I was never prom queen, or any of that in high school, so that's definitely fun to play."[7]

In 2007, during the seventh season, her character is drugged and date raped, which sends her into an emotional tailspin. Her work that season earned Grimes a Gemini award, the Canadian equivalent of an Emmy, for Best Performance in a Children's or Youth Program or Series.

"I felt like, [by the] seventh season, I had the best storylines in the world," Shenae says. "It doesn't get much more challenging than that. I felt like it was time for me to, you know, step off a little bit and let some of the new kids come in, cause it's the pinnacle for young actors."[8]

HOLLYWOOD BECKONS

Shenae Grimes says her professional role model is Natalie Portman. "She is my inspiration, the way her career has gone. It's just been so amazing, and the fact that she went to Harvard University is just beyond me." Shenae acknowledges that being versatile is imperative for any actor who wants to avoid being typecast. "She's done roles of all different types, and that's what I'd love to do, just have a broad spectrum of characters behind me."[9]

Her work on *Degrassi* led to other acting opportunities. After guest spots on *Kevin Hill* and *The Power Strikers,* she was cast to play a teenage Twain again in the TV movie, *Shania: A Life in Eight Albums.* She also had a recurring role on the series *Naturally, Sadie* playing Arden Allcott. But it was Darcy who continued to premiere episode of *The Jay Leno Show,* and began working on material for her next album. She was also linked to rapper-of-the-moment Drake, although she seems content to keep her relationships casual for the time being.

Friends of the singer say she is interested in following Beyoncé's career path and wants to pursue acting. Fashion is also an area of interest and Rihanna acknowledges she'd like to one day "start some companies like a make-up company, a clothing line or maybe a swimsuit line." Whatever challenges she seeks out going forward, Rihanna says the key is to, "Believe in yourself. A dream is but a dream. But if you want it to come true you really have to fight and pursue. I always look to the big picture."[35]

NOTES

1. Grant Rollings. "Rihanna's Star on the Rise," *London Sun,* June 16, 2007, http://barpublish.bits.baseview.com/321907343206042.php.

2. "Rihanna Opens up about Drinking, Drugs and Guns," Filthyrag.com, September 14, 2008, http://www.zimbio.com/Rihanna,+Pon+de+Replay/articles/282/Rihanna+Opens+Up+Drinking+Drugs+Guns.

3. Ibid.

4. Jon Wilde. "Rihanna: Million Dollar Baby," *Daily Mail,* September 14, 2008, http://www.mailonsunday.co.uk/home/moslive/article-1053876/Rihanna-Million-dollar-baby.html.

5. Margeaux Watson. "Caribbean Queen: Rihanna," *Entertainment Weekly,* June 22, 2007, http://www.ew.com/ew/article/0,20043393,00.html.

6 "Talking Shop: Shontelle," BBC.com, February 24, 2009, http://news.bbc.co.uk/2/hi/entertainment/7880732.stm.

7. Wilde, "Rihanna."

8. Grant Rollings. "Daddy Was a Crack Addict," *London Sun,* June 15, 2007, http://www.thesun.co.uk/sol/homepage/showbiz/bizarre/celeb_interviews/237385/Daddy-was-a-crack-addict.html.

9. Wilde, "Rihanna."

10. Amina Taylor. "Move over, Beyoncé," *The Guardian,* November 25, 2005, http://www.guardian.co.uk/music/2005/nov/25/popandrock2.

11. Ibid.

12. Watson, "Caribbean Queen."

13. Ibid.

14. Taylor, "Move over, Beyoncé."

15. *Rolling Stone* review 2005, http://www.people.com/people/rihanna/biography.

16. Watson, "Caribbean Queen."

17. Margeaux Watson. "Rihanna Embracing Her 'Bad' Side," *Entertainment Weekly,* June 21, 2007, http://www.ew.com/ew/article/0,20043289_20043293_20043298,00.html.

18. "Interview: Rihanna,": Ask: Men,: http://www.askmen.com/celebs/interview_200/206_rihanna_interview.html.

19. Ibid.

20. Watson, "Caribbean Queen."

21. "If It's Nuddy That You Want," BBC, October 8, 2006, http://www.bbc.co.uk/totp/news/news/2006/08/10/35553.shtml.

22. Ibid.

23. Monica Corcoran. "Rihanna Reigns," *Cosmopolitan,* 2008, http://www.highbeam.com/doc/1G1-177412946.html. http://www.cosmopolitan.com/celebrity/exclusive/Rihanna-Reigns.

be Shenae's primary showcase and it was only a matter of time before Hollywood producers took notice.

In 2008, she starred as Marissa Dahl in the Lifetime network movie *True Confessions of a Hollywood Starlet.* She also costarred with Ashley Tisdale in ABC Family's *Picture This!* But her life would change irrevocably when she was cast as Annie Wilson on the CW's remake of *Beverly Hills 90210.*

Grimes originally auditioned for two roles: Annie and Silver, currently played by Jessica Stroup. Shenae says she met Jessica at the audition and knew she was perfect for Silver. "So I was like, *All right, Annie is my best bet.*" But then Grimes heard through the Hollywood grapevine that Hilary Duff had been offered the role. The news was disappointing but Grimes was philosophical. "If I've got to lose out to anybody, someone that's as established as Hilary Duff ain't too shabby," she says.[10]

When her agent called a few days later, he did little to improve Shenae's pessimism. "I got what I call the buffer phone call from my agent . . . where he calls and says, 'OK, Shenae, things went real good on this one, but I think it might be time to start looking at other things, start reading other scripts because I don't know how this is going to work out, blah, blah, blah. It's kind of coming down to the wire, so we need to start moving on'." But just 20 minutes later, she received another phone call, "from all of my agents saying, 'Congratulations, Hilary's out, you are in, and you are now Annie on the new *90210'.* I was in shock for a good couple of hours."[11]

In the updated remake, called simply *90210,* Annie is a Kansas City–raised teen who relocates to Beverly Hills with her parents, played by Rob Estes and Lori Loughlin, and her adopted brother Dixon (Tristan Wilds). She attends West Beverly Hills High, where she meets new friends Naomi, Ethan, and Silver, played, respectively, by AnnaLynne McCord, Dustin Milligan, and Jessica Stroup. Shannen Doherty, Jennie Garth, and Joe E. Tata reprise their *Beverly Hills 90210* roles.

The network sent the new cast DVDs of the original show's first four seasons as a gift. "That was awesome," said Grimes. "But I certainly didn't need to watch them again to remember what went on because I remembered the first four seasons in particular like the back of my hand. My mom really raised me on *90210.* That was kind of our mommy-daughter bonding session once a week, *90210* and *Party of Five.* I was one when the show came out, but my mom raised me on it, basically so I was very familiar with the old show."[12]

When asked if perhaps the show wasn't age inappropriate, Grimes insisted she thought it was relevant, even as a very young child. "The drama was something that you hadn't really seen on television before and the issues were real. You felt like that you could finally relate to people that you were seeing on TV. It was serious issues and it showed the serious consequences and it wasn't such a glamorous package put together for everyone's eyes. Yeah, my mom thought it was, I guess, educational in a way and so did I. It was our little bonding."[13]

The excitement of being cast in an anticipated new show was numbingly doused when the Writers' Guild went on strike in November 2007, closing all television production. Instead of leaving for Los Angeles as planned, Shenae passed the time by taking an internship at Fashion Television. But when the strike finally ended in February after three months, Shenae was finally able to leave Toronto for her new life in Los Angeles.

REAL LIFE DRAMA

One of the more bizarre stories that has circulated about Shenae Grimes is that she was briefly kidnapped as a child along with her friend Carolyn Sharf. According to the ZackTaylor.ca website, Shenae and Carolyn were in the fourth grade at Forest Hill Public School when the incident happened. The girls were just leaving school when the father of a casual acquaintance offered to give them a ride.

"We knew her through birthday parties and stuff but we didn't know her father," she says.[14] Carolyn says the three girls thought they were going to a movie together. Instead, the father took them to his house where he refused to let them use the phone to call their parents.

As the hours passed, Carolyn and Shenae started getting nervous and asked to please be taken home. The man put them in the car, leaving his daughter at the house.

"We had no clue what was going on, only that . . . it was getting really late," Carolyn recalled. "I remember the whole car ride we couldn't stop listening to Criptik Souls Crew."[15]

It was around 9:30 when he stopped at a cheese store in Toronto's Greek neighborhood. When he went to get something out of the trunk, Shenae jumped out of the car and ran into a nearby store. She called her father, who in turn called the authorities. The police arrived quickly and apprehended the man. They found a stash of illegal weapons and drugs in his car, Carolyn said. "He was arrested and we never saw his daughter again, she never came back to school."

The girls were released into the custody of Shenae's mom, who had also raced to the parking lot.

Carolyn's parents were relieved to get her back home, but also upset. "I was later grounded for 3 months for getting into a car with a stranger," she says. "The girl who we were friends with never returned to school after that, nor did we ever see her father again. Shenae and me haven't spoken of that day ever since."[16]

Grimes downplayed the incident when asked about it on *E! News*. "Don't believe everything you read. There was a very minor incident that was blown way out of proportion."

Sharf maintains Shenae was a hero. "It happened . . . If Shenae hadn't called her parents, who knows where we would have gone? She may deny it, but she saved my life."[17]

WELCOME TO OZ

The upside of remaking and updating an iconic show is that there's a familiarity about it with the audience. The downside is that people will inevitably compare it to the original. That's true for both the show itself and the actors following in the footsteps of the original cast, even if the characters are different. "The pressure was there but collectively I think we all chose to put it in the back of our minds and keep it there," Grimes says. "From the beginning, we knew we were riding some pretty groundbreaking coattails and wanted to do that justice but at the same time, we knew we were here to do our own thing, our own way, on our own show."[18]

Even so, the buzz swirling around *90210*—which included press conferences, photo shoots, magazine covers, and interviews—gave Grimes pause at what may be in store.

"I don't know what I'm in for," she admitted. "This is my first American gig ever, let alone the crazy phenomenon that it is and is turning out to be . . . For a few weeks there we had one or two photo shoots going on every weekend. That was a little bizarre. I love taking pretty pictures and getting to play dress up and all the rest, but it was like, *What is this all for?* We don't even have a show yet. Get me on a set. Get me doing the real work that I'm here to do. That should just be the icing on the cake, so that was a little bit surreal, to say the least."[19]

Once on the set, which is insulated and isolated from the outside world, Shenae says she felt more settled and comfortable. "The press and the paparazzi and all that kind of stuff, it's a very foreign world to me. Thank God I'm surrounded by the best people, the most grounded and down-to-Earth people around, so we're all leaning on each other and we're all planning on holding each other's hand walking through this madness that's about to ensue."[20]Grimes said that her TV parents had been especially kind, offering her their phone number should she need anything.

Before the show aired, Shenae also stressed that she wasn't going to get lost in a cloud of fame and fall in with hangers-on and wannabes. "I grew up in a very catty area of Toronto, so from a young age I had to establish what an acquaintance was, versus a friend. Thankfully I learned those lessons before I came to Hollywood."[21]

But some things can't be learned except through experience. As anticipated, *90210* quickly became a hit, thrusting its young stars into the white-hot glare of the public eye. It didn't long for stories to appear about Shenae's chain-smoking, weight, and alleged unprofessional conduct on the set such as showing up late and not knowing her lines. Her eating habits, or lack thereof, became an issue after *Gossip Girl* star Penn Badgley suggested Grimes and costar Jessica Stroup eat a double cheeseburger after pictures taken depicted them as near-emaciated.

A *Saturday Night Magazine* writer, though, reported she saw Shenae order a Cobb salad and garlic fries from room service and a diet coke. During the interview, Grimes called Hollywood "terrifying and unsettling." But the experience helped her better identify with her TV character. "We've both had to adjust to this new world of criticism, controversy, and gossip." The negative media attention also created a bond with Doherty, who has had her share of run-ins with the press. "She's advised me to stay strong, keep my head on, and focus on what's real while letting the bullshit slide off. I'm here to do a job and the hype and the scandal should remain irrelevant to it."[22]

When asked how she prepared for the role of Annie Wilson, Shenae laughed. "I'm doing the prep for it right now. I'm riding the wave right along with Annie Wilson. It's a big culture shock. There's no such thing as celebrity back home. Hockey players are a big deal, but actors . . . I didn't get recognized in Canada very often. If I did, nobody would approach me, let alone take my picture when I wasn't looking or anything like that. So this whole crazy hype and everything that's been going on has been a little overwhelming, to say the least, but I'm just rolling with it. I have amazing support here."[23]

Eventually, Shenae became accustomed to the attention, even from the paparazzi. "They're on me every day. They're there . . . it's really not a big deal at all. We exchange little niceties—and then I get in my car and I'm on my way. It's their job. A lot of them have been like, 'I don't want you to be freaked out, but I'm assigned to you'. It is what it is—it's so weird, and it'll never not be weird, but it's not the worst thing in the world."[24]

During her off time from work, Shenae calls herself a shopaholic and music lover. "I use music to inspire me when I'm writing poetry. I'd call them lyrics but I'll refrain as I don't see myself singing on a stage anytime soon."[25] She also enjoys going to see friends perform at small clubs around Los Angeles.

As she adjusts to life in the Hollywood fast lane, Shenae is determined to keep her eye on the prize. "I'm young and my goal as an actor is to experience and portray as many different roles as possible. I thrive off of challenge and change and am definitely a fan of keeping my plate full, but for now I'll try to spread my wings during the off season."[26]

Shenae might want challenges but she swears she won't quit *90210* to get them and that she is in for the long haul. "As long as it's around . . . I'm here—this is my big break man! I'm riding the rollercoaster."[27]

NOTES

1. "90210 Star Shenae Grimes Denies Eating Disorder Rumors," TVGuide.com, November 27, 2008, http://www.tvguide.com/News/Shenae-Grimes-Eating-1000293.aspx.

2. Ibid.

3. "Shenae Grimes," *The Star Scoop,* http://www.thestarscoop.com/2006oct/shenae-grimes.php.

4. "Shenae Grimes on Being 'The New Brenda' (or Not) on 90210," *BuzzSugar,* August 26, 2008, http://www.buzzsugar.com/1892873.

5. "Shenae Grimes," *The Star Scoop.*

6. "Shenae Grimes on Being," *BuzzSugar.*

7. "Shenae Grimes," *The Star Scoop.*

8. "Shenae Grimes on Being," *BuzzSugar.*

9. "Shenae Grimes," *The Star Scoop.*

10. Ian Spelling. "Shenae Grimes Interview," *UGO,* http://www.ugo.com/ugo/html/article/?id=19136&sectionId=25.

11. Ibid.

12. Spoken to the author at a Television Critics Association press tour, July 2008.

13. Ibid.

14. "Former Classmate in Kidnap Drama," *Pop Goes the News,* June 2, 2009, http://popgoesthenews.blogspot.com/2009/06/former-classmate-in-kidnap-drama-claims.htm.

15. Ibid.

16. Ibid.

17. "90210's Shenae Grimes: How Annie Turned Bad," *90210 Media,* http://90210-media.org/?cat=13&paged=43.

18. Carla Thorpe. "90210 Star Shenae Grimes," *Saturday Night Magazine,* http://www.snmag.com/INTERVIEWS/Celebrity-Interviews/90210-Star-Shenae-Grimes.html.

19. Ibid.

20. Spelling, "Shenae Grimes Interview."

21. Complex.com. Shenae Grimes, Mark Echo, http://www.complex.com/CELEBRITIES/Complex-Women/Shenae-Grimes.

22. Thorpe, "90210 Star Shenae Grimes."

23. Spoken to the author at a Television Critics Association press tour, July 2008.

24. Inside TV, "5 Questions with Shenae Grimes," http://television.aol.com/insidetv/2009/01/13/5-questions-with-shenae-grimes/.

25. Thorpe, "90210 Star Shenae Grimes."

26. Ibid.

27. "5 Questions With: Shenae Grimes," *90210 Media,* http://90210-media.org/?cat=13&paged=52.

(AP Photo/Carlo Allegri.)

Despite her all-American, girl-next-door looks, Dakota Fanning has made a career of playing edgy, controversial roles.

13   DAKOTA FANNING

She's never played the all-American girl next door. Her movies are often dark and disturbing, although her characters are inevitably imbued with the strength of resiliency and a spirit that may bend but doesn't break. Her iconic stature doesn't come from pop idolatry; it comes from being considered one of the best actresses of her blossoming generation—a Jodie Foster for Generation Z. So it's ironic that in real life Fanning *is* the blonde-haired, blue-eyed all-American girl next door and not an angst-filled teenager immersed in gothic darkness. As she says, that's why "it's called *acting.*"[1]

AN EARLY START

Conyers, Georgia, is a continent apart from Hollywood and a world away. It is a small town of under 15,000 residents located about a half hour outside Atlanta. The first settler was a blacksmith named John Holcomb who arrived in the early 1800s. Holcomb was opposed to having a railroad run through his property and threatened to shoot anyone who trespassed. Others saw the railroad as a way for the area to prosper. So a banker named Dr. W. D. Conyers persuaded Holcomb to sell his land for $700. Conyers in turn sold the land to the Georgia Railroad. The town of Conyers, a settlement that began as a watering post along the rail line, was incorporated in 1854 and initially had a population of 400.

According to local lore, Conyers was spared from being burnt to the ground during the Civil War because General Sherman allegedly had a friend who lived there. After the war ended, Conyers was both wanton, with 12 bars and five brothels, and respectable, with a college, hotel, and so-called sidewalk churches—Baptist, Methodist, and Presbyterian churches built on Main Street. Eventually, the more religious-minded citizens drove out the bars and brothels and ever since Conyers has prided itself on its traditional family values. While there may not be much traditional about Los Angeles, it shares at least one thing with Conyers: an appreciation for talent.

Hannah Dakota was born on February 23, 1994, the eldest child of Steve and Joy Fanning. Her sister Elle was born four years later in 1998. Both Fanning parents were amateur athletes in their youth. Dad Steve played minor league baseball for the St. Louis Cardinals as a shortstop; mom, Heather Joy Arrington, attended college on a tennis scholarship. Joy's sister Tiffany's life was also informed by sports. But instead of competing, she grew up to be a sportscaster. Known professionally as Jill Arrington, she worked at ESPN for a year as an NFL sideline reporter and currently works for the tennis channel. But then again, athletics runs in Joy's family. Her dad—and Dakota's maternal grandfather—is Rick Arrington, a former professional football quarterback who played for the Philadelphia Eagles from 1970 to 1973.

"My whole family was into sports," Dakota has noted. "I chose acting instead of sports. My sister and I kind of veered off."[2]

She says her first inkling that she wanted to act happened with her dolls. "I collect dolls and I've been doing it my whole life . . . When I was a kid I used to imagine those dolls were my children and I'd act out little stories with them. I think that's when I realized that maybe I could be an actor."[3]

As a young child Dakota—whose family nickname is Kota—would also stage plays at home, giving her sister Ellen supporting parts once she was old enough to walk and talk. Her obvious enjoyment in performing prompted her mom to enroll Dakota in a drama playgroup that would put on a play every week. Dakota, who was five at the time, was a clear standout from the other children.

"The head of the playhouse came up to my mom and said, *Have you ever thought about getting her an agent? Your daughter is the only one who actually tried. She should really consider acting.*"[4]

Three months later, Joy took Dakota to an open casting call at an agency in Georgia. Over the next 10 days, she was cast in three commercials. One, for the Georgia Lottery, paired her with Charles. "I'm on the piano bench with him," she recalls, "and he's singing 'Georgia on My Mind' in a big ballroom."[5]

Her success in Georgia prompted her agent to suggest Joy take Dakota to Los Angeles for the television pilot season, believing her commercial work would lead to series work. The Fannings agreed to try it for six weeks. But Dakota, now six years old, kept getting work, so the six weeks became seven, then eight . . . every time they planned to go home, Dakota would get another job, and during 2000 appeared on *ER, Ally McBeal* (as the young Ally), *Strong Medicine, CSI, The Practice, Spin City,* and a few others.

One of her favorite early jobs was on *Malcolm in the Middle,* where the script called for her to bite Reese, Malcolm's older brother on the leg and arm. "He wanted me to really bite him, so I did!" she laughs, adding, "It was fun."[6]

One of most vivid memories from those early days was meeting her then-idol Britney Spears. "I was in a store and she walked in and my jaw just fell to the floor. I started like sweating. I could not believe that I was meeting her. She told me that I was very cute. And I lost it—I was so excited."[7]

After she was cast in a national Tide detergent commercial, the Fannings relocated to Los Angeles permanently. Although her appearance in a movie was *Tomcat,* it was her role in the film *I Am Sam* opposite Sean Penn, that she considers her true debut. In the film, she plays the daughter of a retarded man (Penn) fighting to retain custody of her. Looking back at the emotionally taxing role, Fanning says she was too excited to worry if it would be hard to do. "I didn't even care if it was hard or difficult I just wanted to do it so bad because I wanted to be an actress really bad." To make herself cry in a scene, Dakota says she imagined her pet goldfish, Flounder, dying. "You use what's real in your life," she says.[8]

Her performance in *I Am Sam* earned Dakota a Screen Actors Guild award nomination, the youngest performer ever so honored. She won the Broadcast Film Critics' Association award for Best Young Actor. It was an auspicious start but it was just the beginning.

FANNING 2.0

Mary Elle Fanning was born on April 9, 1998. She got her break into acting at the age of 11 months, courtesy of being Dakota's younger sister. Her first film appearance was in *I Am Sam* playing the younger version of Dakota's character. She played the young Dakota again in her second job, the television series *Taken,* when she was three. But since then, Elle has established herself as an accomplished actress independent of her famous older sibling both on television and in films, including *Daddy Day Care, The Door in the Floor,* and *Reservation Road.*

In 2007, Elle spent four months in Budapest, Hungary, filming *Nutcracker: The Untold Story,* a musical based on the famous Tchaikovsky ballet. In March 2008, Elle and Dakota were supposed to costar together in *My Sister's Keeper,* but Dakota opted out when she learned she would have to shave her head for the role. (Abigail Breslin and Sofia Vassilieva took over the roles.)

With two underage actors in the family, Joy enlisted her mom Mary Jane to help with her granddaughters' careers. Whenever Dakota and Elle are working at the same time in different locations, Mary Jane accompanies Elle as her guardian while Joy travels with Dakota to her filming locations. But when they're home, Elle says they are like any other two sisters.

"The only time we sort of talk about movies is the experiences we had on the set, about people we met or things we did, like the . . . catering," she laughs. "I love the chicken and the fish. My sister loves Chinese food and sushi."[9]

Elle says her favorite part of acting is "where you do things you probably wouldn't do in your real house, where you flip over food or something . . . I also like to see the wardrobe, all the makeup, the type of character, the name—everything's all wrapped up . . . Also, I get to meet all these different people that I never would have if I didn't do acting."[10]

Joy and Steve, who works as an electronics salesman, deny that they pushed either daughter into acting for the money, saying it was something the girls both loved. "We take pleasure from seeing them do something they enjoy."[11]

THE NEXT JODIE FOSTER

By most standards, Dakota was a prodigy. As a toddler she attended a Montessori school and was reading by the time she was two years old. But while her reputation within the Hollywood film industry as one of its finest young actors continued to grow, so did concerns that she was growing up too fast—a worry she cheerfully shrugged off.

"When I go home, I play with my baby dolls and strollers and diaper bags, and play with my sisters," she said. "I still think of myself as nine years old." For example, she admits that when she was in New York filming *Hide and Seek,* she went to the Empire State Building and had a mini tantrum. "I cried in line for 45 minutes because I didn't want to go up. I've never been up that high before, so I didn't really know what to expect. I pulled my visor down, but I loved it once I was up there . . . the view was spectacular. It was really fun."[12]

Unlike method actors who sweat over backstories and stay in character all day on the set, Dakota has the ability to turn her craft on and off. She also says she doesn't overthink her roles. She reads over the script but doesn't get too familiar with it because inevitably there are changes during filming. "I don't think there's any formal prep work that I ever do," she says. "You're on the set and you have the other actors around you. You're saying these words. You can't help but to sort of fall into it during the take. The moment will take you to that place, and I can't really even help it," she explains, saying it's not a conscious effort. "When they say 'action', I can become [the character]. I know what she'd do in any situation."[13]

What she does focus on is learning from her costars, such as ad-libbing from Sean Penn and a work ethic from Denzel Washington. "I try and learn something new on every movie I do. I try to better myself from everything [and] from everyone on the film and from my characters. I've been very fortunate to play all different kinds. I just try and portray the character and the themes I fell in love with in the script[14] . . . It's an honor even to get to be in movies and have the opportunity to work with the people that I have worked with."[15]

Many of her costars and directors feel the same way about her. *Hide and Seek* director John Polson notes that Dakota arrives on the set with definite ideas about her character. The film is a horror story about a girl with an imaginary friend. "I wasn't dealing with a parent; I was dealing with an actor," he said. "I never felt like her parents had any unhealthy interest in her work, and that makes it much easier for me as a director. She is capable of things she shouldn't be capable of doing at that age . . . She's a very special girl, and nothing is more important than protecting that, protecting her,"[16] he said, referring to the perils of growing up a child actor.

So far, she shows no sign of turning into the next Lindsay Lohan or Britney Spears; the next Jodie Foster, maybe. For her role in *Hide and Seek,* it was reported Dakota took a pay cut in exchange for getting her name above the title next to costar Robert Di Niro's. Fanning's agent, Cindy Osbrink, comments, "I used to say she was 30. Now, after *Hide and Seek,* I say she's 105. She gets more mature and thoughtful and expressive."[17]

Dakota sees it differently. "When people say [how mature I am], I just want to act my age even more! I feel like the age that I am, and not any older." That said, she adds, "It *is* fun to be able to act older sometimes. I think that's what I love about acting, that you can meet people and do things that you would never be able to do in real life."[18] She credits her upbringing for instilling her personal priorities. "I have such a great support system in my family and friends," she says. "I have no choice but to stay grounded because of my family. I've never even been tempted to do anything other than what I've done so far."[19] In addition to family, there is faith.

"I am a Southern Baptist, and I grew up in the south, so every Sunday I went to Sunday school. So I've grown up in a family where that's really important."[20]

Her career is also important. "Acting is what I love to do. I wouldn't trade it for the world. I don't think of it as work. It's really fun for me."[21]

Dakota's agent says that her career plan includes a strategy of alternating film genres, "one fun one, then a serious one, just to keep it fun for her and keep her challenged."[22]

Fun is something Dakota actively seeks out, whether in her work or daily life. One thing she found especially fun was joining the Girl Scouts in September 2005 along with her sister Elle; Dakota was inducted as a Junior Girl Scout and Elle was made a Brownie Scout. Her fellow Girl Scouts quickly learned the perks of having an actress in their midst: the entire troop was treated to a special screening of *Dreamer,* about a girl who tried to bring a broken-down racehorse back to glory.

In typical fashion, Dakota went from the wholesomeness of the Girl Scouts to the most controversial role of her career in the film *Hounddog.* Set in the deep rural south of the 1950s, Dakota plays Lewellen, a young girl living with her single parent, alcoholic father. Lewellen idolizes Elvis and finds comfort in his music. After a local teen rapes her, Lewellen finds the inner strength to get past the trauma and the determination to hope for a better future.

Even before the film was finished filming, the production, and Dakota's parents, were being excoriated by conservative religious group for the rape scene. Ironically, that scene leaves practically everything to the imagination—there is no contact between Dakota and the actor playing the rapist, nor any shots depicting intercourse. All the viewer sees is Dakota's face during the attack and her crying for the Elvis concert tickets she thought he was going to give her.

Hounddog's director Deborah Kampmeier says the film's subject matter did not harm her lead actress. "Dakota doesn't have to hang on to the darkness," she says. "She knows how to goof around with the other kids on the set. That's part of her maturity. But she has a state of presence that usually takes years of meditating to find."[23]

Dakota thinks people are surprised when they work with her because "most people think that kids in the business are brats. You don't have to be a brat to be an actress. I just enjoy it so much that there is no time to do anything like that. And why would I want to when I'm enjoying myself?"[24]

From a professional point of view, *Hounddog* tested Dakota, says agent Osbrink. "It's not just the rape scene; the whole story is challenging Dakota as an actress. And I've never been so proud of her in my life." For her part, Dakota felt the criticism was uncalled for, reactive, and "really stupid . . . The movie wasn't even edited when people started attacking it. It was horrible. Those people should learn not to speak before they've seen something.[25] . . . They were waiting to see something that was shocking and inappropriate, and they weren't going to see it. It was very, very hurtful to be so attacked."[26]

She says the reason she wanted to do the movie was because "it was about such an important issue and something that could help so many, and I know it already has. That's why I love to do movies."[27]

Hounddog was her first experience at negative publicity and she admits it stung. "It's not nice to spread rumors. I learned that it can be very hurtful to talk about others. I read a quote by Oprah Winfrey where she said, 'Turn your wounds into wisdom'."[28] In the process, she would transform from a child actor into teen icon.

BALANCE

After attending preschool and first grade, Dakota was homeschooled for her entire elementary school years. But when she decided she wanted to experience typical teenage rite of passage, Dakota enrolled in a private high school. She says fitting in has not been a problem and that her classmates "realized pretty quickly I am just very normal." She was concerned that some might treat her differently, but says "they really didn't. I've made some amazing friends and some friends that I know I'll probably have forever."[29] As if to prove just how normal she is, Dakota made the cheerleading squad.

> I am a cheerleader. Now everybody always wants me to do cheers. It's so funny. Cheerleading is so much fun, especially at your school because you get such a sense of school spirit and you're proud of your school. I love that. I'm the one that's on top of the pyramid; I'm the flyer, so that's fun too.[30]

Beginning with *Hounddog,* Dakota's roles became noticeably edgier. In *The Secret Life of Bees,* she played a North Carolina teenager named Lily who is haunted by the death of her mother when she was a toddler—during an argument, her parents struggled over a gun. When it fell to the floor, the four-year-old Lily picked it up and it accidentally went off, killing her mother. Lily is befriended by a black woman who helps her discover the truth about her mother's past.

Dakota credits her grandmother with helping her understand life in the segregated South. "My grandmother grew up during this time and had a lot of experiences to tell me about. [She] was raised by black women, just like my mom in the film. Her dad also adopted an African-American boy." The director also screened Spike Lee's documentary *4 Little Girls,* about the horrific bombing of a black Baptist church in Birmingham, Alabama, in 1963, which killed four young girls. "It really impacted me," she says.[31]

Her next film was *Push,* a sci-fi thriller about a group of young people with psychic abilities running from a secret U.S. government agency.

"My character is a true 14-year-old—kind of rebellious. She has a very sassy attitude and that was very fun to get to explore in this film. She says and does things that I never would."[32] Such as, in one scene, Dakota's character, Cassie, gets drunk so she can see the future more clearly. But she says the change in roles was happening organically and wasn't part of a master plan.

> I think that as you get older the roles that you can do kind of are limited and also expanded at the same time. I just try to let it happen naturally and as I get to certain ages some things are right and some things are not. I've been lucky to find the right thing. I have to do what I feel is right for me and grow as an actress. I have to do that no matter what, if I want to continue doing this and I do.[33]

She realizes, though, that not everyone may be comfortable with her growing up. "I can no longer do Lucy in *I Am Sam*. You have to grow up and I am doing it through films. Eventually I'm probably going to play the person that you hate. I think that's the fun part about acting."[34]

Unlike many of her contemporaries, Dakota does not have an adversarial relationship with the media. While she acknowledges that it's hard when mistakes become public knowledge she says, "The attention ultimately comes with acting. The attention is to be expected, and you just live with it. I just try to have a normal life while doing what I love to do."[35]

Now that's she's approaching legal age, Dakota's normal life is starting to include dates. In July 2009, she made gossip column headlines when she was spotted having a dinner date with fellow teen actor Freddie Highmore, best known for *Willy Wonka and the Chocolate Factory*. But her work schedule would make dating, much less having a relationship, difficult to squeeze in.

ALL GROWN UP

Dakota turned 15 in February 2009 and the year would prove to be a turning point in her career, being cast in two high-profile films that allowed her to transform from child actor to young adult star. First, she costarred with *Twilight*'s Kristen Stewart in *The Runaways,* which recounts the formation and early days of the seminal all-girl band. The original members—Joan Jett, Cherie Currie, Lita Ford, Sandy West, and Jackie Fox—were teenagers when they formed the group, which became the first female rock group to sell over one million records. In the movie, Stewart stars as Joan Jett; Dakota as Cherie Currie.

To portray Currie, who was heavily influenced as a teen by David Bowie's glam style, Dakota dons platinum hair and wears ultrahigh platforms. The script also includes a scene where Currie and Jett have a sexual encounter with an onscreen kiss. Stewart said, "Dakota's very controlled and poised. She's going to have to lose herself in this because it's pretty heavy."[36]

Losing herself in a character doesn't seem to be a problem for Dakota. In addition to her role in *The Runaways,* she will team up with Stewart again in

JOAN JETT

In the summer of 1975, Joan Jett began telling people of her desire to form an all-girl rock band. Although only 15, Joan was already a fixture at Hollywood music clubs. She was introduced to drummer Sandy West through mutual acquaintance Kim Fowley. Kim helped Joan and Sandy recruit Micki Steele on bass and Lita Ford on lead guitar. They named the group the Runaways and Kim became their manager. The band played their first gig in the autumn of 1975 at the famed Whiskey A Go-Go in West Hollywood. In November, Joan and Kim met 15-year-old twin sisters Marie and Cherie Currie. When Cherie came to audition for lead singer, she didn't have a song. So on the spot, Joan and Kim wrote "Cherry Bomb." Cherie nailed it and joined the band. Micki left the group and eventually Jackie Fox became the Runaways's bassist.

The band signed with Mercury Records in February 1976 and recorded their first album. They spent much of the year touring in America and overseas. After recording their second album, *Queens of Noise*, The Runaways embarked on their second U.S. tour. In Japan, they were a phenomenon; "Cherry Bomb" hit number one in Japan and their tour there was sold out. The hysteria that greeted the girls was said to be reminiscent of when the Beatles first came to America. But in the midst of their biggest success to date, Jackie quit and returned to the United States forcing Joan to play bass for their performance at the Tokyo Music Festival. Their *Live from Japan* album became one of the biggest imports of the decade.

As soon as they returned to America, they began working on their third album, *Waiting for the Night*—the first album featuring Joan on lead vocals because Cherie Currie left to pursue a solo career. Vickie Blue joined the band as Jackie's replacement. By the end of 1977, the group severed ties with Fowley. They recorded the fourth and final album, *And Now . . . The Runaways*, in 1978. Their last performance was on New Year's Eve at the Cow Palace outside of San Francisco.

Creative differences led the group to disband in 1979. Joan went on to form Joan Jett and the Blackhearts and founded her own music label, Blackheart Records. She continues to perform, occasionally acts, and is executive producing *The Runaways* movie. After leaving the group Cherie Currie also branched off into acting and today is a chainsaw artist and runs an art gallery of her work in Chatsworth, California.

the *Twilight* sequel, *New Moon,* playing bad girl Vampire, Jane Volturi, who has been described as a kind of vampire enforcer. "She's pretty much evil," Dakota laughs. "Yes, she may feel like she's just doing her job by torturing people, but that's evil."[37]

In the film, Dakota and the other actors playing Volturi sported red eyes courtesy hand-painted contacts that *New Moon* director Chris Weitz describes as praying mantis eyes. "You can't really see into them. There's something terribly off-putting about it." Costar Michael Sheen commented in a tweet: "I think Dakota may look the most unsettling. So angelic, yet so weird. As Jane that is, of course. Like an evil red riding hood." Weitz agrees. "She is very strange and very spooky in this movie. I think she wanted to play an evil character for once."[38]

Asked if she's ready for the kind of attention fellow *Twilight* stars Stewart and Pattinson face, Dakota is philosophical. "You have to be able to separate your personal life from playing a character. That's not your real life."[39]

As far as her professional life, Dakota is just enjoying the ride. "Every year a new door opens for roles, so when that time comes . . . I think it's fun just to live in the moment, to take it as it comes and look forward to what you're doing."[40]

NOTES

1. Paul Brennan. "Slack Jawed, Hounddog, and Mr. Donohue (Not) at the Movies," *OC Weekly,* January 24, 2007, http://blogs.ocweekly.com/navelgazing/main/slack-jawed-hounddog-and-mr-do/.

2. Fanning World, http://www.fanningworld.com/viewpage.php?page_id=29.

3. "Dakota Fanning Pushes the Limits," *Parade,* February 2, 2009, http://www.parade.com/celebrity/celebrity-parade/archive/dakota-fanning-pushes-the-limits.html.

4. Queen Latifa. "Dakota Fanning," *Interview,* http://www.interviewmagazine.com/film/dakota-fanning/.

5. Ibid.

6. "War of the World: Dakota Fanning Interview," *Atlantic International,* http://madeinatlantis.com/interviews/dakota_fanning.htm.

7. "Dakota Fanning Pushes the Limits," *Parade.*

8. Latifa, "Dakota Fanning."

9. Thomas DiChiara. "5 Questions With: Elle Fanning," *Moviefone,* March 5, 2009, http://insidemovies.moviefone.com/2009/03/05/elle-fanning-interview-phoebe-in-wonderland/.

10. Cindy Pearlman. "Actress Dakota Fanning, a Veteran at Age 14," *The New York Times Syndicate,* October 12, 2008, http://readingeagle.com/article.aspx?id=109456.

11. Fanning World.

12. Rebecca Murray. "*Uptown Girls'* Young—but Very Mature—Dakota Fanning," *About.com,* http://movies.about.com/cs/mollygunn/a/uptowngirlsdf.htm.

13. Marshall Heyman. "Dakota Fanning: Working Girl," *W,* October 2008, http://www.wmagazine.com/celebrities/2008/10/dakota_fanning.

14. "Dakota Fanning Lives out Her Dreams," *Times Square,* http://timessquare.com/Movies/FILM_INTERVIEWS/Dakota_Fanning_Lives_Out_Her_Dreams/.

15. Murray, "*Uptown Girls'.*"

16. Colleen Long. "'*Hide and Seek'* star Fanning, at 10, already owns acting chops," *Sign on San Diego,* February 4, 2005, http://www.signonsandiego.com/uniontrib/20050204/news_1c04dakota.html.

17. Joel Stein. "Movies: Major League: The Million-Dollar Baby," *Los Angeles Times,* February 27, 2005, http://www.time.com/time/magazine/article/0,9171,1032353,00.html.

18. Adam Robezzoli. "Interview: Dakota Fanning," *Lifeteen.com,* http://www.lifeteen.com/default.aspx?PageID=FEATUREDETAIL&__DocumentId=106317&__ArticleIndex=0.

19. Pearlman, "Actress Dakota Fanning."

20. Robezzoli, "Interview."

21. Long, "'*Hide and Seek'.*"

22. Stein, "Movies."

23. Heyman, "Dakota Fanning."

24. "Dakota Fanning Lives out Her Dreams," *Times Square.*

25. Lloyd Grove. "All Shook Up over Dakota's *Hounddog*," *New York Daily News,* July 20, 2006, http://www.nydailynews.com/archives/gossip/2006/07/20/2006-07-20_ all_shook_up_over_dakota_s_.html.

26. Pearlman, "Actress Dakota Fanning."

27. Heyman, "Dakota Fanning."

28. Long, "*Hide and Seek*'."

29. "I'm a Dead Ringer for a Vampire; Dakota Fanning Goes over to the Dark Side in Her New Movies (Features)." *Daily Record* (Glasgow, Scotland), 2009. HighBeam Research (August 18, 2009). http://www.highbeam.com/doc/1G1-198670861.html

30. "Dakota Fanning Leads the Cheers at New High School," Starpulse.com, September 23, 2008, http://www.starpulse.com/news/index.php/2008/09/23/dakota_fanning_ leads_the_cheers_at_new_h.

31. Pearlman, "Actress Dakota Fanning."

32. "Dakota Fanning Pushes the Limits," *Parade.*

33. "Dakota Fanning Interview," *PUSH,* http://www.moviesonline.ca/movienews_ 15288.html.

34. "Dakota Fanning Pushes the Limits," *Parade.*

35. Pearlman, "Actress Dakota Fanning."

36. Issie Lapowsky. "Kristen Stewart Has a Hot Makeout Scene with Dakota Fanning," *New York Daily News,* July 2, 2009, http://www.nydailynews.com/gossip/2009/ 07/02/2009-07-02_kristen_stewart_has_a_hot_ makeout_scene_with_dakota_fanning_ in_the_runaways_repo.html.

37. Peter McQuaid. "Drama Teen," *New York Times,* August 16, 2009, http://www. nytimes.com/indexes/2009/08/16/style/t/index.html#pagewanted=0&pageName=16seg alw&.

38. *"New Moon* Has Dakota Fanning Seeing 'Red'," *The Kansas City Star,* August 28, 2009, http://docs.newsbank.com/s/InfoWeb/aggdocs/NewsBank/12A60A50F9D9EFC0/ 1083311554222450.

39. McQuaid, "Drama Teen."

40. "Dakota Fanning, Actress," *The Hollywood Reporter,* http://www.hollywood reporter.com/news/dakota-fanning-actress-138277.

(AP Photo/Evan Agostini.)

Even before *Gossip Girl*, Chace was known for his style: He was named Best Dressed in his senior year of high school.

14   CHACE CRAWFORD

If things had gone according to plan, Chace Crawford would have been reporting the news instead of making it. After graduating from high school, he moved to California to attend Pepperdine University in Malibu, studying broadcast journalism. He joined the Sigma Nu fraternity and his future seemed securely mapped out, until Chace's life took an unexpected turn that landed him in New York by way of Hollywood.

LONE STAR

Christopher Chace Crawford was born in Lubbock, Texas, on July 18, 1985. His sister Candice was born a year later on December 16. Their parents, Chris and Dana, were just in their early 20s, with Chris still in school. The family relocated to Minnesota when Chace was six, where Chris served his dermatology internship at Hennepin County Medical and his residency at University of Minnesota, both in Minneapolis. The family lived 15 minutes outside the city in Bloomington, where Chace attended Ridgeview Elementary School.

After Chris completed his training, he brought his family back to Texas to set up his practice. Now a highly regarded physician, Dr. Crawford was named one of the best physicians in Dallas by *Texas Monthly* in 2008. He also serves as the dermatologist for the Texas Rangers baseball team.

Chace's mom Dana was a teacher so education was a priority in the Crawford household. Chace and his sister attended Trinity Christian Academy (TCA), one of the largest single-campus, kindergarten through 12th grade schools in the country. The campus sits on more than 40 acres in Addison, Texas, outside Dallas. More than 1,500 students attend TCA and according to the school's website, 100 percent of graduates attend college. A multidenominational private school, TCA's student body represents more than 137 different churches in the greater Dallas area.

Laid back and charming, Chace had an eye for the ladies from an early age. He got his first girlfriend in fifth grade. "Her name was Kiley Smith and she was my best friend's twin sister." Kiley gave Chace his first kiss, which he calls "one of those super-awkward things. We were at camp, on a lake, really picturesque—it's kind of seared into memory!"[1] Although the youthful romance didn't last, Chace says he and Kiley are still friends.

THE OTHER CRAWFORD

Talk about good genes. Not only did the Chris and Dana Crawford produce a heartthrob son, they also followed up with a beauty queen overachieving daughter. Candice Crawford never had to worry about being in her older brother's shadow because she's been too busy being a golden child in her own right.

She grew up loving sports and in high school at TCA participated in basketball, golf, track, and cross country. After graduating, she attended University of Missouri in Columbia to study journalism. While in college she worked as a personal trainer and was very involved in extracurricular activities, serving on the Homecoming Steering Committee.

"My love for sports journalism derived from my love of playing sports," Candice says.[2] In addition to sports, Candice's competitive nature led her to enter beauty pageants. Her crowning achievement, so to speak, came in 2008 when she was named Miss Missouri USA, beating out 47 other contestants. Crawford also received a special achievement recognition in the swimsuit category.

"Getting up on stage in a swimsuit is not easy," she admits, but credits her broadcast journalism experience with helping her summon the poise required. During the previous semester Candice had interned at a local Columbia television station, which she called excellent practice for the pageant both in her public-speaking skills and overall confidence. Having family there also increased her comfort level. "I had such a great support group . . . They made it easier to walk out there every time." That qualified Candice to participate in the Miss USA pageant, where she earned sixth place in what she indicated was her pageant swan song.[3]

"I think this would be a good ending point for me," she said. "After this is over, I would like to focus again on my career."[4]

After graduating, Candice was hired by the Dallas TV station, 33-TV, to cover local high school sports. She also hosts the Dallas Cowboys weekend sports show, *Special Edition*. Through that show, she met Cowboy quarterback Tony Romo, who she has been linked to romantically.

With her looks and outgoing personality, Candice has been asked if she's interested in trying her hand at acting like her brother. Although she's never thought of actively pursuing acting, she's not counting anything out.

"I'm not opposed to it," Crawford said. "I'm very open."[5]

For a while Chace played football but admits he had neither the size nor the passion for it so he opted for golf. He also spent a lot of time drawing. "I was a nerd," he laughs. "I was in the art department a lot so I was friends with the art kids, the drama kids and the athletes. I was best friends with lots of people so I guess I was popular. It was like a big family—everyone was popular." Less popular was his girlfriend. "I dated a girl from a rival high school and none of the girls from my school liked that."[6]

During the summer, Chace stayed at his grandparents' lake house. "My friends and I have epic stories from the lake," he says. "We'd cruise on the water on Jet Skis, then drive around the country at night. It was the highlight of my high school years."[7]

Back on dry land, Chace dabbled in modeling to make some extra cash, appearing in ads for Hollister, a clothing store aimed at younger teenagers, "so I didn't have to take my clothes off," he jokes.[8] Chace liked the money but not the job. "I didn't like it at all. They treat you like a piece of meat."[9]

He didn't like his job at Abercrombie & Fitch, either. He complained that they played the same three CDs all day long. "They play it so loud you can't even talk in the store and they blast the place with cologne, you can smell it from a block away." Chace was a greeter, welcoming the customers as they entered. "I had to stand out front and time would drag on. I'd beg them to let me work on the cash register."[10]

When he was a senior, the TCA drama teacher suggested Chace audition for a role in a school production of *The Boyfriend*. "I sang the National Anthem," Crawford recalls, and was cast. "It was a good little role and something about it was just fun, but it didn't really trigger anything in me."[11]

Chase graduated from TCA in 2003. He chose to attend Pepperdine in Malibu although in truth, he was unsure what exactly he wanted to do with his life. While his sister had already set her sights on broadcast journalism, Chace, who has jokingly called himself the black sheep of the family, had yet to find himself. It would take the encouragement of his father and the gentle nudging of his mother for Chace to find his way.

CHANGE OF PLANS

Malibu has a unique personality. It is home to both millionaires in beachfront mansions and surfer dudes who hang out in dive bars with peanut-strewn floors, each attracted to the breathtaking natural beauty of the area. Nestled between the Malibu Canyon foothills and the Pacific is Pepperdine University, a private university with a tuition price tag of around $30,000 in 2003. "There were a lot of kids there whose families were very rich," Chace says. "The parents would be on private jets on business trips all the time and, although you could see they loved their kids, they weren't there."[12]

Chace joined the Sigma Nu fraternity and opted to study broadcast journalism, which he enjoyed. But he still felt a lack of direction so he switched to a business major, which led to more anxiety. Even though Chace was good in math, the curriculum required some advanced calculus classes. His parents saw Chace panicking and suggested he take a semester off. Chace gratefully followed their advice. "I was just thinking, *Oh god, I need a little break so I can gear up and kind of tackle that.*"[13]

During his hiatus from class, he lived with some friends and worked as a car valet in Malibu, and says it was one of the best jobs he ever had. "I love cars to begin with. It was right on the beach next to some really nice restaurants, so you got some pretty nice cars. We'd get to just put it to the floor on the Pacific Coast Highway, then we'd have to pull a U-ey and gun it back up, park on the shoulder, and run across the highway."[14]

During that time, one of Chace's friends urged him to meet with his commercial agent but Chace was hesitant—he had hated modeling and assumed doing commercials would be a similar experience. But his friend was persistent and dragged Chace despite his protests. The agent signed Chase that day. He started taking acting classes and continued even when he returned to Pepperdine part-time. Juggling college and acting class and auditions was stretching Chace to his limit.

When his father came for a visit, he saw the stress. Chace told his dad, "Listen, I'm half-assing both things, Dad. I've got to be honest with you. I really need to give one thing my all. I'm really bummed." Chris advised his son to quit school and concentrate on the things he really loved. Chace was relieved and shocked but his dad was adamant and encouraged him to go for it. "That's what it took," Chace says. "He was confident. I don't understand how people do it without some moral and emotional support."[15]

Chace made his professional debut in a 2006 Lifetime movie *Long Lost Son,* where he played a young man kidnapped as a boy from his mother by his father and taken to a Caribbean island. That same year he appeared in his first feature film, *The Covenant.* The film is based on Aron Coleite and Tone Rodriguez's graphic novel. The title refers to a power that is passed generationally from father to son. When an evil force is released during their rite of passage, the four band together to stop it.

Chace played a high school junior named Tyler. "He's kinda the rookie guy that just wants to use the power and be along for the joyride," Chace explains. "It's a fun character, just kind of happy go lucky."[16]

The description could also apply to Chace. He was enjoying his foray into acting and was living life as it came. But that life was about to abruptly change and in the process turn Chace into a household name.

GOSSIP GIRL'S HEARTTHROB

The buzz surrounding *Gossip Girl* started months before the series debuted in 2007. The cast of little known and unknown young actors were enthusiastically looking forward to the experience. "I really don't know what to expect," Chace admitted at the time. It started with his agent sending him a script for the pilot. "I kept auditioning—I think I hit six times. The producers were always nice to me and kept calling me back. So I knew I had a chance."[17]

Despite his relative lack of experience, Chace was chosen to play Nate Archibald. He describes his character as someone "really trying to figure out who he is . . . He doesn't fully accept everything that's been given to him. Overall he's a good guy. He wants to do the right thing." Chace says viewers "live vicariously through Nate. He's always sort of conflicted between his life and who he really is genuinely."[18]

Despite having a very different background than his character, Chace says he understands the kind of pressure an Upper East Side youth can have. "On the East Coast there is a real pressure to go to an elite university," he says. "Nate doesn't want that, and that's how I was. Most kids where I grew up don't leave Texas. That's fine, but that wasn't my thing. I wanted to go and meet other people and I am very fortunate that I could."[19]

Chace admits he was not familiar with the books the series was based on and at first intended to read all 12. "I thought I owed it to the fans to read them. Then I got halfway through the first one and realized, we can do something else; take it where we want it to go. The show is going to stand on its own," so he didn't want to be influenced by the books.[20]

He also does not want to be influenced by newfound fame. "I am trying hard to stay grounded with it," he says. "I don't let it go to my head, but I can see how it could. You hear people say *Yes* all the time and an ego builds up." The loss of anonymity affects all facets of his life. "It can be a bit weird when you are in a restaurant and people are staring. I still get anxious when people stare. It means I stay in a lot and have people over for dinner."[21]

Initially, the actors worked in anonymity. They could shoot in Central Park and be completely ignored by passersby. That changed once the show aired and *Gossip Girl* fans, and paparazzi, started following their every move. Chace said the cast dealt with their newfound notoriety by sticking close together. So close, that Chace and Ed Westwick, who plays the womanizing Chuck, became roommates.

"We didn't know if the show was going to last or not. Ed had never lived away from home, let alone in a different country," Chace says. "We got along and figured it would be a smart move financially. And really, it was also just kind of out of laziness."[22]

Being a heartthrob means having your love life publicly dissected. In 2007, he became romantically involved with country superstar Carrie Underwood. That's when he realized how difficult relationships would be when played out in the public eye. Every move was chronicled, such as when Carrie spent Thanksgiving with Chace at his parents' house in Dallas. By the summer of 2008, the relationship had wilted.

"I met Carrie before *Gossip Girl* had even started and I didn't realize what seeing someone like her would entail. She had a lot of pressure on her and it helped me to learn how to deal with that kind of stuff. She was at a different stage in her career to me and it wasn't a difficult break-up."[23]

His sister Candice painted a slightly different picture. "He was upset about the breakup," she says. "It's always hard when you lose a relationship. But he's doing okay through this whole ordeal. Chace will get through it. We love Carrie, too. They're dolls and they'll both do well."[24]

CARRIE UNDERWOOD

Even before Carrie Underwood won *American Idol* in 2005, she was on her way to becoming America's sweetheart. With her pure voice and down-home charm, she was the girl next door women admired and men adored. Like Chace, she came from a close-knit family rooted in spirituality and values.

Carrie Marie Underwood was born on March 10, 1983—her mom, Carole, actually gave birth to Carrie at home, rather than at a hospital—and is the youngest of three daughters. Her mom is a retired school teacher and her dad Steve is a retired plant worker who now raises cattle. Her older sisters, Shanna and Stephanie, are both elementary school teachers.

Carrie grew up in Checotah, Oklahoma, about an hour's drive from Tulsa. The town has less than 4,000 residents and is so small that it only has one traffic light. It's most famous for being the steer-wrestling capital of the world. The Underwoods lived on a farm, where Carrie developed a love of animals, one reason she became a vegetarian.

From the time she was a little girl she wanted to be a performer. Underwood jokes that she could sing before she could talk. Although normally quiet and polite, when it came to singing Carrie was not shy about letting people know her dreams. "If you were to ask me what I would be when I grow up when I was little I would've been like, I want to be famous."[25]

When she was 13, Carrie went to Nashville to record a demo CD. Carrie sent the demo to radio stations and record labels but it generated no interest. She continued to perform locally but when she left for college, Carrie put her singing aspirations aside—until her friends at college urged her to try out for *American Idol*. Out of the 100,000 people who auditioned that year, Carrie was one of the 193 people chosen who were flown to Hollywood to compete in the next round. On May 25, 2005, Carrie Underwood was named the fourth *American Idol* winner.

Since then, she has become one of country music's most popular performers and one of the most eligible bachelorettes. After winning *American Idol*, Carrie broke up with college sweetheart Drake Clark. In early 2007, she was romantically linked to Dallas Cowboy quarterback Tony Romo for several months, but the relationship broke up over the time demands of his pro football career. In 2008, she dated Dr. Travis Stork, a former *Bachelor* on the ABC reality show who now appears on the syndicated series *The Doctors*. Most recently, she and hockey player Mike Fisher have become a couple.

Despite her success, Carrie says she remains humbled and grateful. "I want people to think of me as a nice person. I really am so blessed. All of this has been a great experience and I thank the American public so much for putting me in this position. I appreciate every second of it."[26]

During his time off from the series, Chace looks to stretch his acting muscles in films such as *The Haunting of Molly Hartley* and *Loaded* but he's most proud of his work in *Twelve*. In the movie he plays a drug dealer and lost 15 pounds off his already-lean frame for the role. "I was pale and scruffy," he says. "No one even recognized me. Everyone had the same small trailer. So it was really a different experience. It was just easier to focus." He particularly enjoyed the less-rigid style of acting. "There were no big master scenes outside. It was more improv." He finished filming right before *Gossip Girl* started production again and the juxtaposition was jarring. "I was so stressed the first day back . . . There were paparazzi guys flying around like wasps . . . it's literally a circus. It definitely drains your focus and energy."[27]

While Chace enjoyed taking on a role diametrically opposed to Nate Archibald, he says it's important to measure one's career moves. "You need to know what your threshold is and what you can take on and what gets to a point where the audience doesn't believe it."[28] In his next film, Chace will see if his fans buy him as a dancer when he stars in the remake of *Footloose,* a role he was cast in after Zac Efron dropped out.

"I know Zac and we're actually friends," Chace says "He's gotta make the best choice for his career at this point and I have to make the best for mine and luckily it worked out for both of us."[29]

The auditions for the film lasted five hours and were physically taxing but Chace says he was up to the challenge and is confident he'll hold his own in the movie because he's always been athletic and has a natural sense of rhythm. That said, he admits, "I'm not a dancer. I need to start stretching now."[30]

MOST ELIGIBLE BACHELOR

While Chace says he's open to finding a girlfriend, he also says he has no plans to settle down anytime soon. Nor will you catch him dating a costar. "*Gossip Girl* creator Josh Schwartz told me to avoid at all costs dating a co-star," he reveals. "We get to shoot in New York and have that as our playground and do the insane things that we get to be a part of. There's a part of me that wants to share that. But I'm having fun living the bachelor life right now. It's a good time to be single."[31]

Maybe so, but he clearly enjoys dating. In May 2009, Chace was seen in the town with 19-year-old *Sports Illustrated* swimsuit model Esti Ginzburg, who costarred in *Twelve* with him. In August 2009, he was photographed with *Twilight* star Ashley Greene. Then in September 2009, several New York papers reported Chace was seeing Bar Refaeli, also a *Sports Illustrated* model and Leonardo DiCaprio's ex.

Chace's reaction to all the speculation is resigned. "I don't like it when my private life is talked about, but it makes me know that I have made it."[32]

That success has been a source of pride for his parents, especially his father. "We've become really close over the past years. He just tries to understand the acting thing so much and has gotten into it while supporting my career. He's always on IMDB and comes to my set and hangs out. He wants to start investing in films and stuff, so we've become closer through all that."[33]

Looking into the future, Chace intends to keep his celebrity in perspective. "Simplicity, that's what it's all about," he says. "I like to keep things simple, from what I wear to who I'm friends with.[34] I actually apply that to my personal life, too. I'm the biggest believer in not talking. I don't Twitter or MySpace or Facebook.

I want to keep to myself. I don't want to be out there. You have to keep some kind of control over who you are."[35]

For as much fun as he's having now, his desire for simplicity will ultimately lead him away from the bustle of New York. "I'll probably settle down somewhere in the country," he says. "It's my roots. It's in my blood."[36]

NOTES

1. Jackie Strause. "Chace Crawford: Summer's Hottest Bachelor," June 17, 2009, http://www.people.com/people/package/article/0,20283823_20285376,00.html.

2. Jordan N. Raubolt. "Crowning Achievement," *Columbia Tribune,* November 16, 2007, http://archive.columbiatribune.com/2007/nov/20071116news006.asp.

3. Ibid.

4. Ibid.

5. Ibid.

6. *OK!* Magazine, July 9, 2008, http://chaceconline.com/press/news.php?newsid=46.

7. Rachhel Chang. "Chace Crawford," *CosmoGirl!,* February 1, 2008, http://www.highbeam.com/doc/1G1-173677887.html.

8. Andrew Williams. "Chace Crawford on Gay Rumors," *Sunday Metro,* June 25, 2008, http://www.metro.co.uk/fame/interviews/article.html?in_article_id=191206&in_page_id=11.

9. Nicole Lampert. "Hot Gossip!" *London Daily Mail,* August 22, 2008, http://www.highbeam.com/doc/1G1-183501005.html.

10. Williams, "Chace Crawford."

11. "Chace Crawford?!" *Wonderland* Magazine, http://coverawards.com/2009/09/16/chace-crawford-is-that-you-in-wonderland-magazine/.

12. Lampert, "Hot Gossip!"

13. Christopher Bollen. "Chace Crawford," *Interview,* September 1, 2009, http://www.highbeam.com/doc/1G1-206533616.html.

14. Ibid.

15. Ibid.

16. Chace Crawford Interview, *MovieWeb,* http://chaceconline.com/press/news.php?newsid=23.

17. Jim Bawden. "Chace Crawford Next Teen Sensation," *Toronto Star,* September 18, 2007, http://www.thestar.com/printArticle/257545.

18. In-person interview with the author, July 2007.

19. Lampert, "Hot Gossip!"

20. In-person interview with the author, July 2007.

21. Lampert, "Hot Gossip!"

22. Bollen, "Chace Crawford."

23. Lampert, "Hot Gossip!"

24. "Candice Crawford: Chace Will Be Alright," *The Hollywood Gossip,* April 3, 2008, http://www.thehollywoodgossip.com/2008/04/candice-crawford-chace-will-be-alright/.

25. Hoda Kotb. "Small Town Carrie Hits Big Time," June 19, 2005, http://www.msnbc.msn.com/id/8245299/.

26. *Q&A: Carrie Underwood,* May 2005, http://www.billboard.com/news/q-a-carrie-underwood-1000944168.story.

27. Bollen, "Chace Crawford."

28. Ibid.

29. Ibid.

30. Tim Stack. "*Footloose* Exclusive: Chace Crawford and Producers Talk about the Upcoming Remake," May 28, 2009, http://hollywoodinsider.ew.com/2009/05/28/footloose-exclu/.

31. "Chace Crawford Likes Being Single," September 9, 2009, http://www.limelife.com/blog-entry/Chace-Crawford-Likes-Being-Single/19839.html.

32. Lampert, "Hot Gossip!"

33. "Chace Crawford Answers 17 Juicy Questions!" *Seventeen,* http://www.seventeen.com/dating/17-questions/chace-crawford-17q#ixzz0Sr8hdpPg.

34. Chang, "Chace Crawford."

35. Bollen, "Chace Crawford."

36. Chang, "Chace Crawford."

(Shea Walsh/AP Images for Sobieski Vodka.)

Aly first gained popularity as a Disney star, but now has successful singing and acting careers.

15 ALY MICHALKA

When CW announced it was planning to air *Hellcats,* a show about cheerleaders filled with young, energetic, and physically gifted performers, it sounded like a typical CW series. What wasn't typical was that the star of the show was a self-avowed creationist Christian who was more apt to be photographed coming out of church than coming out of a Hollywood club. But throughout her career, Aly Michalka had managed to balance her day job with her faith.

Aly says she and her sister Amanda Joy (AJ) have been performing for as long as they can remember—but as young girls they never thought it would become their career. "Ever since I can remember we were putting on music shows when the relatives would come over to the house, and practicing songs our mom would sing at church," Aly told *Christian Music Today* in 2005. "AJ and I wanted to be like her when we were younger, so it really came from that. It's amazing when that trans-forms into something and you think, *Wow, oh my gosh, God had that all planned!*"[1]

Alyson Renae Michalka was born on March 29, 1989, and Amanda Joy was born two years later on April 10, 1991. While AJ was still a baby, the family moved from Torrance, California, outside of Los Angeles, to Seattle, Washington. Their father Mark is a contractor and he ran a construction company. Their mom, Carrie, helped Mark run his business.

When she was younger, Carrie had been a cheerleader at the University of California, Los Angeles, then with the Rams and Raider professional football teams. She also used to sing in a Christian group called the J. C. Band and always encouraged her daughters' love of music. So growing up AJ and Aly's favorite thing to do was sing. After putting on concerts for their pet guinea pig, Brownie, they started singing at church when Aly was five and AJ was three.

Aly briefly attended Mack Elementary School and she and AJ were mostly homeschooled. Since they had each other, they did not feel as if they were missing out on anything by not going to regular school. The sisters also enjoyed having the freedom to pick the subjects they wanted to learn and liked having the teacher's undivided attention.

Being homeschooled also meant avoiding topics such as evolution. In a 2005 interview, Aly and AJ made clear they are creationists. In fact, at one point, Aly asked, surprised, "Wait . . . are they teaching [evolution] in schools now? I think that's kind of disrespectful. Anything that has to do with anybody's beliefs on religion, that should stay out of the classroom. I mean, I think people should be able to pray in school, if people were into that. Everybody should just do their own gig." AJ added, "Evolution is silly. Monkeys? Um, no."[2]

Inspired by their mom's musical skills, Aly and AJ learned to play the piano and the guitar. "We wanted to be like her when we were younger, so it really came from that," Aly explains.

When they got older they started writing songs, mostly for fun but it would eventually lead to a life-altering opportunity.

A PASSION FOR PERFORMING

One day Carrie got a pamphlet in the mail advertising an acting class. As a joke, she put it on her husband's desk. But to Aly, it was no laughing matter—she begged her mom to let her take the class. But Carrie and Mark were both initially hesitant.

"They wanted us to be normal kids," explains Aly. "But AJ and I banded together and we got into it. We had tons of fun."[3]

Agents periodically came to see performances put on by the students and several were impressed with the Michalka girls. Aly remembers the agents encouraging them to move to Los Angeles. As it happened, Mark needed to be back in Los Angeles for his business. So the family packed up and returned to California. Although they still loved music, once back in Los Angeles acting became their focus. Despite being the younger sibling, AJ's career took off before Aly's. Her first job was a TV commercial for a department store and she did some print modeling. Her big acting break came in 2002 when she guest starred on the daytime drama, *Passions*. Over the next three years AJ appeared in several more series.

Things were more difficult for Aly. "I had been auditioning and auditioning," she admitted to *Scholastic*. "But I could never book the jobs because of my braces."[4]

Even so, Aly was happy for AJ. She never got discouraged and kept studying hard because, she says, she had faith she would eventually get her chance. Not long after getting her braces removed, an opportunity presented itself when she auditioned for a new Disney Channel series called *Phil of the Future*.

The audition went well. "I was really proud of myself that I'd gotten that far," Aly recalls.[5] But she was realistic. Unlike AJ, she had no professional acting experience. So when her manager called to say she'd been hired, Aly says she couldn't believe it.

"I was crying and screaming. It was a huge thing for me to accomplish! I was really happy that Disney gave me a chance."[6]

In the series, she played Keely Teslow, Phil's best friend. The show debuted in the summer of 2004. It was an immediate hit.

The girls got their musical break when Hollywood Records, which is owned by Disney, signed the girls to a record deal. "They were sitting on stools, playing five songs they wrote," label president Bob Cavallo recalled to *Blender.* "I signed them on the spot." AJ was especially thrilled. "I grew up loving Disney. And suddenly I was a part of it. It was totally surreal."[7]

They wrote, or cowrote, all the original songs on the album. "It's all things that have happened to us in real life," Aly told *Blender.* "It's stuff that kids can relate to." AJ added, "I think people want to listen to positive music Listening to music that's uplifting is really important, especially for people who are growing up."[8]

Into the Rush was released in August 2005. In the liner notes the first acknowledgement is to "our Bestest Friend and Savior." Aly and AJ said they were not making Christian rock and, indeed, they never sang the word "Jesus," but their music flowed from a Christian perspective. Backstage at Live with Regis and Kelly before a performance of their single "Rush," the sisters, Carrie, the vocal coach, and hairdresser all joined hands to pray for strength.

"We don't ever wanna preach or shove anything down people's throats," Aly was quoted in *The Guide,* "but AJ and I want our music to be inspiring. It's just positive, uplifting messages," AJ added, "We don't want to exclude anybody. If we have a Muslim fan or an atheist fan, that's their thing—I'm gonna love them no matter what."[9]

Their single, "Do You Believe in Magic" was number one on Disney Radio and "No One" was featured in the movie *Ice Princess.* Seemingly overnight, Aly and AJ were working nonstop. When they weren't acting, they were singing. When they got off stage, they went back in front of the camera.

In September 2005, they performed a concert in Hollywood. After that they starred in the movie *Cow Belles,* playing rich sisters forced to work for their father. In November 2005, they filmed *Haversham Hall* for Disney Channel. In the show they played the roles of sisters.

Then Aly and AJ spent December on tour with the Cheetah Girls but the workload was beginning to take its toll. Aly described a typical day on tour to crushable.com. "We wake up in whatever city we're in and usually that's something that I never really know until I ask. We're ready for the day once we get hair and makeup done. Then we come and sound check, and then we have a meet-and-greet, we do touch-ups and pick out our wardrobe. Then we do our band handshake and pray, and kind of just zone out and chill. Then we do the show, get back on the bus, eat dinner and do the same thing the next day."[10]

"We just take it one day at a time," AJ said during a StrScoop.com interview. "When we're on the road, we focus on our music and performing." At home they focused on acting. "We love doing both. I really couldn't pick a favorite. You get two awesome worlds. You can't really compare them."[11]

By the beginning of 2006, *Into the Rush* had sold nearly half a million copies and Aly and AJ would later be nominated for an American Music Awards. Despite their full schedules, they still managed to live full lives, making time to be with friends, relax, go to spas, and rejuvenate. "All of this stuff is, to me, being a normal kid," Aly commented to *Scholastic.* "I always find time to relax. Go into my bedroom and read a book. Or talk to a friend on the phone. It's fun because I've always enjoyed doing a lot of activities. I get bored really easily."[12]

Although Aly is openly devout, she doesn't want to be labeled a Christian singer. Similarly, although she loved Disney, she didn't want to be typecast as a teen idol. She just wanted to be a performer everyone could enjoy.

"I don't ever want to put myself in a box," Aly commented to *Netscape Celebrity* in 2006. "I definitely want to do a wide range of things." At the same time, she stressed the importance of staying grounded. "I have been blessed to be a part of [this career] yet it's not your whole life."[13]

Aly told *Christian Music Interviews* that it was never her or AJ's intention to become rock stars or famous actors. "We didn't focus on any of that, but it really came from a passion—and God being able to bless those passions for some reason. The TV shows and movies just came, and we just so happened to get a record deal and it was not contrived. We call it a God thing. God has shown us favor and we want to be positive role models for others. We take that really seriously and responsibly."[14]

Aly understands celebrities who shy away from the responsibility of being role models. "But if I put myself in a situation where I'm seen by millions of kids, I have some sort of responsibility no matter what. There's no excuse to [behave poorly], because people are looking up to you. That just comes with the territory."[15]

In late 2006, Aly and AJ also released a Christmas album, *Acoustic Hearts of Winter;* in 2007, they released their second album, *Insomniatic.* Aly continued to costar on *Phil of the Future* until it went out of production in 2008.

In 2009, Aly announced on her MySpace page that she had been cast in her first feature film, *Bandslam,* about a battle-of-the-bands competition. In the movie, Aly played Charlotte Banks, the lead singer and guitarist in a band formed by a group of friends. The movie gave Aly the chance to channel some of her musical influences, which include Heart, the Police, the Beach Boys, Seal, U2, and gospel and country music.

In *Cinema Source,* Aly described Charlotte as a "kind of a version of me and that girl that you want to be your best friend because she's so fun, like let's fly by the seat of our pants and have a good time and forget about thinking and just live life the fullest. She's really passionate about what she does and she loves her music."[16] Aly also said she particularly liked that Charlotte was not a caricature as is often found in typical teen movie characters.

Normally, Aly preferred to keep her music life separate from her acting life. "I have always said that. But this script in itself was really different. I had a special personal connection with it and I said, hey, forget about it." She added to *Cinema Source,* "I fully believe in being able to combine the two since it's a natural talent that I feel comfortable with, but at the same time, I want to be able to separate my music from my acting."[17]

Although Aly was still performing with AJ, they were maturing as artists and decided that their "Aly and AJ" image needed to be updated so they adopted a new band name: 78violet.

In the summer of 2009, Aly told *Cinema Source,* "I definitely feel like it's a natural progression for us, really to be able to grow up. But in a way that's graceful, not pushed or forced, like hey, we're older, you know. I am 20 now and AJ's 18, which means our fans are now 17 and 18 and 19 and they are with us and we've been able to gain older fans as well. The music will speak for itself and it sounds like a revamped version of what Aly and AJ used to be."[18]

She also said 78violet's first album would be released sometime in 2010. "We're really taking our time just setting it up and really releasing it properly. We got to work with some amazing artists that I loved ever since I was young like Nancy Wilson from Heart, we got to write with her, and it was such an incredible experience. She's like a mentor and an aunt, which is so crazy to think of because I was such a big fan. I was kind of nervous to write with her at first."[19]

Although *Bandslam* failed to make such noise at the box office, it received positive reviews and gave producers a chance to see Aly outside her Disney persona. Her next project would complete her transformation from kid star to young adult actor.

HELLCATS

In 2010, the CW network announced it had cast Aly Michalka and *High School Musical* honey Ashley Tisdale in the series *Hellcats,* which is set against a backdrop of competitive cheerleading. The series is described as a coming-of-age story. Aly plays Marti Perkins, a prelaw student at Lancer University in Memphis, Tennessee. But when she loses her scholarship, the only way she can stay in school is by winning a place on Lancer's legendary cheerleading team, the Hellcats. To nearly everyone's surprise, Marti makes the squad, and, according to the production notes, "is thrust into a world of camaraderie, backstabbing and the intersection of sports, backroom academia and big money." Tisdale plays Marti's new roommate, Savannah Monroe, who is also on the squad.

During a press interview, Aly was enthusiastic about her new role. "Cheerleading is badass," she says. "These people are athletic. These people work out like crazy. These people are trustworthy people because they are there to catch you when you are up in the air, flying. They are there to have your back. It's this team effort."[20]

Michalka said that even though she had no previous cheerleading experience, "My mom has that background. So I guess I have it in my blood. But I've never had an interest to be on a squad, probably because there's no home-schooling cheerleading squads," she joked.[21]

At an age when many young performers consider taking time off to attend real college rather than just play a college student on the small screen, Aly said higher education is probably not in her plans.

"College is obviously something that I've thought about a little bit, but I'm so happy with what I'm doing now," she explained to crushable.com. "I feel like college is an avenue for you to find what you want to do; what you want to have as your career; finding yourself as a person. If I wanted to go there for fun and have a good time and be on my own I would do that for sure, but I already know what I want to do."[22]

NOTES

1. Andy Argyrakis, *Away from the Rush,* Christian Music Today, http://www.chris tianitytoday.com/music/interviews/2005/alyandaj-1105.html.

2. "Tweenage Riot," *Blender* Magazine, June 2006, http://www.blender.com/guide/articles.aspx?id=1937.

3. Christian Activities Youth Ministries, *Sister Duo Aly & AJ,* http://www.christian activities.com/youth/story.asp?id=5024.

4. MSN, *Scholastic Interview,* November 2004, http://groups.msn.com/Philofthe Future/amscholastic.msnw.

5. Ibid.

6. Ibid.

7. "Tweenage Riot."

8. Ibid.

9. Grace Norwich. *Amped Up: Aly & AJ, The Official Biography,* New York: Penguin, 2007.

10. *Aly & AJ in Concert,* The Disney Channel, 1995.

11. StarScoop.com, http://www.thestarscoop.com/2006oct/aly_and_aj.php.

12. MSN, *Scholastic Interview.*

13. Stacy Jenel Smith. "The Sister Act That Plays Together: Aly & A.J.," http://web centers.netscape.compuserve.com/celebrity/becksmith.jsp?p=bsf_michalka_rstar.

14. Maximizing Music and Media in Youth Ministry, *Aly & AJ,* http://www.inter linc-online.com/artists/index.html?p=2&id=183PHPSESSID=cd380d6731eebd6519e56c 1925cad101.

15. Andy Argyrakis. "Away from the Rush," *The Fish,* http://www.thefish.com/music/interviews/11617908/Away-from-the-Rush/.

16. Rocco Passafuime. "Aly Michalka," *Cinema Source,* August 21, 2009, http://www.thecinemasource.com/blog/interviews/aly-michalka-interview-for-bandslam/.

17. Ibid.

18. Aly Michalka interview for *Bandslam,* http://ja-jp.facebook.com/note.php?note_id= 107330452823.

19. See Ashley Boyer, *A Voice for This Generation,* http://www.briomag.com/briomag azine/entertainment/a0007094.html.

20. Press conference interview with the author, July 2010.

21. Ibid.

22. Nikki Katz. "Aly Michalka Interview," http://crushable.com/entertainment/aly-michalka-interview/.

Following a successful stand-up career and starring in her own sitcom, Ellen found new success with her talk show, winning the best daytime talk show Emmy in 2008.

16 ELLEN DEGENERES

Ellen DeGeneres never set out to be the poster child for the lesbian community; she just wanted to be funny. She also wanted to live her personal life in relative privacy and have people treat her as kindly as she tried to treat others. She wanted what most people strive for—a fulfilling life and someone special to share it with. But her decision to publicly acknowledge that she was gay in 1997 put her squarely in the forefront of an often bitter and angry debate over the acceptance of gays in mainstream society. One would be hard-pressed to think of a less-likely personality to be at the center of a media and social controversy than Ellen, who throughout her career projected a girl-next-door persona and an easy-to-get-along-with disposition that by all accounts accurately reflected who she was offstage as well.

Once she was officially out of the closet, DeGeneres's sexual orientation became the thing that defined her, especially in media reports. Instead of being viewed as a comedian who happened to be gay, she became a gay comedian. Although many in the gay community wanted DeGeneres to take on the role of activist, she stressed her sole intent was to express who she was as an individual and not become the new lesbian standard-bearer. But in doing so she managed to upset both those who disapproved of her lifestyle choice and those who shared it.

The fallout was swift. For almost three years, her career languished, a victim of not just her personal admission but the breathless play it received in the media and the concern by those running networks and studios that Ellen would no longer be accepted into mainstream American homes by viewers. What got lost in all the hoopla was that Ellen was the same funny and gracious woman she always was. But there was a tacit assumption by less-forward thinkers that DeGeneres was destined to become a cautionary footnote in Hollywood lore as the gifted performer whose career couldn't survive the queer label.

But a funny thing happened on the way to obscurity—talent won out. Television once again came calling and offered DeGeneres the chance to host her own daytime talk fest. *The Ellen DeGeneres Show* has proven to be the ideal format to showcase her unique talents and personality. A bona fide hit, the show has earned the comedian a new legion of fiercely loyal fans who have embraced Ellen as a welcome guest in their homes—and as a comedian who just happens to be gay. It also gives Ellen a pulpit from which to spread the message of tolerance. She has become a teen icon because her humor and humanity cross generational lines and because she's living proof to anyone bullied because of their sexual orientation that it really does get better.

Much of Ellen's appeal is that she really *is* the girl next door. It's just that this girl prefers other girls. Even those who disagree with her lifestyle on moral or ethical principles can still identify with her obvious compassion and be seduced by her endearing charm.

The thing about second chances is that by definition they follow on the heels of loss or struggle. To better understand how Ellen was able to turn personal adversity into a professional rebirth it's necessary to look back at her life and put the events that shaped and informed her personality and humor in big-picture perspective. And if there is one lasting legacy to be gleaned from Ellen's life story, it's that we love who we love because we are who we are. And by staying true to who she is, Ellen has prevailed and come out on top.

CHILDHOOD

DeGeneres was born at Ochsner Hospital in the New Orleans suburb of Metairie, Louisiana, on January 26, 1958. Like many people who find their way into comedy, Ellen's early childhood, while not hell on earth, wasn't exactly the stuff of dreams, either. Her dad, Elliott DeGeneres, worked as an insurance salesman while her mom Elizabeth Jane, who everyone called Betty, was an administrative assistant in addition to taking care of the house and minding after Ellen and her brother Vance, who was four years older. Being a devout, religious man, Elliott expected his children to behave in a certain way and for the most part, they did. Both Ellen and Vance were polite and respectful to their elders and stayed out of trouble.

Although it was the first marriage for Elliott, Betty had been briefly married once before to a young military man named George M. Simon. Shortly after she and Simon divorced, Betty met Elliott in church. A devout Christian Scientist, Elliott was not flashy or flamboyant, but he was steady and reliable. Ellen calls him very religious and very honest and says he never once raised his voice to her.

Ellen and her family lived in Metairie until she was in third grade, when Elliott moved them uptown to the Audubon Park section of New Orleans, a quiet, sleepy area five miles north of the French Quarter. Unlike the striking antebellum-style homes in the Garden District with their sprawling grounds and lush foliage, the DeGeneres' white-collar, middle-class neighborhood offered more foundations of neatly arranged cinder blocks.

Growing up, Ellen's idols were naturalists Jane Goodall and Dian Fossey, and she fantasized about leaving New Orleans to become a naturalist. However, Ellen also remembers being fascinated by certain performers she saw on television.

According to her parents, Ellen was a tomboy who also loved frilly dresses, dolls, and babies. Unlike some comics who are born clowns, Ellen was on the quiet side and didn't make efforts to stand out among any crowd. In fact, a former classmate from La Salle Elementary School remembers Ellen as being rather unremarkable.

"She wasn't a show-off or a class clown or even all that funny, really just sort of average," says Debbie, now a homemaker in the New Orleans area. "La Salle was a small neighborhood school, the kind of place where everybody knew everybody. We'd go over to each other's house for birthday parties or to play, and Ellen's family was no different from the rest. There was nothing that made them stand out in your memory."[1]

As a kid, Ellen grew up in the shadow of her older brother, Vance. She has made wry comments about how many pictures her parents took of Vance growing up, while they seemed to take none of her. But she's quick to add that she was in awe of her brother, not jealous.

Ellen often felt uprooted as a child, moving several times because of her father's work and being forced to go to a different school almost every year. "I never really kind of adjusted or fit in," she says, "so I was just frustrated."[2]

Years later, in her early act, Ellen would use those feelings of isolation to make people laugh.

As a kid, I used to wander around the woods, because my parents had put me there . . . I was coming home from school from kindergarten . . . well, they told me it was kindergarten. I found out later I had been working in a factory for ten years. It's good for a kid to know how to make gloves.[3]

Ellen's parents separated in April 1972. Vance was already out of high school and living on his own while Ellen and her mom moved to an apartment in Metairie. Ellen says coming from a broken home helped her realize how important humor was. Whenever she saw her mom was feeling blue, Ellen could make her laugh.

"As a thirteen-year-old kid, to realize that you can manipulate somebody and make them happy is a really powerful thing. To know that I could make my mom feel good started pushing me toward comedy; that's when I started working on it."[4]

Ellen's cousin, Buddy DeGeneres, says she's just a chip off the DeGeneres' entertainer block. "Talent runs in our family. There are a lot of musicians among us. For example my dad was in the group John Fred and the Playboys, and they had a hit record Judy in Disguise. Also, everyone in the family has a good sense of humor. You should hear the one-liners when we all get together. So it's no real surprise that someone from the family is a famous comedian."[5]

People always ask me, "Were you funny as a child?" Well, no, I was an accountant.[6]

At Grace King High School, Ellen was an average, and not particularly avid, student, meandering her way through classes. By the time she was 16, Ellen had grown into an attractive young woman who tended to hang out with older friends of both sexes. Although her social life was better in high school than it has been in middle school, Ellen still felt like an outsider. "Back then in New Orleans I didn't have any hangouts; I moved around too much for that. I had a lot of different friends, but all the time I was trying to find myself. I didn't know who I really wanted to be, or what I wanted to be."[7]

As soon as the divorce from Elliott was final, Betty jumped into another marriage with salesman Roy Gruessendorf, who made it clear he didn't approve of Ellen's crowd. Because of the disapproval she felt from Roy, Ellen tended to stay out even more than she otherwise might have, preferring to be anywhere but home. So Betty and Roy decided Ellen needed to be removed from the bad influence of her friends and announced they were moving to Texas—immediately. Ellen wouldn't even be allowed to finish out her junior year. So they moved to Atlanta, Texas, which Ellen has described as having a downtown a block long.

The move was traumatic. She left behind a sophisticated, culturally rich city in New Orleans for a small rural town located in the middle of nowhere. She was also leaving her brother, Vance. Betty worked hard to make the move seem positive. Although Ellen could have stayed with her maternal grandmother, who lived in New Orleans, she didn't want to make that break from her mother.

For all her rebellion, Ellen adored her mother, and the thought of being separated from Betty made her feel worse than leaving her friends. Although she still wasn't happy, Ellen was determined to get through it. The move also provided her with one advantage: She would be able, in a way, to reinvent herself in this new town where nobody knew her. She could become whoever she wanted to be, and she was going to make sure not to slip back into her former wallflower mode. Plus, it was only a year and a half until her high school graduation and she was counting the days.

DEEP IN THE HEART . . .

Atlanta, Texas, is a short car ride to the point where Texas, Arkansas, and Louisiana meet. Pine trees flourish in and around Atlanta, a quiet town nestled squarely in the Sun Belt. The area enjoys moderate weather year round, with temperatures in the winter rarely dropping below 50 degrees. As in New Orleans, the summers were hot, but the Texas air was sandpaper dry.

In 1975, the population of Atlanta was a mere 5,000 people, and its small size was initially a bit intimidating to Ellen. Being the new kid in town was difficult because it was a place where everyone already knew everybody. Instead of the vibrant 24-hour-a-day energy of New Orleans, Atlanta had one movie theater and, being in the days before cable, three TV channels, all with spotty reception. No building was taller than one story, and the only place to hang out was the local Dairy Queen. But there were plenty of churches and many of the town's young people participated in activities organized by the local churches, which ranged from Bible study classes to field trips to the very popular youth choruses.

Ellen used her humor to fit in, even though being outgoing didn't come naturally then. She had arrived in Atlanta on the chubby side, having been consoling herself with food ever since learning about the pending move to Texas. And at five feet eight she was taller than most of her female classmates, which made her feel awkward. She was also still suffering bouts of depression and homesickness. But even when she didn't feel like it, Ellen willed herself to be outgoing, cheerful, and funny—but only to a point.

"I was not the class cutup," Ellen says. "I really am uncomfortable with being the focus. So it was more a way of me just dealing with life. Humor was part of my personality. I was funny around my friends, but I was never confident enough to stand up and be loud and obnoxious. I wouldn't have called that kind of attention to myself, to try to be funny and try to get that approval. It was only with my friends."[8]

Ellen spent most of her free time involved in school activities. She particularly liked singing in the chorus and was also a varsity tennis star for the school team, the Rabbits; her first year there, she won the team's Outstanding Player award.

Then in her junior year, she became romantically involved with Ben Heath, who was both a top student and a star of the high school football team. They shared an interest in sports and both loved *Saturday Night Live*. By the time their senior year was drawing to a close, Ellen fantasized about becoming Ben's wife. On one hand he was just as eager to settle down but at the same time, Ben didn't want to rush into marriage since he was going away to college.

"I wanted to marry Ben desperately," Ellen admits. "But he told me he thought we should wait."[9]

According to the woman who eventually did marry Heath, it broke Ellen's heart. But his rejection forced Ellen to acknowledge and confront her attraction to women. Some gay women know from childhood that they have absolutely no sexual or emotional attraction to men, but Ellen's journey to self-realization wasn't so definitive.

"There are certain people who know early on that that's who they are. But I didn't know at all," explains Ellen. "People make choices all the time. Ben's now the mayor of some small town in Texas. I could be the mayor's wife. You know, I'm sure I'd have a nice place with Ben somewhere and we'd have kids and I wouldn't have known. I could have chosen to live my life in a way just to fit into society. But," she adds quietly, "I would not be happy."[10]

That realization would be vividly brought home when she was 18 and became physically intimate with her best girlfriend. As opposed to being a sexual epiphany, the affair mostly confused Ellen at first and she resisted contemplating the implications of the relationship.

"The first time it happened, it was not my idea," Ellen recalls. "She told me she loved me. I just thought, *What is this? Where is this coming from? What are you talking about?* I was freaked out even by the thought of it. I was scared."[11]

But not *that* scared. She and her friend, whom Ellen refuses to identify other than to say the woman is married, continued their sexual relationship for many months under the noses of friends, family, and boyfriends.

"We both had boyfriends and were double-dating, and yet we were together. But nobody knew. We didn't know what we were doing. It was this fun little experience that I guess some people have. I didn't think about being gay. I just thought it was just her; it was just because we really were best friends and liked each other a lot, and then I went on dating men. And then I met someone else later and that came up again and that freaked me out again. So for a while, I just tried to ignore it. Clearly, it was just me still fighting it."[12]

Perhaps one of the reasons Ellen had been so desperate to marry Ben was that she was trying to keep her attraction to women buried so she wouldn't have to acknowledge who she really was. Considering her family background and religion and the conservative environment of Atlanta, Texas, it would have been so much simpler to conform. Marrying Ben, or any other man, would have guaranteed Ellen acceptance. But it would have also entrapped her in a life that would have ultimately stifled her.

TREADING WATER

Now that Ellen's romance with Ben was over, the future was a question mark. She had absolutely no idea what she wanted to do with her life. She would have loved to become a professional tennis player but knew she wasn't good enough. She also liked golf but didn't think she could make a living at it. Singing was something else Ellen enjoyed immensely, but she seriously doubted that anyone was going to pay to hear her do that. And although she had once fancied becoming a naturalist, reality had curbed that dream.

So, as her high school graduation approached, Ellen felt rudderless. She had no desire to go to college, had no career she yearned to pursue nor, quite frankly, did she have any goals. The idea of being a secretary or an assembly-line worker certainly didn't hold much appeal for her. It wasn't a case of Ellen feeling she was above such jobs; she just knew they didn't match her personality, because she had already tried.

"I worked in a glove factory for about a day and a half. My mother worked there, too, and I remember midday the second day I said, *I'm not feeling well. I'm going to go home.* She said, *You're not coming back, are you?* I said, *No.* And so I never came back. I worked jobs like that, for just a day or two."[13]

Ellen's malaise and lack of concrete goal did not sit well with Roy. But the more he kept after Ellen to buckle down and get a job, the more depressed she became about her future and the more she tuned him out. She stayed out late as much as possible to avoid Roy—they couldn't argue if they weren't in the same room.

Betty tried without success to make things right between Roy and Ellen but what she didn't know was that Ellen was harboring a dark secret—in 1975, Roy had sexually molested her. Ellen didn't tell her mom because at the time Betty was recuperating from a mastectomy and she didn't want to upset her. Ellen later realized that was the absolutely wrong decision. "I should have [told her] right away," she admitted to *The Advocate*.[14]

Years later Betty would discuss the abuse in her book *Love Ellen*. Looking back now, DeGeneres says, "The statistics are that one in three women have been molested in some way and there should be more people talking about it; it shouldn't be a shameful thing. It *never* is your fault. So I don't mind talking about it. And that's the lesson: don't ever stay silent when something like this happens. You should always, *always,* tell somebody."[15]

Eventually, Ellen decided it was time to leave Texas, so she made arrangements to go back to New Orleans as soon as she finished high school and move in with her grandmother until she could afford a place of her own. The night of her graduation, Ellen packed all her belongings into her yellow Volkswagen. The next morning, she got up early and had breakfast with her mother before getting in her car and driving away to an uncertain future.

JACK OF ALL TRADES

Ellen spent one semester as a communications student at the University of New Orleans, mostly because everyone she knew was going to college. But it didn't take long for her to realize she was wasting her time. So during the day she looked for work; at night she hung out with friends at bars. Increasingly, Ellen found the company of women stimulating, deep, and honest. She began to spend more and more time in gay bars as her comfort level increased. She would dance and flirt and talk and laugh and feel as if she belonged. After years of resisting the label, "I realized I was definitely gay."

Ellen was evolving personally, but her future was still vague. She took a succession of jobs in what she calls an odd-job binge, holding each one for months, weeks, or hours, depending on how quickly she became bored, restless, and self-conscious. She was an employment counselor, baby-sat, worked at a car wash, wrapped packages in a department store, did accounting for a man who owned a wig store, took a job as a clothing salesperson, tended bar, shucked oysters, painted houses, sold vacuum cleaners, and worked as a waitress. Her job as a landscaper lasted four hours. None of these jobs struck her as anything she would like to do the rest of her life.

COMING OUT

Once Ellen had been honest with herself, she felt compelled to be honest with her mother. Ellen didn't want to deceive Betty, nor did she want to have to live a lie around her. The right time presented itself when Ellen was 19. She and her mother were in Pass Christian, Mississippi, where Betty's sister lived and where the entire family had congregated for a gathering.

"We were walking along the beach with our pants rolled up and barefoot, and the water was coming in," Ellen recalls. "I said, *I'm in love.* And she said, *That's great.* Then I said, *It's with a woman.*"[16]

Ellen started to cry, both out of relief and because she knew this wasn't what her mother had dreamed for her. She was desperate for her mother's approval, or at least her acceptance.

Betty wept, too, out of confusion and deep worry. "I was shocked. I had no inkling that she might be gay. I guess I said, *Are you sure? How do you know?* All those things. I came from a time where you grew up, you got married, you had a husband and he took care of things. Period."[17]

Betty later admitted to Diane Sawyer, "One of my frivolous thoughts when she told me was, *Oh, her engagement picture will never be in the paper. I'll never be the mother of the bride.*"[18]

"The most ironic thing about this was that her whole fear was, *You're not going to meet a man? Who's going to take care of you?*" Ellen says wryly.[19]

The rest of the family wouldn't know Ellen's secret for many years to come, except for her father. Unfortunately, Ellen's decision to be honest with him resulted in a painful rejection. Although Ellen assumed all along that he would have a hard time with it because he was religious, she was not prepared for the reaction she got from her father and stepmother, who she was living with at the time.

"After I told them," Ellen says, "they asked me to move out of the house. I mean, they just thought it would be better for me to live somewhere else because the woman he married had two daughters. Even though I didn't acknowledge it for years, that was bad, because they loved me and I loved them, and yet they didn't want me in the house. They didn't want that to be around her little girls."[20]

Despite the intense hurt and sense of betrayal Ellen felt, she still found it in her heart to accept her father's position without rejecting him in return. She understood it was ignorance on their part and refused to let his rejection keep her from loving him and including him in her life whenever possible.

Ellen knew she could have chosen not to live her life honestly and date men she was not sexually attracted to and ignore her emotional and sexual feelings for women. But she could not choose not to be attracted to women. That was part of her. That was who she was. It was, quite simply, how she was born.

While coming to terms with who she was, Ellen still had no clue what she wanted to do with her life. The months turned into years, and at 21 she was still in the same directionless rut she'd been in the day she graduated from high school. She needed to put her life in perspective and was given a boost when Betty took a leave of absence from her job in Atlanta and came to New Orleans to be with Ellen.

Betty stayed with her mom and Ellen shared a furnished apartment with Kathy "Kat" Perkoff. Blonde and pretty, Kat was a poet, and Ellen thought she had found her life mate. Spurred by her relationship with Kat, Ellen wrote comedy stories in her free time, though she didn't come up with anything she liked enough to send out to editors. But at whatever job she happened to have, she would engage others through humor. Coworkers encouraged Ellen to try her hand at stand-up. Eventually, the opportunity presented itself in 1980 when Ellen was asked to participate in a luncheon benefit. The thunderous applause took her completely by surprise, as did having someone in the audience come up to her after the show and ask her to work at a coffeehouse at the University of New Orleans.

The panic didn't hit her until she was driving home. When she walked into her apartment, she and Kat looked over the stack of things she'd been writing, and suddenly Ellen's confidence soared. All those days of writing were about to pay off.

The stories and observations that never quite worked as humor pieces for a magazine were perfectly suited to be delivered from a stage behind a microphone. She quickly wrote some additional material to round out her routine.

For Ellen, the night was an unqualified success: The audience loved her, and she got paid $15.

After that, she was asked to appear at small venues at other colleges, such as Loyola or Tulane. After a few more gigs, Betty believed her daughter had finally found a calling and told her comedy was what she was meant to do. Inspired by her mother's encouragement, Ellen busied herself perfecting the material she already had and writing new routines.

But her life was about to come to a screeching, emotional halt.

COMEDY CATHARSIS

Ellen and Kat had hit a rough spot in their relationship after DeGeneres discovered Perkoff had cheated on her.

> We were living together and I moved out to teach her a lesson so I was staying with someone else at the time, but always thinking that I'd go back. My brother's band was performing that night, and I saw her at the club. It was really loud, and she kept saying, *When are you going to come home?* And I kept acting like I couldn't hear her, like the music was too loud. She left first, and then I left.[21]

On the way home, Ellen passed a horrifying accident on the interstate, with a car split in two. At 6:00 A.M. the next morning, Kat's sister showed up where Ellen was staying and told her Kat had been killed the night before in a car accident. Ellen realized that was the accident she had passed. She hadn't recognized the car because Kat's friend had been driving. In an instant, her life turned upside down.

"It was a pretty devastating event in my life because I felt tremendously guilty," Ellen recalled to *The Advocate*. "I was 20 years old, and it was my first taste of knowing that somebody could be gone like that; you could be talking to them and then by the next day you will never see them again. And it made me start living a different way and realize what's important."[22]

Numb with grief and unable to pay the rent by herself, Ellen moved into a place where the surroundings reflected her mental state: a squalid, flea-ridden two-room hellhole with only a mattress to sleep on. But like so many artists, her pain became material.

She wrote a bit about calling God and asking him why there were fleas in the world. Ellen promised herself she would perform the skit one day on TV. Looking back, Ellen says she coped with the tragedy of Kat's death through comedy. And it saved her. It allowed Ellen to get on with her life and gave her a sense of purpose.

Ellen continued to hold down odd jobs during the day and performing at night whenever and wherever she could. Even though she was only paid pocket change, Ellen was having fun, and she had finally found a place where she felt she belonged: up on stage, making people laugh. Then, she got her first break at a most unexpected time from a most unexpected source.

Clyde's Comedy Corner in the French Quarter wasn't just the humor showcase in New Orleans. It was literally the *only* showcase where local comic talents could try out their routines and hone their skills. When the club opened in December 1980, Ellen was one of the first stand-ups hired by owner Clyde Abercrombie. Ellen agreed to do one show a night during the week and two a night on Fridays and Saturdays. She was so astounded that Clyde even knew of her, much less wanted to hire her that she would have probably worked for free. But she didn't.

"I was getting paid like three hundred dollars a week, enough so that I didn't have to work a regular job."[23]

Her style evolved into observational humor and a quirky way of seeing things. "I try to appeal to all ages, and for that reason I stayed away from youth-oriented routines that older people might not relate to. I don't insult people, either. No one's going to be offended by my humor, and I won't be embarrassed if my parents happen to be there."[24]

By late 1981, Ellen had made a name for herself as a local talent with tons of potential and a potential national career.

GOING NATIONAL

In 1982, Ellen moved to San Francisco, which had many more comedy clubs. Although Ellen was able to get some spots at a number of them, she was suddenly a small fish in a very big pond—an outsider who had no reputation, no local buzz, no heat, and not enough bookings to make ends meet. So she ended up back in New Orleans. In the interim, Clyde's had closed and suddenly Ellen had no venue and had to go to work in a law firm.

Then Showtime sponsored a contest to find the funniest person in America. All anyone had to do to enter was send in a videotaped performance. Ellen did and to her utter amazement, she was named funniest person in Louisiana. Showtime then notified Ellen that she was a finalist for the national competition. She and the other finalists performed their routines on a Showtime special. And Ellen won.

The prize was $500 and a TV special, which they showed in two-minute snippets between movies. But the national exposure convinced her it was time to go on the road. So, in 1983, she bought a van, attached a large nose above the front bumper, and once again headed to California.

For the next several years, Ellen traveled the country and built her reputation as a stand-up. She was eventually invited to appear on the *Tonight Show,* which brought her even more acclaim. She made Los Angeles her home and inevitably, Hollywood came calling.

In 1987, she was cast in a small role on the sitcom *Open House,* which was on the air for two and a half years. In 1991, she appeared in a Canadian-produced documentary called *Wisecracks,* which focused on the world of female stand-up comics. Although reviews of the film were mixed, Ellen was singled out as a bright spot. That led to a role on the series *Laurie Hill.* The show was critically panned and was canceled after five weeks.

Early in the spring of 1993, Ellen signed a deal for her own show, *These Friends of Mine,* which debuted in March 1994. The series was eventually renamed *Ellen.* The popularity of the show meant more media attention, which meant more questions about her private life. Although it was no secret within the entertainment industry that Ellen was gay, the public at large did not know. While Ellen didn't lie, she also avoided answering questions about her love life.

COMING OUT ON *ELLEN*

In her heart Ellen had to know that it was only a matter of time before her life would play out in the papers and that it probably wouldn't be pretty. So in the summer of 1996, Ellen invited her writing staff to her house and asked what they thought about having her series character come out as a lesbian. By having Ellen Morgan come out of the closet, she would lead the way for Ellen DeGeneres to do the same. And once set into motion, there would be no turning back.

"I made a decision during the summer that I wasn't going to live my life as a lie anymore," she said later. What took her so long to finally muster the courage was "the shame. I know what it feels like to try to blend in so that everybody else will think you're okay and they won't hurt you. I decided that this was not going to be something I was going to live the rest of my life ashamed of. You are bombarded early on that what you're supposed to do in life, if you're a girl, is meet a nice guy and get married and have kids and be accepted." In other words, be the girl next door, except, as Ellen notes: "I'm the girl on the other side of you."[25]

Ellen's coming out made TV history, but she initially paid a price. After the series went off the air after its fifth season, Ellen's career stalled. But within two years, she was back in demand. She was booked for a national stand-up tour that would end in New York and be taped for an HBO special. She was also working with CBS on a new sitcom. And she hosted the post 9/11 Emmy Awards to universal acclaim.

In April 2002, it was announced Ellen would have her own daytime talk show. By the summer of 2002, she was in demand everywhere. She was receiving rave reviews for her new *Here and Now* stand-up act, she was finishing up voice-over work on Pixar's *Finding Nemo* and had been signed by Simon & Schuster to write a new book of comic essays, *The Funny Thing Is . . .,* which would be published to coincide with the debut of her talk show.

The Ellen DeGeneres Show was a hit right out of the box when it debuted in 2003 and was nominated for 12 Daytime Emmys its first year. It is now a fixture, with a thriving accompanying website.

Jim Paratore echoes those sentiments. "I knew if we could get her on the air, viewers would see what her humor is all about. This is a great American comeback story. And it is someone who has a huge heart and is a terrific person and really deserves it. It shows she's succeeding because she's a talent. Viewers know she's gay, but that doesn't matter. She's good. Now it's a sweet victory for us all."[26]

Ellen has also found stability in her private life, having married partner Portia de Rossi in August 2008. Because of the challenges she has faced professionally and personally Ellen can savor her journey.

"Nothing has been easy," she told journalist Stone Phillips. "Not one step of the way has been easy. I'm really proud that I'm strong, because I didn't think I was strong. There's a moment in *Finding Nemo* when Dory starts crying and says, *I feel like I'm home.* That's what I feel like. I feel like I am finally home with everything."[27]

NOTES

1. Interview with the author.

2. James Robert Parish, *Hollywood Book of Breakups,* Hoboken, NJ: John Wiley & Sons, 2006.

3. HBO Comedy Special, *Women of the Night,* 1987.

4. Suzanne Lavin. *Women and Comedy in Solo Performance,* London: Psychology Press, 2004.

5. Interview with the author.

6. HBO Comedy Special, *Women of the Night.*

7. July Wieder. "Ellen: Born Again," *The Advocate,* March 14, 2000.

8. Kathleen Tracy. *The Real Story of Ellen DeGeneres,* New York: Pinnacle Books, 2005.

9. Ibid.

10. Ibid.

11. Ibid.

12. Ibid.

13. *Larry King Live,* CNN.com, September 2007, http://transcripts.cnn.com/TRAN SCRIPTS/0409/07/lkl.01.html.

14. Wieder, "Ellen."

15. Ibid.

16. Ibid.

17. Diane Sawyer interview, *20/20*, ABC, April 30, 1997.

18. Ibid.

19. Ibid.

20. Tracy, *The Real Story.*

21. Ibid.

22. Wieder, "Ellen."

23. Tracy, *The Real Story.*

24. Ibid.

25. Stone Phillips. *MSN Newsmakers*, November 11, 2004, http://www.msnbc.msn.com/id/6430100/ns/dateline_nbc-newsmakers/t/catching-ellen-degeneres/.

26. Ben Fong-Torres, *Parade,* October 31, 2004, http://news.google.com/newspapers?nid=1980&dat=20041031&id=ZMiAAAAIBAJ&sjid=HK8FAAAAIBAJ&pg=4991,5225495.

27. Phillips, *MSN Newsmakers.*

Lady Gaga got her start by performing in funky New York music clubs. She returned to her hometown to make an appearance on MTV's *Total Request Live* show in August 2008, filmed in Manhattan's Times Square.

17 LADY GAGA

Frank Sinatra, Elvis, the Beatles, Madonna . . . once every generation or so a musical performer comes along who not only taps into the collective consciousness of the day's youth, but also transforms the music industry both artistically and culturally. These performers' careers also span decades, giving them an iconic status whose influence transcends generations. Whether Lady Gaga has the staying power to join this pantheon of performers remains to be seen but her string of chart-topping hit records proves she is no one-hit wonder and that behind the outrageous costumes is a unique talent that is a distinct product of her times.

Lady Gaga's story begins in Manhattan's upper West Side. Stefani Joanne Angelina Germanotta was born on March 28, 1986. Her father Joseph owned an IT company that installed wireless systems in hotels; her mom Cynthia was a vice president at Verizon before leaving and working at her husband's business.

The Germanottas stressed education and sent Stefani and her younger sister Natali, born in 1992, to Sacred Heart, a Catholic girls' school near the Guggenheim Museum. The oldest independent school in New York, Sacred Heart was a favorite among Manhattan's social elite. As a result, many of Stefani's classmates were from uber-rich families—among the school's alumni include Nicki and Paris Hilton and several of the Kennedys.

"Sacred Heart may have been prestigious, but there were lots of different kinds of girls," Gaga later recalled to *New York* magazine. "Some had extreme wealth, others were on welfare and scholarship, and some were in the middle, which was my family. All our money went into education and the house."[1]

Music was a part of Stefani's life from a young age. One of her favorite memories was participating in a piano concert at Sacred Heart when she was eight years old. She recalls being one of twenty young girls sitting in a row in dresses, getting up to play one by one. Not one for false modesty, she also recalls already being quite good at the piano.

When she was 11, Stefani began attending acting classes on Saturdays that lasted all day long. By the time she reached eighth grade, Stefani figured out that acting was a good way to meet boys. She started auditioning for plays with Sacred Heart's all boys' brother school, Regis High School, and typically was cast in the lead female role. Her performances included Adelaide in *Guys and Dolls* and Philia in *A Funny Thing Happened on the Way to the Forum.*

In a foreshadowing of things to come, during plays she didn't want to be called by her real name backstage. She would stay in character and insist of being addressed by that name.

Looking back, Gaga told *In Touch,* "I was a bit insecure in high school. I used to get made fun of for being either too provocative or too eccentric, so I started to tone it down. I didn't fit in, and I felt like a freak."[2]

A good student, Stefani occasionally ran afoul of the teachers because she was a little too free showing off her décolletage. She says she was 15 to 20 pounds heavier than her adult weight and would wear shirts that were low-cut. The teachers would tell her the shirts were inappropriate. She would argue that other girls were wearing the same thing. The difference was, they were flat-chested while Stefani was not, hence the nickname, *Big Boobs McGee.*

However, her classmates remember Stefani being generally popular and not suffering any undue bullying at the hand of classmates. Even then, though, she did have an eclectic fashion sense that may have been a provocative nudge at her posh schoolmates. While the other girls were sleek and designer stylish, Stefani was partial to black hair, heavy eye makeup, and form-fitting clothes.

But she had an eye for the finer things as well. Stefani was one of the few girls in her school to have a part-time job, working as a waitress at an Upper West Side diner. She saved up and one of the first things she bought herself was a Gucci purse. "I was so excited because all the girls at Sacred Heart always had their fancy purses, and I always had whatever," she admitted to *New York.* "My mom and dad were not buying me a $600 purse."[3]

Known for being a little bit boy crazy, singing was already her primary passion. A fan of Pink Floyd and the Beatles, she formed a classic rock cover band, performing at open-mike nights at the Songwriters Hall of Fame. She also bought a fake ID, which gave her entrée into clubs.

Around this time she began dating a 26-year-old waiter from the restaurant where she worked. "That's part of why I needed a job after school, too," she commented to writer Vanessa Grigoriadis. "My dad wouldn't give me money to go out on the weekends because he knew I was going downtown and being bad."[4] It was during that time she got her first tattoo: a G clef on her lower back.

After graduating from high school, Stefani enrolled at New York University's Tisch School of the Arts and moved into a campus dorm. But the school ended up not being a good fit. Stefani felt she was artistically more advanced than what the classes were offering her. During her sophomore year, Stefani told her parents that she was going to drop out of college and pursue a career as a rock star.

Although not thrilled, her dad agreed to help her financially for one year *if* she agreed to go back to school if her music didn't pan out. Stefani agreed and rented the cheapest apartment she could find on the Lower East Side, furnishing it with a futon and a Yoko Ono album that was mounted on the wall over her bed. She dyed her hair black and straightened her naturally curly hair.

In September 2005, she started the Stefani Germanotta Band with some friends from New York University and within a couple of months they began working on a five-track demo, *Words,* with producer Joe Vulpis.

Guitarist Calvin Pia recalled on the website *Shine,* "We used to rehearse at this really dingy practice space on the Lower East Side, like, under some grocery store, where you'd have to enter through those metal doors on the sidewalk, and she had this huge keyboard that she'd wheel down the street from her apartment on Rivington and Suffolk. Stefani had a following of about fifteen to twenty people at each show."[5]

Pia described Stefani as "very bubbly, very eccentric, very driven," but adds, "The high art thing? I did not see any hints of that!"[6]

One of her acquaintances from the time told the *New York Post,* "She was a very suburban, preppy, friendly, social party girl. There was nothing that would tip you off that she had this Warhol-esque, new art extremism . . . Her 'crazy' outfit was putting suspenders on her jeans."[7]

Frankie Fredericks, her manager at the time, added, "We'd kick it, jam, get drunk. She said she wanted to have a record deal by the time she was 21."[8]

The Stefani Germanotta Band recorded their first EP, *Red and Blue,* in March 2006 but the group disbanded a few months later when her bandmates became too busy with school. By that time Stefani was integrating herself into the East Village music scene, where she would begin to find her musical voice.

Not long after dropping out of college, Stefani met and became friends with Wendy Starland, a singer-songwriter who knew Rob Fusari, a producer known for his work with Whitney Houston and Destiny's Child. After seeing Stefani perform, Starland called Rob and suggested he arrange a meeting.

His first impression? "She was a little overweight," he recalled in a *New York Post* interview. "She looked like something out of *Goodfellas,* like she was ready to make pasta any minute. She had on leggings and some strange cut-up shirt, a hat that looked like it was out of Prince's *Purple Rain.*"[9]

But after Stefani sang, his attitude changed. "I'm telling you, it was, like, 10 seconds in and I'm texting my management. I'm like, I need a contract—*immediately.*"[10]

Fusari felt Stefani was on a fast track to nowhere so he told her they were not going in the right direction; her music wasn't something kids could relate to. So they made her sound less rock and more dance, with a Euro flavor. Stefani also knew that her name was not radio, or record label, friendly. But there are several versions of how the name Lady Gaga was adopted and who coined it remains in debate. In one story, it was inspired by Fusari's tendency to sing Queen's "Radio Ga Ga" when Stefani walked into the studio; Fusari has claimed he accidentally made it up when writing a text message; and Starland says it came out of a brainstorming session.

However, it came to be, and once Stefani Germanotta adopted the Lady Gaga persona, there was no turning back.

OVERCOMING ADVERSITY

Lady Gaga and Wendy Starland collaborated on writing rock songs for four months, but the response from friends and associates was tepid. Gaga and her inner circle knew they needed a new direction. So after Fusari read an article on how producer Timbaland had rebranded Nelly Furtado from a folk artist into a sultry dance diva, he suggested Gaga also delve into dance music.

She, in a word, freaked. She accused Fusari of not believing in her or her music. But eventually, Gaga calmed down and took Fusari's advice to heart and they started working on music with a beat. They also began a romantic relationship, which led to a sometimes volatile relationship. She had a thin skin when he criticized any of her writing and he also pushed her to not only be an artist but to present the image of one as well—at all times in public. Unschooled to the world of fashion, Gaga slowly developed her look, leaving the sweatpants and off-the-shoulder tops behind in favor of a more eclectic style.

The energy and flashiness of the dance music scene proved to be a perfect fit for Gaga, who was more showman that crooner, and soon she was ready to showcase her new persona, believing that to truly get her as a performer, prospective managers and labels needed to see her perform live.

She was invited to a meeting with L.A. Reid at Island Def Jam, near Times Square. Reid listened to Gaga play the piano and announced that she was a star. She signed a deal with Reid's label for $850,000 and produced several tracks. Then just as suddenly she was out. Reid canceled three business dinners and soon after the label dropped Gaga.

Fusari says Gaga was crushed. The only bright spot was that she had refused part of the advance in order to maintain ownership of her master demos. That move would prove to be a stroke of business genius. But at the time, it seemed small consolation and for the first time, Stefani considered the possibility that she might not succeed.

"I went back to my apartment on the Lower East Side, and I was so depressed," she says. "That's when I started the real devotion to my music and art."[11]

It was 2007 and Gaga immersed herself in the hard rock scene. Her romance with Fusari having run its course, she fell in love with the manager of St. Jerome's, a rock bar. It was there she met Lady Starlight, a DJ/go-go dancer who says she introduced Gaga to many people and places in the underground music scene. And her style of dress had begun to have a costume-esque flair—skin-tight leopard pants, red pumps with six-inch heels, and lots of spandex unitards.

"The Lower East Side has an arrogance, a stench," Gaga says. "We walk and talk and live and breathe who we are with such an incredible stench that eventually the stench becomes a reality. Our vanity is a positive thing. It's made me the woman I am today."

Gaga started performing her songs with Starlight at small clubs and opening for a local glam band. Fusari came to one of their shows and was horrified, saying it was Rocky Horror meets eighties band.

In the spring of 2007, Fusari arranged a meeting for Gaga with Interscope through his friend Vincent Herbert, who was now working with the label as an A&R rep. They flew to Los Angeles to meet Jimmy Iovine, who ran the label. After listening to a few of her master demos, he signed her and had her writing songs for other performers, such as Pussycat Dolls and Britney Spears.

In the meantime, Herbert worked to create a marketable image for Gaga, such as dying her hair blond. Around that time, Gaga was introduced to the art of artist Andy Warhol and devoured books about him. His philosophy about stardom and celebrity—that they were just another art form—clicked with her and was the impetus for the true transformation from Stefani Germanotta to Lady Gaga. She embraced dance music, seeing it as inclusive and joy giving.

R&B singer Akon, a fellow Interscope artist, heard one of her tracks, "Just Dance," and raved about it to Iovine, who decided it was time to groom her as a solo act. Gaga first performed at small venues, including many gay clubs. Her outfits became more eccentric and her following grew.

In 2007, Lady Gaga released her first album, *The Fame,* but despite the catchy melodies and lyrics of her first singles, radio stations in the United States by and large bypassed including her music in their song rotations.

"They would say, *This is too racy, too dance-oriented, too underground. It's not marketable.* And I would say, *My name is Lady Gaga, I've been on the music scene for years, and I'm telling you, this is what's next.* And look . . . I was right."[12]

It would take a while for the radio industry to realize it but *The Fame* would eventually go on to be multiplatinum, selling more than 14 million copies worldwide with two number one singles: "Just Dance" and "Poker Face." The album also earned her six Grammy nominations and two wins. With that album, Lady Gaga became the first artist in history to claim four number one hits from a debut album ("Just Dance," "Poker Face," "LoveGame," and "Paparazzi").

In 2009, the album was rereleased with eight new tracks, including "Telephone" with Beyoncé, as a two-disk set called *The Fame Monster,* which became the best-selling album of 2010, with sales nearing six million. Gaga is also possibly the most viewed artist ever online, reaching one *billion* views of her music videos. The single "Born This Way," set a new iTunes speed record for going to number one in less than three hours.

Success opened many doors for Gaga and prompted her to close others. Rob Fusari, who sued Gaga for $30 million, a case which was ultimately settled out of court, says she has left people behind, changing phone numbers so that old friends can no longer reach her.

Brendan Sullivan, aka DJ VH1, who worked with her on some early show says, "You know, she used to send texts out in New York inviting everyone on the Lower East Side to her shows, and not too many people would come. And after the vocal coach, dieting, exercising, and all the rest, now everyone wants to go.

She has gotten annoyed by that: *Why didn't they come before?* You know, once she blew up, and everyone wanted a piece of her, we stopped calling her Gaga. We started calling her Stef again."[13]

Her inner circle includes her team, which she calls Haus of Gaga. "In this industry, you get a lot of stylists and producers thrown at you, but this is my own creative team, modeled on Warhol's Factory. Everyone is under 26 and we do everything together." They understand she performs not to just entertain but to provoke. "How do I make pop, commercial art be taken as seriously as fine art? That's what Warhol did. How do I make music and performances that are thought-provoking, fresh and future? We decide what's good and, if the ideas are powerful enough, we can convince the world that it's great."[14]

She has toured almost nonstop since the release of *The Fame*—grossing $170 million from 137 shows in 22 countries from May 2010 to May 2011—all the while becoming an icon of outsiders everywhere—affectionately calling her fans little monsters—and a vocal advocate on behalf of the gay community. In October 2009, she participated in the National Equality March in Washington, D.C., walking shoulder to shoulder with the masses.

"I will never turn my back on my friends," she said at the rally. "Today is not a one-off performance."[15]

FAME MONSTER

Lady Gaga is right where she always believed she would be. Rather than relax and savor her success, she seems even more driven, saying her art is her entire life. "I had to suppress it for so many years in high school because I was made fun of but now I'm completely insulated in my box of insanity and I can do whatever I like."[16]

"Every minute of this is a completely brilliant and wonderful moment that I cherish. And it's like, now you have everybody watching, GaGa, you'd better be f***ing great."[17]

She accepts the pressure. "You know, I have such an appreciation for where I am in my life because I've struggled and because I couldn't get signed, and because I couldn't get played on the radio. There are times when it can be a lot to deal with but always when I get up in the morning I try to find that very joyful place that reminds me that I would die if someone took it all away. If someone did that I wouldn't be a person anymore."[18]

Perhaps the key to her popularity is that her music is layered, enabling listeners to find their own level to relate to.

"I have found that my work has to be both deep and shallow," she says. "All of my songs have meaning, all of my clothing has iconography buried into it. But by the same token, it's just as special if you look at it in its shallowest form: a quick moment of melody, a beautiful dress. People think, *Gaga's so sweet* or *Gaga sucks*. The point is that it's memorable. For commercial art to be taken seriously as fine art is a very unusual and difficult task. I think that a lot of people don't get it and a lot of people don't know what to make of me. And, you know what? I'm OK with that."[19]

NOTES

1. Vanessa Grigoriadis. "Growing Up Gaga," *New York,* March 28, 2010, http://nymag.com/arts/popmusic/features/65127/.

2. "Lady Gaga Was Surprisingly Normal!" *In Touch,* http://www.intouchweekly.com/2009/12/in_touch_exclusivelady_gaga_wa.php.

3. Grigoriadis, "Growing Up Gaga."

4. Ibid.

5. "Lady Gaga's Former Band Mates: She Didn't Always Have this Persona," *Shine,* http://shine.yahoo.com/channel/beauty/lady-gagas-former-band-mates-she-didnt-always-have-this-persona-521402.

6. Ibid.

7. Maureen Callahan and Sara Stewart. "Who's That Lady?" *New York Post,* January 21, 2010, http://www.nypost.com/p/entertainment/music/who_that_lady_CBlHI927dRlLmIwjVfGrwK.

8. Ibid.

9. Callahan and Stewart, "Who's That Lady?"

10. Ibid.

11. Grigoriadis, "Growing Up Gaga."

12. Fiona Sturges. "Lady Gaga: How the World Went Crazy for the New Queen of Pop," *The Independent,* May 16, 2009, http://www.independent.co.uk/arts-entertainment/music/features/lady-gaga-how-the-world-went-crazy-for-the-new-queen-of-pop-1684375.html.

13. Grigoriadis, "Growing Up Gaga."

14. Hattie Collins. "Lady GaGa: The Future of Pop?" *The Sunday Times,* December 14, 2008, http://www.thesundaytimes.co.uk/sto/culture/music/article137332.ece.

15. Dan Zak. "Lady Gaga, Already a Gay Icon, Shows She's an Activist Too," *Washington Post,* October 12, 2009, http://www.washingtonpost.com/wp-dyn/content/article/2009/10/11/AR2009101101892.html?hpid=topnews&sid=ST2009101101924.

16. Callahan and Stewart, "Who's That Lady?"

17. Ruby Warrington. "Lady Gaga: Ready for Her Close-Up," *The Sunday Times,* February 22, 2009, http://entertainment.timesonline.co.uk/tol/arts_and_entertainment/music/article5746827.ece.

18. Sturges, "Lady Gaga."

19. Ibid.

Shaun White celebrates after winning the men's snowboard half-pipe competition at the Vancouver 2010 Olympics in Vancouver, British Columbia.

18 SHAUN WHITE

Sport is inherently challenging. It requires athletes to push their bodies beyond normal endurance and also demands near-superhuman mental toughness. Nobody embodies this more than Shaun White. But when he was born on September 3, 1986, in San Diego, his parents Roger and Cathy weren't fantasizing about his future as a world-class athlete because they feared their infant may not live to celebrate his first birthday.

Shaun was born with a congenital heart defect called tetralogy of Fallot, which restricts blood flow to the lungs so the body does not get enough oxygen. Doctors performed surgery when he was six months old to fix the defect. Roger worked at the San Clemente Water Department and Cathy was a waitress; so the medical bills were a challenge. Their finances became more strapped when Shaun needed another surgery when he was 18 months old.

"It was hard because my daughter had to have brain surgery at the same time," Cathy recalls. "Both could have died. It made us realize how short life is, how precious your children are."[1]

Some parents may have become overly protective of their child who had been a sickly infant, but Cathy and Roger encouraged his activities. So just a few years later when he was six, Shaun picked up his first skateboard after watching his older brother Jesse skateboard at the local YMCA.

In their backyard, the Whites installed a skateboard mini-ramp and a trampoline. Shaun would watch Jesse jump off the back of the ramp and land on the trampoline. Shaun would then take it one step further—he would add a back-flip before landing. Perhaps some of it is genetic—his grandparents were in Roller Derby.

A short time later, Shaun also discovered snowboarding and immediately started jumping. His love of speed prompted his mom to restrict Shaun to board backward.

That parental rule enabled him to master that skill in a way few do. His family made regular trips to Big Bear where Shaun honed his skills.

When he was seven, Shaun won the race and half-pipe events at the Southern California Conference finals in the 12-and-under category. Encouraged by his success, he entered more competitions. Shaun, his parents, brother, and sister Kari would sleep in their 1964 van at events, cooking on the stove in back. At times Shaun hiked up the half-pipe because he couldn't afford to buy tickets. But the family seemed to thrive and uniformly supported Shaun.

From his first competition, Shaun stood out because he always went full out, fearless. "You know the best thing about competition? There's this whole strategy game, and when it all works out it's like solving that hard math equation," he explains. "You finally get the answer and you're so happy. Whenever I'm at the top of the hill and I know I only have one more run, I don't back off, I get stoked by it. When some guy does a really hard trick and my run is right after, you know I'm going to go bigger."[2]

Shaun considers falling part of the sport. "I started at 6, so I've been in the air a long time. It doesn't bother me. When I'm learning something, I don't care if I slam. I always ask myself, *How hard can I really fall?*"[3]

Actually, really hard. His worst fall happened when he was 11 after a collision on the vert ramp. "I was skating doubles with Bob Burnquist at the 1997 MTV Sports and Music Festival," White recalls. "Our lines got messed up and we hit midair."[4] Shaun broke his right hand, right foot, fractured his skull, and was knocked unconscious. But as soon as he recuperated, he was right back on his board.

At the time, snowboarding was in its commercial infancy. So the money for Shaun's travel and competition came out of his parents' pockets, costing as much as $20,000 a year.

"When I started snowboarding there were no Olympics, no X games, no money or anything in the sport, they just basically knew I had a talent and went for it." White goes on to say "I had some heart conditions when I was first born so going from that struggle to now letting me go out there and do all these things . . . you put a dream in front of somebody and you're so young and it just seems so close and I said I can do this and I just took every step towards it."[5]

Once he had won nearly every amateur competition available, Shaun turned pro in 1999 when he was 13, picking up Burton as a sponsor. He won his first major title in 2001 at the Arctic Challenge but it was more than the win that was earning him a reputation. From the beginning, he pushed the envelope, putting tricks together in innovative ways and achieving unprecedented air.

In 2003, Shaun dominated every competition he entered, culminating with the Winter X Games, where he won gold medals in the slopestyle and the superpipe. He was also won the best-athlete award. A few weeks later, Shaun became the youngest snowboarder to ever win the United States Open Slopestyle Championship.

Most of the time, Shaun's parents traveled with him, which was fine with him. "For the most part I like having my parents there. My dad is rad, and when my mom's there I don't have to worry about anything," laughs. "I'll make it to the contest on time, and everything is going to be taken care of." Being the youngest snowboarder made for some awkward situations. "For me it was weird, 'cause at 14 I wasn't down with the whole party scene. So seeing all these guys getting drunk and coming home with random girls was super strange to me." But overall the experience was positive. "When I started traveling, seeing all the other cultures and how tough some people have it made me pretty grateful. I mean, I get to travel around the world, snowboard, and they pay me for it."[6]

Despite being a fulltime athlete, White was determined to earn his high school diploma, in part because he was aware he was becoming a role model.

> I thought there'd be all these other kids saying, *Look at Shaun, he didn't go to high school.* I didn't want that, and I didn't want to see people on a plane and have to tell them I dropped out. That's not cool no matter what. But there were times when I didn't want to do it. I'm in a hotel room in Japan with all these flashing lights outside, and I'm supposed to close the curtains and study algebra?[7]

Most athletes find it challenging enough to excel in one sport. White set his sights on dominating two. He made his professional skateboarding debut at the 2003 Slam City Jam, finishing fourth in the vert half-pipe. That qualified him for the 2003 X Games, where he finished sixth in the vert competition.

It is estimated there are less than 40 world-class vert skaters and many of them were around when the X Games started. Now in their 30s, they are possessive of the sport and some are pained that it has been commercialized. They form a kind of clique that does not necessarily welcome new, young talent with open arms, especially when that young rider is turning the sport on its rollers.

In 2005, Shaun won the first Dew Tour event and placed second at the X Games. In 2006, he won the Dew Tour event in Denver. The older skateboarders considered him an intruder and treated him accordingly.

"When I won that event, it shook things up," Shaun admits. "Breaking into that group is tough. And to break in as the guy who snowboards all year . . . some of them had a hard time with it." Shaun's brother Jesse explains, "It's normal hazing, like the old quarterback to the young quarterback. He probably gets more of it than the others, but it's not like they're egging the house or anything."[8]

What the skateboarders did not seem to realize is that Shaun wasn't competing against them. "For me, it's all about an internal competition. I have been this way since I was a tiny little kid competing on the soccer field. It's not about beating anyone else out there; it's just about being better than myself,"[9] he says. "I've always thought that if I tried to beat someone, then I could only get as good as they are. If I try to be as good as I can be, there's no telling where that might lead."[10]

Shaun was officially a two-sport threat. He was also a marketer's dream. By 2006, Shaun had amassed millions of dollars in sponsorship money from companies like Target, Volcom clothing, and the IMG sport agency. And it would only grow.

In December 2005, he qualified for the 2006 Winter Olympics in half-pipe and won the gold medal in an exhilarating come-from-behind victory, becoming known as the Flying Tomato. Again, his biggest competition was himself. "I know that I gave it my all at the Olympics," he says. "If someone had beat me it would have been disappointing, but I would have been okay because I know that I gave it my all. Everyone was riding great that day; I was stoked for everyone and honestly was blown away by the level of riding."[11]

Shaun continued switching back and forth between sports. At the 2007 Summer X Games, he won the gold medal in the vert, becoming the first and only person to win gold medals at both the Summer and Winter Games. He was also the first to win consecutive gold medals in the Winter X Games superpipe competition (2008 and 2009). And Shaun is the only athlete to win both Summer and Winter Dew Cups. And in 2010, he won his second snowboarding gold medal.

Shaun believes that each sport makes him better in the other. "I think skating just keeps it fresh for me. I don't think about snowboarding all year, so when I come back to it I'm excited to get back onto the hill. That has helped me keep focused and push myself a little bit harder."[12]

Shaun says the ideas for his innovative moves sometimes come in dreams but often happen when he's relaxing with music.

> Music has been a thing which really defines the moods and situations that I'm in. I actually competed in a competition where I won a guitar. It just gave me a whole new love for music and appreciation, and it really turned me on to different bands and different groups. And from there I just got more inspired and more motivated. I think everybody can agree that you can hear a certain song and it will put you in a certain mood, and that's just the beauty of music and I am so inspired by that.[13]

The irony is that by proving himself as champion in both snowboarding and skateboarding, he feels slightly removed from both worlds. "Because I'm the guy that does both sports, I'm not really embedded in either. Even the guys from snowboarding hang out all the time, after the season. But I disappear, I go skateboard and I don't really see a lot of those guys too much."[14]

The difference for Shaun is that he basically skateboards for fun and passion. "I never wanted any sponsors, I just wanted to compete. I could have gone out and got skateboarding sponsors or whatever but I didn't want it. I skate for Birdhouse but that's it. A lot of the guys that see me at the ramp are like, 'you don't even need to be here' because of my success with snowboarding. But that's even more reason to be there I find, just for the hell of it. Just for the fun of it. That's what I'm all about right now, having a good time and doing what I like."[15]

NOTES

1. Allison Glock. "Shaun White, Snowboarding's Hottest Star, Is Set to Blow Up in Skateboarding, Too," http://sports.espn.go.com/espnmag/story?id=3246499.

2. Ibid.

3. Tim Keown. "A Darker Shade of White," http://sports.espn.go.com/espnmag/story?id=3247400.

4. Glock, "Shaun White."

5. "Shaun White: From Open Heart Surgery to Olympic Hero," GlobalGrind.com, February 24, 2010, http://globalgrind.com/channel/gossip/content/1414069/shaun-white-from-open-heart-surgery-to-olympic-hero.

6. Ash Marshall. "2010 Winter Olympics: My Interview with USA Gold Medalist Shaun White," February 19, 2010, http://bleacherreport.com/articles/348717-2010-winter-olympics-my-interview-with-us-gold-medalist-shaun-white.

7. Keown, "A Darker Shade."

8. Ibid.

9. Rick Baker. "Shaun White Interview," July 29, 2010, http://www.popmag.com.au/home/news/shaun-white-interview.aspx.

10. Keown, "A Darker Shade."

11. Baker, "Shaun White Interview."

12. Ibid.

13. Marshall, "2010 Winter Olympics."

14. Tom Eagar. "Shaun White Interview," October 29, 2010, http://www.huckmagazine.com/features/shaun-white-interview/.

15. Ibid.

SELECTED BIBLIOGRAPHY

Bawden, Jim. "Chace Crawford Next Teen Sensation," *Toronto Star,* September 18, 2007, http://www.thestar.com/printArticle/257545.

Brinton, Jessica. "Fancy Man: Robert Pattinson," *The Sunday Times,* December 14, 2008, http://women.timesonline.co.uk/tol/life_and_style/women/celebrity/article530 7734.ece.

Chang, Justin, "Taylor Lautner," *Daily Variety,* November 4, 2004.

Clarke, Liz. "New Face of Gymnastics," *The Washington Post,* March 1, 2008, http://www.highbeam.com/doc/1P2-15425660.html.

Coleman, Judy. "At Sweet 16, Lovato's Ready for Her Close-Up." *Boston Globe,* September 23, 2008, p. 8SID.

Cyrus, Miley. *Miles to Go.* New York: Disney Hyperion, 2009.

Freydkin, Donna. "Lea Michele Never Stopped Believing," *USA Today,* May 10, 2010, http://docs.newsbank.com/s/InfoWeb/aggdocs/NewsBank/12FA1BDFF4BD7318/108 3311554222450?p_multi=USTB&s_lang=en-US.

Glock, Allison. "Shaun White, Snowboarding's Hottest Star, Is Set to Blow Up in Skateboarding, Too," http://sports.espn.go.com/espnmag/story?id=3246499.

Grigoriadis, Vanessa. "Growing Up Gaga," *New York,* March 28, 2010, http://nymag.com/arts/popmusic/features/65127/.

Kent, Brittany. *Miley Cyrus: This Is Her Life,* New York: Berkley Trade, 2008.

McQuaid, Peter. "Drama Teen," *New York Times,* August 16, 2009, http://www.nytimes.com/indexes/2009/08/16/style/t/index.html#pagewanted=0&pageName=16segalw&.

Norwich, Grace. *Amped Up: Aly & Aj, The Official Biography,* New York: Penguin, 2007.

Parvis, Sarah. *Taylor Swift,* Riverside, NJ: Andrews McMeel Publishing, 2009.

Rader, Dotson. "Shia LaBeouf: I'm Proud of Growing Up Poor," *Parade,* May 29, 2009, http://www.Parade.com/celebrity/2009/06/shia-labeouf-growing-up-poor.html.

Roberts, Sheila. "Kristen Stewart Interview: The Messengers." *Movies Online*, http://www.moviesonline.ca/movienews_11136.html.

Robin, Emily. *Blake Lively: Traveling to the Top,* New York: Scholastic, 2009.

Ross, Jerry. "How Vanessa Hudgens Went to the Top of the Class," *USAToday Weekend,* January 28, 2007, http://www.usaweekend.com/07_issues/070128/070128vanessa_hudgens.html.

Ryals, Lexi. *Taylor Swift: Country's Sweetheart,* New York: Price Stern Sloan, 2008.

Tan, Michelle. "Is Selena Gomez . . . the Next Miley Cyrus?" People.com, http://www.people.com/people/archive/article/0,20203953,00.html.

Tracy, Kathleen. *The Real Story of Ellen DeGeneres,* New York: Pinnacle Books, 2005.

Watson, Margeaux. "Caribbean Queen: Rihanna," *Entertainment Weekly,* June 22, 2007, http://www.ew.com/ew/article/0,20043393,00.html.

INDEX

ABOUT THE AUTHOR

A journalist for over 20 years, Kathleen Tracy's writing has been featured in magazines including *A&E Biography, The Herald, KidScreen, VideoAge,* and *TV Times.* She is currently a special issues contributor to *Daily Variety* and is also the author of over 70 books including *Sacha Baron Cohen* (St. Martin's), *The Boy Who Would Be King* (Dutton), *Jerry Seinfeld: The Entire Domain* (Carol Publishing), *Don Imus: America's Cowboy* (Carroll & Graf), *The Girl's Got Bite: A Look at Buffy's World* (St. Martin's), *Morgan Freeman: A Reluctant Treasure* (Barricade Books), *Tennessee Williams* (Mitchell-Lane), and *Judy Blume* (Greenwood).